ISBN 978-1-331-27467-4
PIBN 10167653

This book is a reproduction of an important historical work. Forgotten Books uses
state-of-the-art technology to digitally reconstruct the work, preserving the original format
whilst repairing imperfections present in the aged copy. In rare cases, an imperfection in
the original, such as a blemish or missing page, may be replicated in our edition. We do,
however, repair the vast majority of imperfections successfully; any imperfections that
remain are intentionally left to preserve the state of such historical works.

1 MONTH OF
FREE
READING

at

www.ForgottenBooks.com

By purchasing this book you are eligible for one month membership to ForgottenBooks.com, giving you unlimited access to our entire collection of over 700,000 titles via our web site and mobile apps.

To claim your free month visit:

www.forgottenbooks.com/free167653

English
Français
Deutsche
Italiano
Español
Português

www.forgottenbooks.com

Mythology Photography **Fiction**
Fishing Christianity **Art** Cooking
Essays Buddhism Freemasonry
Medicine **Biology** Music **Ancient**
Egypt Evolution Carpentry Physics
Dance Geology **Mathematics** Fitness
Shakespeare **Folklore** Yoga Marketing
Confidence Immortality Biographies
Poetry **Psychology** Witchcraft
Electronics Chemistry History **Law**
Accounting **Philosophy** Anthropology
Alchemy Drama Quantum Mechanics
Atheism Sexual Health **Ancient History**
Entrepreneurship Languages Sport
Paleontology Needlework Islam
Metaphysics Investment Archaeology
Parenting Statistics Criminology
Motivational

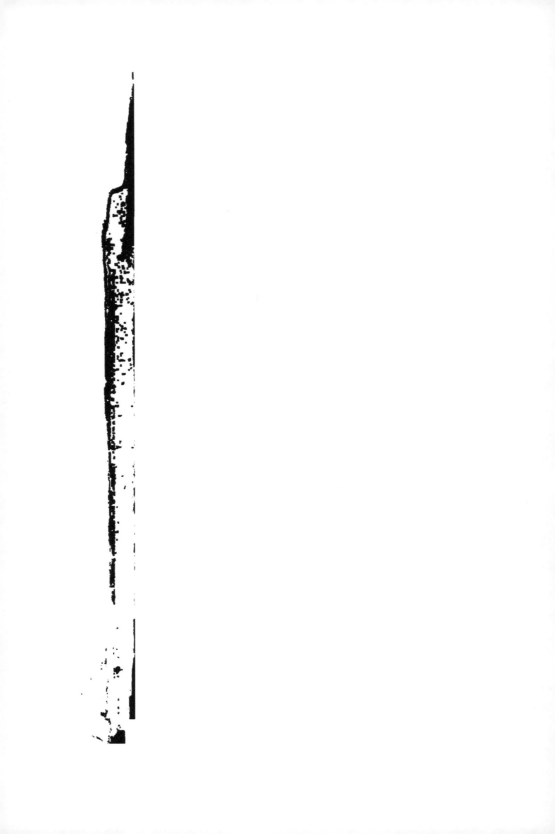

REYNOLDS' HANDBOOK

OF THE

MINING LAWS

OF THE

UNITED STATES AND CANADA

Arranged with reference to

Alaska and the Northwest Territories .

Also including the laws of

BRITISH COLUMBIA AND ONTARIO

Forms and Glossary

PARTS I AND II.

By

JOSEPH WARD REYNOLDS
OF THE MINNESOTA BAR

CHICAGO - - **NEW YORK**

W. B. Conkey Company

1898

PREFACE.

THE purpose of this book is to furnish, in the smallest possible compass and at the lowest possible price, an authoritative exposition of the law relating to mines and mining in the United States and Canada, as it exists at this date. The scope of the work includes the whole mining law to date of the two countries, arranged particularly with reference to Alaska, the Northwest Territories, British Columbia, Ontario and the Rainy Lake Districts. The statutory enactments are not extensive in either country, but the great body of the mining law exists in the "regulations" of the Departments of the Interior, and the judicial decisions of the respective countries. This book contains all the statutes and governmental "regulations" on the subject, in both countries, together with reference to all the judicial and departmental decisions construing such statutes or regulations or settling important principles of mining law.

Where there is conflict of authority upon any question the author has not hesitated to state what he regards as the correct principle.

It includes all necessary "forms" for proceedings under the mining laws of both countries.

A glossary of facts pertinent to Alaska and the Northwest Territories is also added, which may be of interest, if not benefit, to the reader. In short,

it is endeavored to make this work a safe and re-
liable guide to the one interested, or expecting to
be interested, in mines or mining in the United
States or Canada and especially in Alaska, Northwest Territories, British Columbia and Ontario.

Part I contains all general and local laws and
governmental regulations respecting mining in force
in Alaska.

Part II contains all general and local laws and
governmental regulations in force in the Northwest
Territories, British Columbia and Ontario.

JOS. WARD REYNOLDS.

MAY 1, 1898.

PART I.

MINING LAWS

OF THE

UNITED STATES AND ALASKA.

PART I.

THE RELATIVE EFFECT OF LAWS, REGULATIONS AND RULES.

Subject of Part I.—It will be observed that the primary purpose of Part I. of this book is to state the law respecting mines and mining now in force in *Alaska.* In fulfillment of that purpose, the arrangement of the text, upon each point discussed, is as follows:

1. The provisions of the United States statutes.

2. The regulations of the Department of the Interior.

3. The law of the State of Oregon in force May 17, 1884, and the acts of Congress applicable to Alaska.

4. The author's exposition of the principles involved, and

5. The Judicial and Departmental Decisions on the point under consideration.

The Text.—The general provisions of the **United States statutes** in reference to **"Mineral Lands and Mining Resources,"** being **Chapter Six of Title XXXII,** are taken as the guide in the discussion of the law, and are considered with reference to each particular subject legislated upon. Consequently, where a section of the statutes refers to only one subject it is discussed as a whole, but where more than one subject is involved in a section, they are considered in their order and the text of the section divided accordingly.

Citations.—The citation of departmental regulations, the laws applicable to Alaska and the decisions of the judiciary or departments, is strictly confined in each instance to the precise subject under consideration.

Conflict of Laws.—The provisions of the United States statutes must prevail, when brought in conflict with departmental regulations, local laws or miners' rules. Departmental regulations have, however, the same force and effect as the statutes in pursuance of which they are adopted, if they are within the authority granted. In determining the effect of the federal statutes on the subject of mineral lands it should always be kept in mind that, in many respects, they do not purport to be exclusive, but rather contemplate that they shall be supplemented by local legislation in the various States and Territories, or by miners' rules adopted in the mining districts. The United States statutes on this subject may properly be regarded as monuments fixing the bounds beyond which, in any State or Territory, regulations, legislation or rules shall not go, and within which such regulations and local laws and rules may be adopted as shall appear to be necessary or convenient, and as shall subserve the general purpose of the federal legislation. Properly speaking, Alaska has no local laws, because it has no legislature, but Congress, by adopting the laws of Oregon in force May 17, 1884, has made those laws, so far as applicable, exactly equivalent in importance to acts of Congress and must be so regarded and construed, when not in conflict there-with. Consequently, the "local laws" of Alaska are the acts of Congress of local application.

A UNITED STATES LAND OFFICE ESTAB-LISHED FOR ALASKA.

Alaska a Land District.—That the said District of Alaska is hereby created a land district, and a United States land office for said district is hereby located at Sitka. § 8, 23 S. L. 24, I Supp., 430.

REGISTER AND RECEIVER AND SURVEYOR GENERAL.

Appointment of Surveyor General.—That there shall be appointed by the President, by and with the advice and consent of the Senate, a surveyor-general for the District of Alaska, embracing one surveying district.

Salary.—That the surveyor-general of Alaska shall receive a salary at the rate of two thousand dollars per annum.

Division of Territory Into Two Land Districts.—The President is authorized and empowered, in his discretion, to divide said Territory into two land districts and to designate the boundaries thereof.

Additional Officers.—And he is also authorized and empowered to appoint, by and with the advice and consent of the Senate, a register of said additional land office and receiver of public moneys therefor, and in case of the creation of such additional land district the surveyor-general shall serve in both districts.   § 8, Id., as amended.

Laws of United States Relating to Mining Claims Extended to Alaska.—And the laws of the United States relating to mining claims, and the rights incident thereto, shall, from and after the passage of this act be in full force and effect in said district, under the administration thereof herein provided for, subject to such regulations as may be made by the Secretary of the Interior, approved by the President.   § 8, Id.

Possession of Indians Not Disturbed.—Provided, That the Indians or other persons in said district shall not be disturbed in the possession of any lands actually in their use or occupation or now claimed by them, but the terms under which such persons may acquire title to such lands is reserved for future legislation by Congress.   § 8, Id.

Existing Rights of Miners Recognized.—And provided further, That parties who have located mines or mineral privileges therein under the laws of the United States applicable to the public domain, or who have occupied and improved or exercised acts of ownership over such claims, shall not be disturbed therein, but shall be allowed to perfect their title to such claims by payment as aforesaid.   § 8, Id.

General Land Laws Not in Force in Alaska.—But nothing contained in this act shall be construed to put in force in said district the general land laws of the United States.   § 8, Id.

STATUS OF ALASKA COURT.

Anomalous Court.—The United States District Court of Alaska is the "Supreme Court of the Territory" from which appeals lie to the United States Circuit Court of Appeals for the Ninth Circuit or to the United States Supreme Court, as the case may be. Coquitlam v. U. S., 16 S. C. R. 1117, 163 U. S. 346.

Court of Appeals.—Cases in the Alaska courts "arising under the Patent laws, under the Revenue laws and under Criminal laws and in Admiralty cases," are reviewable only in the United States Circuit Court of Appeals for the Ninth Judicial Circuit, the determination of which court is final. §§ 6, 15, 26 S. L. 826, I Supp. 903-5.

Supreme Court.—In all other cases, at law and in equity, the final judgments and decrees of the Supreme Court of the Territory, in cases where the nature of the matter in dispute, exclusive of costs, to be ascertained by the oath of either party, or of other competent witnesses, exceeds five thousand dollars, may be reviewed in the United States Supreme Court, by writ of error, in cases of trial by jury, and by appeal in other cases. §§ 691-2, 702 R. S. U. S.; 18 S. L. 27, I Supp. 7; 23 S. L. 443, I Supp. 485.

Supreme Court.—The last paragraph does "not apply to any case wherein is involved the validity of any copyright, or in which is drawn in question the validity of a treaty or statute of or an authority exercised under the United States, but in all such cases an appeal or writ of error may be brought without regard to the sum or value in dispute." 23 S. L. 443, I Supp. 485; § 6, 26 S. L. 826, I Supp. 901.

FEDERAL LAWS PREVAIL.
PROVISIONS OF UNITED STATES STATUTES.

Laws of United States Relating to Mining Claims Extended to Alaska.—And the laws of the United States relating to mining claims, and the rights incident thereto, shall, from and after the passage of this act, be in full force and effect in said district, under the administration thereof herein provided for, subject to such regulations as may be made by the Secretary of the Interior, approved by the President. § 8, 23 S. L. 24, I Supp. 430.

Existing Rights of Miners Recognized.—And provided further, That parties who have located mines or mineral privileges therein under the laws of the United States applicable to the public domain, or who have occupied and improved or exercised acts of ownership over such claims, shall not be disturbed therein, but shall be allowed to perfect their title to such claims by payment as aforesaid. § 8, Id.

General Land Laws Not in Force in Alaska.— But nothing contained in this act shall be construed to put in force in said district the general land laws of the United States. § 8, Id.

Laws of Oregon Supplementary to, Not Amend-

atory of, Acts of Congress.—It is the purpose of the organic law of Alaska to continue the Federal legislation as paramount in the Territory, and not to treat the laws of Oregon, thereby adopted, as amendatory thereof, but, rather, as supplementary thereto.

LAWS OF OREGON MADE APPLICABLE THERETO.

Laws of Oregon Adopted.—"**That the general laws of the State of Oregon now in force are hereby declared to be the law in said district, so far as the same may be applicable and not in conflict with the provisions of this act or the laws of the United States." 23 S. L. 24, I Supp. 430.**

Organic Act.—The foregoing provision is part of the Organic act, "Providing a Civil Government for Alaska," adopted by Congress May 17, 1884.

Laws of Oregon—How Construed.—It will be observed that the language of the section quoted is not *retroactive* and that the laws thus applied to Alaska were those in force at the date of the passage of the act, viz., May 17, 1884. Subsequent repeals or amendments of those laws, or the passing of new ones, by the legislature of Oregon do not affect the laws of Alaska, which are those which were in force in Oregon on the date mentioned. Oregon was given by the act mentioned no authority to legislate for Alaska in the future and what laws have been adopted in that state since May 17, 1884, are immaterial so far as their application to Alaska is concerned.

"Applicable" Defined.—In using the word "applicable" in the above quoted statute, Congress has furnished to the courts a veritable puzzle for their solution, as the question will be involved wherever a law of Oregon is invoked in actions arising in Alaska. The construction of the above statute thus far adopted seems to indicate that the words "may be applicable" as thus used mean rather "should be applied" than "may be applied," and that in determining what laws of Oregon are applicable, the courts should consider Alaska's anomalous condition, the absence of fee ownership in lands, and the policy of the general government, in retaining absolute control over it. [1]

ASSERTION OF OWNERSHIP OF MINERAL LANDS BY THE UNITED STATES GOVERNMENT.

PROVISION OF U. S. STATUTES.

Mineral Lands Reserved.—In all cases lands valuable for minerals shall be reserved from sale, except as otherwise expressly directed by law. § 2318, R. S. U. S. 1878. 2d Edition.

Primary Source of Title.—Under the laws of

---

[1] For the cases construing the act of May 17, 1884, see: U. S. v. Mosely, 8 F. 688; U. S. v. Savaloff, 2 Sawy. 311; U. S. v. Stephens, 12 F. 52; Kie v. U. S., 27 F. 351; U. S. v. Nelson, 29 F. 202; In re Can-ah-can-qua, 29 F. 687; Nelson v. U. S., 30. F. 112; McAllister v. U. S., 11 S. C. R 949, 141 U. S. 174; Ex parte Cooper, 12 S. C. R. 453, 143 U. S. 472; Ex parte Kie, 46 F. 485; U. S. v. Clark, 46 F. 633; Miller v. Blackett, 47 F. 547; Ex parte Emma, 48 F. 211; U. S. v. Warwick, 51 F. 280; Finn v. Hoyt, 52 F. 83; U. S. v. Hillyer, 58 F. 678; In re Moore, 66 F. 947; Decker v. Williams, 73 F. 308; U. S. v. Ash, 75 F. 651; Holden v. Williams, 75 F. 798; Carroll v. Price, 81 F. 137; Bennett v. Harkrader, 15 S. C. R. 863, 158 U. S. 441; Carroll v. Price, 81 F. 137; Meydenbauer v. Stevens, 78 F. 787; Callsen v. Hope, 75 F. 758; Haltern v. Emmons, 46 F. 452.

England, the King, by the royal prerogative, was entitled to all mines of gold and silver, whether found in crown lands or in the lands of a subject, and was, in fact, regarded as the original proprietor of all lands in the Kingdom, and the primary source of title.

In the United States, Grant of Lands Includes Mineral.—The same principle has been adopted in this country, except that Congress has never asserted ownership in mines discovered in the lands of a subject where the Government has parted with the title without reservation. [2]

Patent Conveys Mineral Rights Notwithstanding Statutory Reservation.—"The land department in this very case, as in cases of patents to preemptioners, homestead claimants and other purchasers of the public lands, have acted, and, I think, correctly, upon the idea that patents to lands, not known to be mineral lands at the time the patent issued, carry the title to all mines subsequently discovered in the lands, notwithstanding the reservation from sale of mineral lands in the acts of Congress." Davis v. Wiebbold, 11 S. C. R. 628, 139 U. S. 507.

INDIVIDUAL TITLE TO MINERAL LANDS MAY BE ACQUIRED.
PROVISIONS OF U. S. STATUTES.
Mineral Lands Open to Purchase by Citizens.—All valuable mineral deposits in lands belonging

---

[2] Wight v. Dubois, 21 F. 693; Steel v. St. Louis S. & R. Co., 106 U. S. 447, 1 S. C. R. 389.

to the United States, both surveyed and unsurveyed, are hereby declared to be free and open to exploration and purchase, and the lands in which they are found to occupation and purchase, by citizens of the United States and those who have declared their intention to become such, under regulations prescribed by law, and according to the local customs or rules of miners in the several mining districts, so far as the same are applicable and not inconsistent with the laws of the United States. § 2319, Id.

LAND OFFICE REGULATIONS.

Different Kinds of Claims.—Mining claims are of two distinct classes: Lode claims and placers. § 1, circular, Dec. 15, 1897.

Meaning of Regulations.—It will be observed that the statute makes "regulations prescribed by law," of equal force with the statute itself. "Regulations prescribed by law" means the rules of procedure defined by statute or adopted by the executive branch of the Government, viz.—by the Secretary of the Interior, or by the Commissioner of the General Land Office, or by the Surveyor General, under the Secretary's direction.

"The Secretary of the Interior is charged with the supervision of public business relating to the following subjects: * * * * The public lands, including mines." § 441, R. S.

"The Commissioner of the General Land Office shall perform, under the direction of the Secretary of the Interior, all executive duties appertaining to the surveying and sale of the public lands of the United States, or in any wise respecting such public lands; and, also, such as relate to private claims of land, and the issuing of patents for all (grants) of land under the authority of the Government." § 453, Id.

Citizenship and Miners' Rules.—The subject of "citizenship" and of "the local customs or rules of miners in the several mining districts," mentioned in the foregoing statute, is elsewhere herein discussed.

Mining Rights Are Property.—The rights secured by the location of mining claims pursuant to the provisions of statute and the land office regulations are property rights, and are recognized and protected as such by law. Such property may, without infringing the title of the United States, be sold, transferred, mortgaged and inherited, but, prior to patent, mining claims are not subject to the wife's dower. [8]

Legal Status of Mining Claims.—"It has therefore been repeatedly held that mining claims are property, in the fullest sense of the word, and may be sold, transferred, mortgaged and inherited with-

[8] Forbes v. Gracey, 94 U. S. 762; Black v. Elkhorn M. Co., 16 S. C. R. 1101, 163 U. S. 445; Harkrader v. Carroll, 76 F. 474; Carson C. G. & S. M. Co. v. Norton S. M. Co., 73 F. 597; Doe v. Waterloo M. Co., 54 F. 935, 70 F. 455; Hamilton v. Southern N. G. & S. M. Co., 33 F. 562; Wakeman v. Norton, 49 P. 283, Col.; Patchin v. Keeley, 19 Nev. 404, 14 P. 347; Crossman v. Pendery, 8 F. 693; Union C. M. Co. v. Taylor, 100 U. S 42; Hopkins v. Noyes, 4 Mont. 550, 2 P. 280; Milton v. Lombard, 51 Col. 258; Harris v. Equator M. & S. Co., 8 F. 863.

out infringing the' title of the United States, and that when a location is perfected it has the effect of a grant by the United States of the right of present and exclusive possession." Manuel v. Wulff, 14 S. C. R. 651, 152 U. S. 505.

Locator's Interest.—"The interest in a mining claim, prior to the payment of any money for the granting of a patent for the land, is nothing more than a right to the exclusive possession of the land based upon conditions subsequent, a failure to fulfill which forfeits the locator's interest in the claim. We do not think that under the federal statute the locator takes such an estate in the claim that dower attaches to it." Black v. Elkhorn M. Co., 16 S. C. R. 1101, 163 U. S. 445.

Limitation of Placer Claims.—No such location (placer) shall include more than twenty acres for each individual claimant. § 2331, R. S.

LAW OF ALASKA.

Limitation of Lode Claims.—And the discoverer of any new lead or vein not previously located upon shall be allowed one additional claim for the discovery thereof. Nothing in this section shall be so construed as to allow any person not the discoverer to locate more than one claim upon any one lead or vein. Laws of Oregon, Oct. 24, 1864, § 3829 H. A. L. O. 1887.

Restrictions Upon Right of Acquisition.—By the foregoing provision of the laws of Oregon each locator on a vein or lode is restricted to one location, except the discoverer, who may have two, which, it will be observed, is in accordance with the policy of the federal legislation in reference to placer locations; but any person, otherwise qualified, is entitled to the benefit of the law, regardless of age or sex.

LENGTH OF LODE CLAIMS FIXED BY LAW.
PROVISION OF U. S. STATUTES.

Length of Mining Claims Upon Veins or Lodes. —Mining claims upon veins or lodes of quartz or other rock in place bearing gold, silver, cinnabar, lead, tin, copper, or other valuable deposits, heretofore located, shall be governed as to length along the vein or lode by the customs, regulations, and laws in force at the date of their location. A mining claim located after the tenth day of May, eighteen hundred and seventy-two, whether located by one or more persons, may equal, but shall not exceed, one thousand five hundred feet in length along the vein or lode. § 2320, Id.

LAND OFFICE REGULATIONS.

Prior Rights Not Affected.—The status of lode claims located or patented previous to the 10th day of May, 1872, is not changed with regard to their extent along the lode or width of surface; but the claim is enlarged by Sections 2322 and 2328, by investing the locator, his heirs or assigns, with the right to follow, upon the conditions stated therein, all veins, lodes, or ledges, the top or apex of which lies inside of the surface lines of his claim. § 2, circular, Dec. 15, 1897.

Rights of Prior Adverse Claimants Not Impaired.—It is to be distinctly understood, however, that the law limits the possessory right to veins, lodes or ledges, *other* than the one named in the original location, to such as were not *adversely claimed on May 10, 1872,* and that where such other vein or ledge was so adversely claimed at that date the right of the party so adversely claiming is in no way impaired by the provisions of the Revised Statutes. § 3, Id.

Provision Defined.—From and after the 10th May, 1872, any person who is a citizen of the United States, or who has declared his intention to become a citizen, may locate, record and hold a mining claim of *fifteen hundred linear feet* along the course of any mineral vein or lode subject to location; or an association of persons, severally qualified as above, may make joint location of such claim of *fifteen hundred feet*, but in no event can a location of a vein or lode made subsequent to May 10, 1872, exceed fifteen hundred feet along the course thereof, whatever may be the number of persons composing the association. § 4, Id.

LAW OF ALASKA.

Length 1,500 Feet.—"Any person or company of persons establishing a claim on any quartz lead containing gold, silver, copper, tin, or lead, or a claim or a vein of cinnabar, for the purpose of mining the same, shall be allowed to have, hold, and possess the lead or vein, with all its dips, spurs and angles, for the distance of fifteen hundred feet in length and three hundred feet in width on each side of such lead or vein." Laws of Oregon, Oct. 25, 1880, § 3827, H. A. L. O. 1887.

Not a Subject for Miners' Rules.—So far as Alaska is concerned the *length* of a lode claim is thus fixed by law at 1,500 feet, and it cannot be changed by "Miners' Rules."[4]

Length May Be 1,500 Feet Regardless of Local Laws or Rules.—"If discovered from the surface, the discoverer might, under Rev. St., § 2320, claim 'one thousand five hundred feet in length along the vein or lode.'" "It (the local law as to length) was superseded by the legislation of Congress, as found in the Revised Statutes." Enterprise M. Co. v. Rico-Aspen M. Co., 17 S. C. R. 762, 167 U. S. 108.

DISCOVERY THE INITIAL ACT IN THE ACQUISITION OF MINING RIGHTS.
PROVISION OF U. S. STATUTES.

No location until discovery.   * * * * **No location of a mining claim shall be made until the discovery of the vein or lode within the limits of the claim located. § 2320, Id.**

LAND OFFICE REGULATIONS.

No Location Before Discovery.—No lode claim shall be located until after the discovery of a vein or lode within the limits of the claim, the object of which provision is evidently to prevent the appropriation of presumed mineral ground for speculative purposes to the exclusion of bona fide prospectors, before sufficient work has been done to determine whether a vein or lode really exists. § 10, circular, Dec. 15, 1897.

Confirming Discovery.—The claimant should, therefore, prior to locating his claim, unless the vein can be traced upon the surface, sink a shaft, or

4 Meydenbauer v. Stevens, 78 F. 787

run a tunnel or drift, to a sufficient depth therein to discover and develop a mineral-bearing vein, lode or crevice; should determine, if possible, the general course of such vein in either direction from the point of discovery, by which direction he will be governed in marking the boundaries of his claim on the surface. § 11, Id.

LAW OF ALASKA.

Discovery Protected Thirty Days.—To establish a valid claim, the discoverer or person wishing to establish a claim shall post a notice on the lead or vein, with the name or names attached, which shall protect the claim or claims for thirty days, and before the expiration of said thirty days he or they shall cause the claim or claims to be recorded as hereinafter provided, and describing as near as may be the claim or claims and their location, but continuous working of said claim or claims shall obviate the necessity of such record. Laws of Oregon, Oct. 24, 1864, § 3828 H. A. L. O. 1887.

Preference to Discoverer.—And the discoverer of any new lead or vein not previously located upon shall be allowed one additional claim for the discovery thereof; nothing in this section shall be so construed as to allow any person not the discoverer to locate more than one claim upon any one lead or vein. Laws of Oregon, Oct. 24, 1864.

Advantage to Discoverer.—By the foregoing "Law of Alaska" the discoverer of a lode may locate two claims thereon, while others are restricted to one.

Discovery and the Discoverer's Rights.—The important questions under the foregoing provision of the U. S. statutes are, what constitutes *discovery*,[5] and what are the *rights of the discoverer?*[6]

For all practical purposes the following stated principles will be found to be sufficient answers thereto: "Discovery," as applied to lode claims, means the disclosing or detecting of mineral bearing rock in place; and the discoverer, who is on the ground prosecuting with reasonable diligence the necessary explorations to ascertain definitely the position and strike of the lode, by posting on the vein notice of his discovery and intention, is protected in his right to make his proper location for a reasonable time, which is fixed, as to Alaska, at the period of thirty days.

Miners' Rules.—Where these questions are involved the Miners' Rules of the different localities, if subsisting and generally recognized, may also be of importance in their solution.

No Priority of Right Until Discovery.—Of course, until the discovery of the vein or lode the rights of all prospectors are equal, and the mere finding of favorable indications, is not a "discovery," within the meaning of the statute.

Discovery the Inception of Rights.—The loca-

---

5 O'Reilly v. Campbell, 6 S. C. R. 421, 116 U. S. 48; Meydenbauer v. Stevens, 78 F. 787; Migeon v. Montana C. Ry. Co., 77 F. 249; Book v. Justice M. Co., 58 F. 106; Waterloo M. Co. v. Doe, 56 F. 685; Cheesman v. Shreeve, 40 F. 787; Hyman v. Wheeler, 29 F. 347; Erhardt v. Boaro, 8 F. 692; Crossman v. Pendery, 8 F. 693; Zollars v. Evans, 5 F. 172; North N. M. Co. v. Orient M. Co., 1 F. 522; McShane v. Kenkle, 44 P. 979, Mont.; Walsh v. Mueller, 40 P. 292, Mont.; Davidson v. Bordeaux, 40 P. 1075, Mont.; Watson v. Mayberry, 49 P. 479, Col.; Riste v. Morton, 49 P. 656, Mont.; Dobbs Placer, 1 L. D. 565; Kahn v. Old T. M. Co., 2 U. 174: Mt. Diablo M. & M. Co. v. Callison, 5 Sawy. 439; Book v. Justice, 58 F. 106; Sullivan v. Iron S. M. Co., 143 U. S. 431; Stevens v. Williams, 1 McCrary 480; Harrington v. Chambers, 3 U. 94, 1 P. 362.

6 Guillim v. Donnellan, 5 S. C. R. 1110, 115 U. S. 45; Richmond M. Co. v. Rose, 5 S. C. R. 1055, 114 U. S. 576; Doe v. Waterloo M. Co., 54 F. 935, 55 F. 11, 70 F. 455; Jupiter M. Co. v. Bodie C. M. Co., 11 F. 666; Patterson v. Tarbell, 37 P. 76 Or; Wight v. Tabor, 2 L. D. 738; North Noonday M. Co. v. Orient M. Co., 6 Sawy. 299; Jupiter M. Co. v. Bodie C. M. Co., 7 Sawy. 96.

tion, when completed, relates back to the time of
the discovery, and the title when acquired is regarded in law as having its inception at the same
date.   Notwithstanding the provision of statute, if
the location is made prior to discovery, the entry
will be valid, if other rights have not intervened.

Notice of Discovery.—As soon as the prospector
has discovered the lode or vein, as a precautionary
means, though perhaps not required by law, he
should at once post conspicuously thereon a notice
or warning, duly signed and dated, indicating his
intention to claim the same.   Form I, appendix.

Lode.—" 'The Miners,' to use his (a witness') language, 'made the definition first.'   As used by
miners, before being defined by any authority, the
term 'lode' simply meant that formation by which
the miner could be led or guided.   It is an altera-
tion of the verb 'lead,' and whatever the miner
could follow, expecting to find ore, was his lode.
Some formation within which he could find ore, and
out of which he could not expect to find ore, was his
lode.   The term 'lode star,' 'guiding star' or 'north
star,' he adds, is of the same origin.   *   *   *   A
fissure in the earth's crust, an opening in its rocks
and strata made by some force of nature, in which
the mineral is deposited, would seem to be essential
to the definition of a lode, in the judgment of
geologists.   But to the practical miner, the fissure
and its walls are only of importance as indicating
the boundaries within which he may look for and
reasonably expect to find the ore he seeks."   Eureka
M. Co. v. Richmond M. Co., 4 Sawyr. 302.

Indications.—"Under the requirements above quoted a valid location of a mining claim may be made whenever the prospector has discovered such indications of mineral that he is willing to spend his time and money in following, in expectation of finding ore, and that a valid location may be made of a ledge deep in the ground, and appearing at the surface not in the shape of ore, but in vein matter only." Harrington v. Chambers, 1 Pac. 375.

Value.—"Nor is it necessary that the ore shall be of economical value for treatment. It is enough if it is something ascertainable, something beyond a mere trace, which can be positively and certainly verified as existing in the ore." Stevens v. Gill, 1 Morr. M. R. 576.

Extent.—"A vein or lode authorized to be located is a seam or fissure in the earth's crust filled with quartz, or with some other kind of rock, in place, carrying gold, silver or other valuable mineral deposits named in the statute. It is not enough to discover detached pieces of quartz or mere bunches of quartz not in place.

"The vein, however, may be very thin, and it may be many feet thick or thin in places—almost or quite pinched out, in miners' phrase—and in other places widening out into extensive bodies of ore. So, also, in places it may be quite or nearly barren, and at other places immensely rich. It is only necessary to discover a genuine mineral vein or lode, whether small or large, rich or poor, at the point of discovery within the lines of the claim located, to entitle

25

the miner to make a valid location, including the vein or lode. It may, and often does, require much time and labor and great expense to develop a vein or lode, after discovery and location, sufficiently to determine whether there is a really valuable mine or not, and a location would be necessary before incurring such expense in developing the vein to secure to the miner the fruits of his labor and expense in case a rich mine should be developed.'' Jupiter M. Co. v. Bodie M. Co., 11 Fed. 666.

Continuity.—''Certainly the lode or vein must be continuous in the sense that it can be traced through the surrounding rocks, though slight interruptions of the mineral-bearing rock would not be alone sufficient to destroy the identity of the vein. Nor would a short partial closure of the fissure have that effect if a little further on it recurred again with mineral-bearing rock within it. And such is the idea conveyed in the previous part of the charge. 'On the other hand,' said the judge, 'with well-defined boundaries, very slight evidence of ore within such boundaries will prove the existence of a lode. Such boundaries constitute a fissure, and if in such fissure ore is found, although at considerable intervals and in small quantities, it is called a lode or vein.' '' Iron Silver M. Co. v. Cheesman, 116 U. S. 538.

Demarkation.—''An impregnation, to the extent to which it may be traced as a body of ore, is as fully within the broad terms of the act of Congress as any other form of deposit. * * * It is true that a lode must have boundaries, but there seems

26

to be no reason for saying that they must be such as can be seen. There may be other means of determining their existence and continuance, as by assay and analysis." Hyman v. Wheeler, 29 Fed. 347.

First in Time, First in Right.—"In all such cases, the first in time in the commencement of proceedings for the acquisition of the title, when the same are regularly followed up, is deemed to be the first in right." Shepley v. Cowan, 91 U. S. 330.

Discoverer Protected Against Intruders.—"They (the discoverers) could not be deprived of their inchoate rights by the tortious acts of others; nor could the intruders and trespassers initiate any rights which would defeat those of the prior discoverers. * * * And whenever preliminary work is required to define and describe the claim located, the first discoverer must be protected in the possession of the claim until sufficient excavations and development can be made, so as to disclose whether a vein or deposit of such richness exists as to justify work to extract the metal. Otherwise, the whole purpose of allowing the free exploration of the public lands for the precious metals would in such cases be defeated, and force and violence in the struggle for possession, instead of previous discovery, would determine the rights of claimants. * * * There must be something beyond a mere guess on the part of the miner to authorize him to make a location which will exclude others from the ground, such as the discovery of the precious metals in it, or in such proximity to it as to justify a reasonable belief in their existence. Then protection will be afforded to the locator to make the necessary excavations and prepare the proper certificate for record.'' Erhardt v. Boaro, 113 U. S. 527.

SIDE LIMITS OF LODE CLAIMS.
PROVISIONS OF U. S. STATUTES.

Width of Claims.—No claim shall extend more than three hundred feet on each side of the middle of the vein at the surface, nor shall any claim be limited by any mining regulation to less than twenty-five feet on each side of the middle of the vein at the surface, except where adverse rights existing on the tenth day of May, eighteen hundred and seventy-two, render such limitation necessary. § 2320, Id.

LAND OFFICE REGULATIONS.

Extent of Surface.—''With regard to the extent of surface ground adjoining a vein or lode, and claimed for the convenient working thereof, the Revised Statutes provide that the lateral extent of locations of veins or lodes made after May 10, 1872, shall in no case exceed 300 feet on each side of the middle of the vein at the surface, and that no such surface rights shall be limited by any mining regulations to less than twenty-five feet on each side of the middle of the vein at the surface, except where adverse rights existing on the 10th of May, 1872, may render such limitation necessary; the end lines

28

of such claims to be in all cases parallel to each other.

Lateral Limit 300 Feet.—Said lateral measurements cannot extend beyond 300 feet on either side of the middle of the vein at the surface, or such distance as is allowed by local laws. For example: Four hundred feet cannot be taken on one side and 200 feet on the other. If, however, 300 feet on each side are allowed, and by reason of prior claims but 100 feet can be taken on one side, the locator will not be restricted to less than 300 feet on the other side

Middle of Vein—How Determined.—And when the locator does not determine by exploration where the middle of the vein at the surface is, his discovery shaft must be assumed to mark such point. § 5, circular, Dec 15, 1897.

Effect of Statute—Parallelogram.—By the foregoing it will be perceived that no lode claim located after the 10th of May, 1872, can exceed a parallelogram 1,500 feet in length by 600 feet in width, but whether surface ground of that width can· be taken depends upon the local regulations or State or Territorial laws in force in the several mining districts; and that no such local regulations or State or Territorial laws shall limit a vein or lode claim to less than 1,500 feet along the course thereof, whether the location is made by one or more persons, nor can surface rights be limited to less than fifty feet in width unless adverse claims existing on the 10th day of May, 1872, render such lateral limitation necessary. § 6, Id.

LAW OF ALASKA.

Width 600 feet.—"Any person or company of persons establishing a claim on any quartz lead containing gold, silver, copper, tin, or lead, or a claim or a vein of cinnabar, for the purpose of mining the same, shall be allowed to have, hold and possess the land of vein, with all its dips, spurs and angles, for the distance of fifteen hundred feet in length and three hundred feet in width on each side of such lead or vein.'' Laws of Oregon, Oct. 25, 1880.

Not Subject to Regulation by Miners' Rules.—It will be seen, from the foregoing provision of the laws of Oregon, that the "width" of lode claims is not a subject for miners' regulations in Alaska, it being fixed at 300 feet on each side of the middle of the vein.

Attention is also directed to the construction placed on the above provision of the U. S. statutes by the U. S. Land Office. It is, in effect, that the width of a claim on either side of the middle cannot exceed 300 feet, no matter what may be the width on the other side. [7]

Middle of Vein to Be Designated.—It will be presumed that the discovery shaft marks the middle of the vein, unless it has been sufficiently developed to show where it is in fact, and that point designated in the location notice.

END LINES SHALL BE PARALLEL.

PROVISION OF U. S. STATUTES.

End Lines.—The end lines of each claim shall be parallel to each other. § 2320, Id.

There is no technical rule rendering locations void

[7] Lakin v. Roberts, 53 F. 333, 54 F. 461; Jupiter M. Co. v. Bodie C. M. Co., 11 F. 666; North N. M. Co. v. Orient M. Co., 1 F. 522.

because the end lines are not parallel. There may be cases when it will be found impracticable to observe the rule.

The serious consequence of the failure to observe the rule is the deprivation or jeopardizing of the locator's extra-lateral rights. [8]

End Lines May Become Side Lines.—"When a claim is located across, instead of along, the lode, its side lines must be treated as its end lines, and its end lines as its side lines." King v. Amy C. M. Co., 152 U. S. 222.

Parallelism Essential to Extra-Lateral Rights.—"Under the act of 1866, parallelism in the end lines of a surface location was not required, but where a location has been made since the act of 1872, *such parallelism is essential to the existence of any right in the locator or patentee to follow his vein outside of the vertical planes drawn through the side lines.* His lateral right by the statute is confined to such portion of the vein as lies between such planes drawn through the end lines, and extended in their own direction; that is, between paralleled vertical planes. It can embrace no other portion." Iron S. M. Co. v. Elgin Co., 118 U. S. 196.

Modification of Foregoing Doctrine.—"That the end lines are not parallel cannot be the basis of an objection, because their convergence, when extended in the direction of the dip of the vein, would give defendant less, instead of more, than the law

---

[8] Walrath v. Champion M. Co., 63 F. 552, 72 F. 978; Doe v. Waterloo M. Co., 54 F. 935; Chessman v. Hart, 42 F. 98; Montana Co. v. Clark, 42 F. 626.

provides for." Carson C. G. & S. M. Co. v. North
S. M. Co., 73 Fed. 597.

**Location Contemplated Is in Form a Parallelo-
gram.**—"A claim located in conformity with the
provisions of this section would take the form of a
parallelogram, if the course or strike of the vein or
lode should run in a straight line; but such veins
and lodes are often found, upon explorations, to run
in a course deviating at different points from such
line, and from this circumstance much difficulty
often arises in determining the lateral rights of the
locators." King v. Amy & S. C. M. Co., 14 S. C.
R. 510, 152 U. S. 222.

EXTRA-LATERAL RIGHTS SECURED BY LOCATIONS ON LODES.

PROVISION OF U. S. STATUTES.

**Locators' Rights of Possession and Enjoyment.
—The locators of all mining locations heretofore
made, or which shall hereafter be made, on any
mineral vein, lode or ledge, situated on the public
domain, their heirs and assigns, where no adverse
claim exists on the tenth day of May, eighteen
hundred and seventy-two, so long as they comply
with the laws of the United States, and with
State, territorial, and local regulations not in conflict with the laws of the United States governing
their possessory title, shall have the exclusive
right of possession and enjoyment of all the surface included within the lines of their locations,
and of all veins, lodes and ledges throughout their**

entire depth, the top or apex of which lies inside of such surface lines extended downward vertically, although such veins, lodes or ledges may so far depart from a perpendicular in their course downward as to extend out-side the vertical side lines of such surface locations.

Limits of Possession of Outside Veins.—But their right of possession to such outside parts of such veins or ledges shall be confined to such portions thereof as lie between vertical planes drawn downward as above described, through the end lines of their locations, so continued in their own direction that such planes will intersect such exterior parts of such veins or ledges. § 2322, Id.

LAND OFFICE REGULATIONS.

Locations Confined to Public Domain.—The rights granted to locators under Section 2322, Revised Statutes, are restricted to such locations on veins, lodes or ledges as may be "situated on the *public domain.*" In applications for lode claims where the survey conflicts with the survey or location lines of a prior valid lode claim and the ground within the conflicting surveys is excluded, the applicant not only has no right to the excluded ground, but he has no right to that portion of any vein or lode the top or apex of which lies within such excluded ground, unless his location was prior to May 10, 1872. His right to the lode claimed terminates where the lode, in its onward course or strike, intersects the exterior boundary of such excluded ground and passes within it. The end line of his survey should not, therefore, be established beyond such intersection. § 7, circular, Dec. 15, 1897.

Lines of Conflicting Surveys—How Established.
—Where, however, the lode claim for which survey
is being made was located prior to the conflicting
claim, and such conflict is to be excluded, in order
to include all ground not so excluded the end line
of the survey may be established within the conflicting lode claim, but the line must be so run as
not to extend any farther into such conflicting claim
than may be necessary to make such end line
parallel to the other end line and at the same time
embrace the ground so held and claimed. The
useless practice in such cases of extending *both* the
side lines of a survey into the conflicting claim, and
establishing an end line wholly within it, beyond a
point necessary under the rule just stated, will be
discontinued. § 8, Id.

The portion of the federal statutes above quoted
involves, principally, the question of the *extra-
lateral rights* of locators on veins or lodes. The
manner of making the location is considered under
another paragraph.

The principle here discussed seems to be in process
of evolution, and while in conflict with some of the
decisions, the true interpretation of the statute would
appear to lead to these conclusions:[9]

1. The U. S. statute contemplates locations in the
form of right angled parallelograms, lengthwise of
the veins or lodes, and upon their apexes.[10]

[9] Iron S. M. Co. v. Elgin M. S. Co., 6 S. C. R. 1177; Iron S. M. Co. v.
Chessman, 6 S. C. R. 481, 116 U. S. 529; Flagstaffs S. M. Co. v. Tarbet. 98
U. S. 463; Catron v. Old, 48 P. 687, Col.; Contra Fitzgerald v. Clark, 42 P.
273, Mont.; Walrath v. Champion M. Co., 63 F. 552, 72 F. 978; Doe v.
Waterloo M. Co., 54 F. 935, 70 F. 455; Book v. Justice M. Co., 58 F. 106;
Amadon M. G M. Co. v. South S. H. G. M. Co., 36 F. 668; Hymar v.
Wheeler, 29 L. D. 347.

[10] Meydenbauer v. Stevens, 78 F. 787; Book v. Justice M. Co., 58 F.
106; Bi-Metallic M. Co., 15 L. D. 309.

2. Prima facie, the locator is entitled to only the mineral lying within the planes of the boundary lines of his claim, extended vertically to the earth's center. [11]

3. The burden of proof is on the locator to show that his location is on the apex of the vein or lode which he seeks to follow on its dip outside of his side lines. [12]

4. A location made upon the dip of a vein carries with it no extra-lateral rights, though it is probably valid against a subsequent location on the apex of the same vein; and, being valid, terminates such subsequent locator's extra-lateral rights to whatever extent it conflicts therewith. [13]

5. Locations upon blanket veins or mere deposits, though consisting of rock in place, have no extra-lateral rights. [14]

6. Where veins unite below the surface, and locations have been made on the apexes of both veins, to the prior location belongs the right to follow the merged veins beyond the place of union. [15]

7. If the location is so made that the vein or lode intersects one end line and one side line, the location is voidable, until patented, beyond the point

---

11 Book v. Justice M. Co., 58 F. 106; Meydenbauer v. Stevens, 78 F. 787; Cheesman v. Shreeve, 37 F. 36; Driscoll v. Dunwoody, 16 P. 726, Mont.

12 Meydenbauer v. Stevens, 78 F. 787; Book v. Justice M. Co., 58 F. 106; Walrath v. Champion M. Co., 63 F. 552, 72 F. 978.

13 Meydenbauer v. Stevens, 78 F. 787; Book v. Justice M. Co., 58 F. 106; Bi-Metallic M. Co., 15 L. D. 309; Iron S. M. Co. v. Murphy, 368; Colorado S. C. M. Co. v. Turck, 50 F. 888, 54 F. 262; Androaeda Lode, 13 L. D. 146; Eilers v. Boatman, 3 U. 59, 2 P. 66.

14 Tabor v. Dexter, 9 Mor. M. R. 614.

15 Walrath v. Champion M. Co., 63 F. 552, 72 F. 978; Little Josephine M. Co. v. Fullerton, 58 F. 521; King v. Thomas, 12 P. 865, Mont.; Dorner v. Richards, 151 U. S. 658.

of intersection on the side line, at which point a new end line is thereby established parallel to the other end line, but the locator's right to follow the dip of his lode beyond the side lines as thus limited is unimpaired.[16]

8. If the location is made crosswise of the vein or lode, so that the same intersects both side lines, new end lines are thereby established drawn through said respective points of intersection at right angles to the side lines, the location is voidable, until patented, outside of said new end lines; if the distance between said new end lines is less than the width of the claim as located, they are to be regarded in law as new side lines, and the locator may follow the dip of his lode laterally beyond said new side lines; but if the distance between said new end lines is greater than the width of the claim as located, the lines do not become shifted by the fact that the vein or lode intersects both original side lines, but the right of the locator to follow the dip of his lode laterally beyond the original side lines as thus limited by the new end lines, remains, to that extent, unimpaired.[17]

Space forbids discussion of the conclusions above stated further than to say that it is believed that such a construction of the statute is logical, just and correct.

---

[16] Waterloo M. Co. v. Doe, 82 F. 45; Republican M. Co. v. Tyler M. Co., 79 F. 733; Mining Co. v. Sweeney, 54 F. 284; Last Chance M. Co. v. Tyler M. Co., 61 F. 557, 157 U. S. 683, 15 S. C. R. 733, 71 F. 848; Consolidated W. G. M. Co. v. Champion M. Co, 63 F. 540; Del Monte M. & M. Co. v. New York L. C. M. Co., 66 F. 212; Carson C. G. S. M. Co. v. North Star M. Co., 73 F. 597; Walrath v. Champion M Co., 63 F. 552, 72 F. 978; Col. C. C. M. Co. v. Turek, 50 F. 888; Catron v. Old, 48 P. 687, Col. contra.

[17] Argentine M. Co. v. Terrible M. Co., 7 S. C. R. 1356, 122 U. S. 478; New Dunderberg M. Co. v. Old, 79 F. 598; Tyler M. Co. v. Sweeney, 79 F. 277; Tyler M. Co. v. Last C. M. Co., 71 F. 848.

Conflict of Opinion.—The last, and perhaps also the seventh, proposition is undoubtedly in direct conflict with the decision referred to below in King v. Amy & S. C. M. Co., 14 S. C. R. 510, 152 U. S. 222; and, indeed, it would seem that Justice Field, of the U. S. Supreme Court, the most eminent of all authorities on questions of mining law, was committed to the doctrine, that a *locator had no extra-lateral rights unless his vein or lode intersected both end lines* of the claim as located on the ground; but granted that such may be the expressed position of that great jurist, the fact remains that his opinion can be regarded as scarcely more than personal, as is indicated by the case of Last Chance M. Co. v. Tyler quoted below, and that the U. S. Supreme Court considers the correct construction of the statute an unsettled question.

The Safe Course.—*Safety demands, however, that the locator should adopt the construction of the statute which requires the location to be marked on the ground in the form of a parallelogram so that both end lines will cross the vein.* A location in any other form may result in depriving the locator of valuable extra-lateral rights.

Correct Construction in Doubt.—"According to the orginal location of the Tyler claim the vein enters through an end and passes out through a side line, while by the amended location it passes in and out through end lines. Of course, if the latter is a valid location, the owner of the claim would unquestionably have the right to follow the vein on its dip beyond the vertical plane of the side line. But if it were not, and the original location was the only valid one, has the owner the right to follow the vein outside any boundaries of the claim extended downward? It has been held by this court in the cases heretofore cited that where the course of a vein is across, instead of lengthwise of the location, the side lines become the end lines, and the end the side lines; but there has been no decision as to what extra territorial rights exist if a vein enters at an end and passes out at a side line. Is that a case for which no provision has been made by statute? Are the parties left to the old rule of the common law—that the owner of real estate owns all above and below the surface, and no more? Or may the court rely upon some equitable doctrine, and give to the owner of the vein the right to pursue it on its dip, in whatever direction that may go, within the limits of some equitably created end lines?

If the common law rule as to real estate obtains in such a case, then, of course, on the original location the owners of the Tyler claim would have no right to follow the dip of their vein outside the vertical planes of any of its boundary lines, and even if the amended application was perfectly valid the question would arise whether the rights acquired under it related back to the date of the original location, or arose simply at the time of the amendment, in which case there would be no doubt of the fact that the owners of the Last Chance had by years a prior location. However, in the view we have taken of the other question, it is unnecessary to consider this." Last Chance M. Co. v. Tyler M. Co., 15 S. C. R. 733; 157 U. S. 683.

Apex May Be Line of Great Length.—"The apex of a vein is not necessarily a point, but often a line of great length, and any portion of the apex on the course or strike of the vein found within the limits of 'a claim is a sufficient discovery to entitle the locator to obtain title." Larkin v. Upton, 12 S. C. R. 614, 144 U. S. 19.

Where the Vein Intersects Both Side Lines They Are Legally Transmuted to End Lines, Regardless of Their Length [669 feet] After Transmutation, as Compared With the Original Width of the Claim [491 feet].—"In the Amy claim, the lines marked as side lines cross the course of the strike of the vein, and do not run parallel with it. They therefore constitute end lines. * * * Applying this doctrine to the case before us, it follows that the vein in controversy, the apex of which was within the surface lines of the Amy claim, did not carry the owner's right beyond the vertical plane drawn down through the north side line of that claim. The Amy claim had no lateral-right by virtue of the extension of the vein through what was called the 'north side' of its claim, as that side line so-called was, in fact, one of its end lines." King v. Amy & S. C. M. Co., 14 S. C. R. 510, 152 U. S. 222.

LOCATOR ENTITLED TO UNDISTURBED POSSESSION OF SURFACE OF HIS CLAIM.

PROVISION OF U. S. STATUTES.

Not Authorized to Enter Upon Surface of Another's Claim.—And nothing in this section shall authorize the locator or possessor of a vein or lode which extends in its downward course beyond the vertical lines of his claim to enter upon the surface of a claim owned or possessed by another. § 2322, Id.

Effect of Compliance with the Law.—It is also provided in the same section of the statutes as that from which the above extract is taken, that locators "shall have the exclusive right of possession and enjoyment of all the surface included within the lines of their locations," so long as they comply with the laws. [18]

The result of the foregoing provisions may be summed up as follows:

1. **The locator of a valid mining claim** enjoys the same protection in his possession thereof as any owner of real estate.

2. **No one may enter thereon adversely** while the claimant is complying with the law, and such an intruder can acquire no rights therein even by excluding the rightful claimant therefrom until he is in default.

3. **Even for public purposes,** or under the power of *eminent domain*, the claimant's use or possession

[18] Meydenbauer v. Stevens, 78 F. 787.

cannot be interfered with, except by due compensation for the injury.

PRIORITY OF LOCATION CONTROLS OWNERSHIP OF LODE INTERSECTIONS.

PROVISION OF U. S. STATUTES.

Where Veins Intersect, Etc.—Where two or more veins intersect or cross each other, priority of title shall govern, and such prior location shall be entitled to all ore or mineral contained within the space of intersection; but the subsequent location shall have the right of way through the space of intersection for the purposes of the convenient working of the mine. And where two or more veins unite, the oldest or prior location shall take the vein below the point of union, including all the space of intersection. § 2336, Id.

Intersection of Veins, Not of Claims.—By reason of the preceding provision of law guaranteeing to the owners of valid mining claims "the exclusive right of possession and enjoyment of all the surface included within the lines of their location and of all veins, lodes and ledges throughout their entire depth the top or apex of which lies inside of such surface lines," it has been contended that in case of the intersection of veins the prior location took all of the intersecting vein lying within its boundary lines. The plain words of the statute are the sufficient refutation of that argument, for it expressly limits the right of the prior location to "all ore or mineral contained within the space of *"intersection"* of *"two or more veins,"* not of two or more claims.[19]

Where veins merge into one, the united vein belongs to the first location.

MINING TUNNELS, MANNER OF LOCATION AND RIGHTS SECURED THEREBY.

PROVISION OF U. S. STATUTES.

Owners of Tunnels, Rights of.—Where a tunnel is run for the development of a vein or lode, or for the discovery of mines, the owners of such tunnel shall have the right of possession of all veins or lodes within three thousand feet from the face of such tunnel on the line thereof, not previously known to exist, discovered in such tunnel, to the same extent as if discovered from the surface; and locations on the line of such tunnel of veins or lodes not appearing on the surface, made by other parties after the commencement of the tunnel, and while the same is being prosecuted with reasonable diligence, shall be invalid. § 2323, Id.

LAND OFFICE REGULATIONS.

Effect of Statute Defined.—The effect of this is simply to give the proprietors of a mining tunnel run in good faith the possessory right to 1,500 feet of any blind lodes cut, discovered or intersected by such tunnel, which were previously not known to exist, within 3,000 feet from the face or point of commencement of such tunnel, and to prohibit other

---

19 Book v. Justice M. Co., 58 F. 106; Little Josephine M. Co. v. Fullerton, 58 F. 521; Chessman v. Hart, 42 F. 98.

parties, after the commencement of the tunnel, from prospecting for and making locations of lodes on the *line thereof* and within said distance of 3,000 feet, unless such lodes appear upon the surface or were previously known to exist. § 19, circular, Dec. 15, 1897.

"Face" Means Point of Entrance.—The term "face," as used in said section, is construed and held to mean the first working face formed in the tunnel, and to signify the point at which the tunnel actually enters cover; it being from this point that the 3,000 feet are to be counted upon which prospecting is prohibited as aforesaid. § 20, Id.

Proprietors Must Give Notice of Location.—To avail themselves of the benefits of this provision of law, the proprietors of a mining tunnel will be required, at the time they enter cover as aforesaid, to give proper notice of their tunnel location by erecting a substantial post, board or monument at the face or point of commencement thereof, upon which should be posted a good and sufficient notice, giving the names of the parties or company claiming the tunnel right; the actual or proposed course or direction of the tunnel; the height and width thereof, and the course and distance from such face or point of commencement to some permanent well known objects in the vicinity by which to fix and determine the *locus* in manner heretofore set forth applicable to locations of veins or lodes. § 21, Id.

Must Erect Stakes or Monuments.—And at the time of posting such notice they shall, in order that miners or prospectors may be enabled to determine whether or not they are within the lines of the tunnel, establish the boundary lines thereof, by stakes or monuments placed along such lines at proper intervals, to the terminus of the 3,000 feet from the face or point of commencement of the tunnel, and the lines so marked will define and govern as to the specific boundaries within which prospecting for lodes not previously known to exist is prohibited while work on the tunnel is being prosecuted with reasonable diligence. § 21, Id.

Notice Must Be Recorded.—At the time of posting notice and marking out the lines of the tunnel as aforesaid, a full and correct copy of such notice of location defining the tunnel claim must be filed for record with the mining recorder of the district, to which notice must be attached the sworn statement or declaration of the owners, claimants or projectors of such tunnel, setting forth the facts in the case; stating the amount expended by themselves and their predecessors in interest in prosecuting work thereon; the extent of the work performed, and that it is *bona fide* their intention to prosecute work on the tunnel so located and described with reasonable diligence for the development of a vein or lode, or for the discovery of mines or both, as the case may be. This notice of location must be duly recorded, and, with the said sworn statement attached, kept on the recorder's files for future reference. § 22, Id.

Compliance Urged.—By a compliance with the foregoing much needless difficulty will be avoided, and the way for the adjustment of legal rights acquired in virtue of said Section 2323 will be made much more easy and certain. § 23, Id.

Speculative Locations Prohibited.—This office will take particular care that no improper advantage is taken of this provision of law by parties making or professing to make tunnel locations, ostensibly for the purposes named in the statute, but really for the purpose of monopolizing the lands lying in front of their tunnels to the detriment of the mining interests and to the exclusion of *bona* *fide* prospectors or miners, but will hold such tunnel claimants to a strict compliance with the terms of the statutes; and a *reasonable diligence* on their part in prosecuting the work is one of the essential conditions of their implied contract. Negligence or want of due diligence will be construed as working a forfeiture of their right to all undiscovered veins on the line of such tunnel. § 24, Id.

Locator's Peril.—It is apparent that one who locates a claim on the line of a tunnel in process of construction, does so at his peril, unless the vein was known to exist before the location of the tunnel site, for if the tunnel reaches such vein within 3,000 feet of its face, it is appropriated to the tunnel proprietor.[20] FORM 5.

Right of Way.—Tunnels undoubtedly have right of way, for purposes of discovery, but where injury is caused to prior claimants, due compensation must be made.

Doctrine of Relation, Time of Location, Length of Claim, Location May Be All or Partly on One Side.—"If discovered from the surface, the discoverer might, under Rev. St., § 2320, claim 'one thousand five hundred feet in length along the vein or lode.' The clear import of the language, then, is to give to the tunnel owner discovering a vein in the tunnel, a right to appropriate 1,500 feet in length of that vein. * * * The discovery in the tunnel is like a discovery on the surface. Until one is made, there is no right to locate a claim in re-

[20] Glacier M. S. M. Co. v. Willis, 8 S. C. R. 1214, 127 U. S. 471; Back v. Sierra N. C. M. Co., 2 I 386, 17 P. 83.

spect to the vein, and the time to determine where and how it shall be located arises only upon the discovery—whether such discovery be made on the surface or in the tunnel. * * *

"We hold, therefore, that the right to a vein discovered in the tunnel dates, by relation, back to the time of the location of the tunnel site, and also that the right of locating the claim to the vein arises upon its discovery in the tunnel, and may be exercised by locating that claim the full length of 1,500 feet on either side of the tunnel, or in such proportion thereof on either side as the locator may desire." Enterprise M. Co. v. Rico-Aspen M. Co., 17 S. C. R. 762, 167 U. S. 108.

Failure to Mark on Surface.—"Does the failure to mark on the surface of the ground the point of discovery and the boundaries of the tract claimed destroy the right of the tunnel owner to the veins he has discovered in the tunnel? * * * The conditions surrounding a vein or lode discovered in a tunnel are such as to make against the idea or necessity of a surface location. * * * But, without determining what would be the rights acquired under a surface location based upon a discovery in a tunnel, it is enough to hold, following the plain language of the statute, that the discovery of the vein in a tunnel, worked according to the provisions of the statute, gives a right to the possession of the vein to the same length as if discovered from the surface, and that a location on the surface is not essential to a continuance of that right." Campbell v. Ellet, 17 S. C. R. 765, 167 U. S. 116.

Posting Notice of Claim.—"We do not mean to hold that such right of possession can be maintained without compliance with the provisions of the local statutes in reference to the record of the claim, or without posting in some suitable place, conveniently near to the place of discovery, a proper notice of the extent of the claim—in other words, without any practical location; for in this case notice was posted at the mouth of the tunnel, and no more suitable place can be suggested, and a proper notice was put on record in the office named in the statute." Campbell v. Ellet, 17 S. C. R. 765, 167 U. S. 116.

ABANDONMENT OF TUNNELS.

PROVISION OF U. S. STATUTES.

Failure to Work for Six Months, Abandonment. —But failure to prosecute the work on the tunnel for six months shall be considered as an abandonment of the right to all undiscovered veins on the line of such tunnel. § 2323, Id.

LABOR ON TUNNEL IS LABOR ON CLAIM.

Tunnels, Cost of—How Treated. —That Section 2324 of the Revised Statutes be, and the same is hereby, amended so that where a person or company has or may run a tunnel for the purpose of developing a lode or lodes, owned by said person or company, the money so expended in said tunnel shall be taken and considered as expended on said lode or lodes, whether located prior to or since the passage of said act; and such person or company shall not be required to perform work on the surface of said lode or lodes in order to hold the same as required by said act. § 2324, Id., 18 S. L. 315.

LAND OFFICE REGULATIONS.

Fraudulent Tunnel Locations.—This office will take particular care that no improper advantage is taken of this provision of law by parties making or professing to make tunnel locations, ostensibly for the purposes named in the statute, but really for the purpose of monopolizing the lands lying in front of their tunnels to the detriment of the mining interests and to the exclusion of *bona fide* prospectors or miners, but will hold such tunnel claimants to a strict compliance with the terms of the statutes; and a *reasonable diligence* on their part in prosecuting the work is one of the essential conditions of their implied contract. Negligence or want of due diligence will be construed as working a forfeiture of their right to all undiscovered veins on the line of such tunnel. § 24, circular, Dec. 15, 1897.

Six Months' Abandonment.—Locations made on the line of a tunnel after six months' cessation of work thereon, upon lodes not discovered by means of the tunnel, are valid.[20]

AUTHORITY OF MINERS TO ADOPT AND ENFORCE RULES AND REGULATIONS.

Regulations Made by Miners.—The miners of each mining district may make regulations not in conflict with the laws of the United States, or with the laws of the State or Territory in which the district is situated, governing the location, manner of recording, amount of work necessary to hold possession of a mining claim, subject to the following requirements: § 2324, Id.

LAND OFFICE REGULATIONS.

Miners' Rules as to Recording.—The location notice must be filed for record in all respects as required by the State or Territorial laws and local rules and regulations, if there be any. § 13, circular, Dec. 15, 1897.

LAW OF ALASKA.

Miners' Rules and Customs Provable as Facts.— On the trial of an action to recover the possession of a mining claim, the customs, usages or regulations established and in force in the mining district or diggings in which such claim is situated not in conflict with any law of the United States or of this State, so far as they may be pertinent and applicable to the issue to be tried, may be proven as facts, and when so proven shall be deemed the law governing the rights of the parties thereto. Laws of Oregon, Oct. 21, 1864, § 2181, H. A. L. O. 1887.

Right of Purchase Limited by Miners' Rules.— Any person may hold one claim by location, as hereinafter provided, upon each lead or vein, and as many by purchase as the local laws of the miners in the district where such claims are located may allow. Laws of Oregon, Oct. 24, 1864, § 3829, H. A. L. O. 1887.

Organizing Mining Districts.—It shall be the duty of the county clerk of any county, upon the receipt of notice of a miner's meeting organizing a miner's district in said county, with a description of the boundaries thereof, to record the same in a book to be kept in his office as other county records, to be called a "book of record of mining claims;"

and upon the petition of parties interested, he may appoint a deputy for such district who shall reside in said district or its vicinity, and shall record all mining claims and water rights in the order in which they are presented for record, and shall transmit a copy of such record at the end of each month to the county clerk, who shall record the same in the above mentioned book of record, for which he shall receive one dollar for each and every claim. It shall further be the duty of said county clerk to furnish a copy of this law to his said deputy, who shall keep the same in his office, open at all reasonable times for the inspection of all persons interested therein. Laws of Oregon, Oct. 21, 1864, § 3831, H. A. L. O. 1887.

Scope of Miners' Rules.—Miners shall be empowered to make local laws in relation to the possession of water rights, the possession and working of placer claims, and the survey and sale of town lots in mining camps, subject to the laws of the United States. Laws of Oregon, Oct. 24, 1864, § 3832, H. A. L. O. 1887.

Primitive Legislation.—The provision of the federal statute above quoted deserves to be characterized as primitive legislation.

When the law was enacted, it undoubtedly was proper enough to recognize the rights and titles which had accrued prior thereto under the regulations adopted by the miners, but to authorize the continuance of miners' legislation was to subject those engaged, or to engage, in that business, to perpetual uncertainty as to their rights, and to discredit the industry as a legitimate pursuit.[21]

---

[21] Glacier M. S. M. Co. v. Willis, 8 S. C. R. 1214, 127 U. S. 471; Jennison v. Kirk, 98 U. S. 453; Meydenbauer v. Stevens, 78 F. 787; Jupiter M. Co. v. Bodie C. M. Co., 11 F. 666; North N. M. Co. v. Orient M. Co., 1 F. 522; Strong v. Ryan, 46 Cal. 33.

Restrictions on Right to Purchase Claims.—The provision of the laws of Oregon authorizing miners to restrict individual purchases would, undoubtedly, be held void, so far as it conflicts with § 2326, R. S. U. S., which provided that, "Nothing herein contained shall be construed to prevent the alienation of the title conveyed by a patent for a mining claim to any person whatever."

Before patent such restrictions might be valid, being authorized by law, but they could have no force outside of the district for which they were adopted. [22]

BOUNDARIES OF CLAIM MUST BE MARKED ON GROUND.

PROVISION OF U. S. STATUTES.

Location Must Be Marked.—The location must be distinctly marked on the ground so that its boundaries can be readily traced.   § 2324, Id.

LAND OFFICE REGULATIONS.

Importance of Due Location.—Locators cannot exercise too much care in defining their locations at the outset, inasmuch as the law requires that all records of mining locations made subsequent to May 10, 1872, shall contain the name or names of the locators, the date of the location and such a *description of the claim or claims* located, by reference to some natural object or permanent monument, as will identify the claim. § 9, circular, Dec. 15, 1897.

Discovery Precedes Location.—No lode claim

[22] English v. Johnson, 17 Cal. 108; Prosser v. Parks, 18 Cal. 48; Table M. T. Co. v. Stranahan, 20 Cal. 209; Patterson v. Keystone M. Co., 23 Cal. 576; Hess v. Winder, 30 Cal. 355.

shall be located until after the discovery of a vein
or lode within the limits of the claim, the object of
which provision is evidently to prevent the appropriation of presumed mineral ground for speculative purposes to the exclusion of *bona fide* prospectors, before sufficient work has been done to determine whether a vein or lode really exists. § 10, Id.

How Marked.—The claimant should, therefore,
prior to locating his claim, unless the vein can be
traced upon the surface, sink a shaft, or run a tunnel or drift, to a sufficient depth therein to discover
and develop a mineral-bearing vein, lode or crevice; should determine, if possible, the general
course of such vein in either direction from the point
of discovery, by which direction he will be governed
in marking the boundaries of his claim on the surface. His location notice should give the course
and distance as nearly as practicable from the discovery shaft on the claim to some permanent, well
known points or objects, such, for instance, as stone
monuments, blazed trees, the confluence of streams,
point of intersection of well known gulches, ravines
or roads, prominent buttes, hills, etc., which may
be in the immediate vicinity, and which will serve
to perpetuate and fix the *locus* of the claim and
render it susceptible of identification from the description thereof given in the record of locations in
the district, and should be duly recorded. § 11, Id.

Stakes and Monuments.—In addition to the foregoing data, the claimant should state the names of
adjoining claims, or, if none adjoin, the relative
positions of the nearest claims; should drive a post
or erect a monument of stones at each corner of his
surface ground, and at the point of discovery or discovery shaft should fix a post, stake or board, upon
which should be designated the name of the lode,
the name or names of the locators, the number of

52

feet claimed, and in which direction from the point of discovery; it being essential that the location notice filed for record, in addition to the foregoing description, should state whether the entire claim of 1,500 feet is taken on one side of the point of discovery or whether it is partly upon one and partly upon the other side thereof, and in the latter case, how many feet are claimed upon each side of such discovery point. § 12, Id.

Only Marking Actually Required.—'' Rev. St., § 2324, merely requires that the locations shall be distinctly marked on the ground, so that their boundaries can be readily traced.'' Haws v. Victoria C. M. Co., 16 S. C. R. 282, 160 U. S. 303.

There is no law applicable to Alaska requiring more than this, but, perhaps, expensive litigation and great loss, as well as all contention and question, can be avoided by following the directions given below:[28]

Relocation by Owner.—In case development proves that the supposed discovery in the discovery shaft, tunnel, drift or adit is a false lead, but the true vein is elsewhere discovered on the claim before adverse rights accrue, it is probable that the location would not be void, but the claimant should adopt the safe course and relocate the claim.[24]

Claim May Be Marked by Stakes and Identified

---

[28] Meydenbauer v. Stevens, 78 F. 787; Cheesman v. Shreeve, 40 F. 787; Brown v. Levan, 46 P. 661, Idaho; Howeth v. Sullenger, 45 P. 841, Cal., Willeford v. Bell, 49 P. 6, Cal.; Richmond M. Co. v. Rose, 5 S. C. R. 1055; 114 U. S. 576; Carroll v. Price, 81 F. 187; Gird v. California O. Co., 60 F. 531; Crœsus M. M. & S. Co. v. Colorado L. & M. Co , 19 F. 78; Taylor v. Parenteau, 48 P. 505, Col.

[24] Cheesman v. Shreeve, 40 F. 787; Fuller v. Harris, 29 F. 814; McEvoy v. Hyman, 25 P. 596; Fisher v. Seymour, 49 P. 30, Col.; Philpotts v. Blasdell, 8 Nev. 61.

by Reference to Another Claim.—"A reference to some natural object or permanent monument is named for that purpose. Of course, the section means when such reference can be made. Mining lode claims are frequently found where there are no permanent monuments or natural objects other than rocks or neighboring hills. Stakes driven into the ground are, in such cases, the most certain means of identification. Such stakes were placed here, with a description of the premises by metes, and, to comply with the requirements of the statute as far as possible, the location of the lode is also indicated by stating its distance south of 'Vaughan's Little Jennie Mine,' probably the best known and most easily defined object in the vicinity." Hammer v. Garfield M. & M. Co., 9 S. C. R. 548, 130 U. S. 291.

Indefinite Description May Not Invalidate Certificate.—"Conceding the indefiniteness of the description in the certificate, it does not follow that it is absolutely void, for, as said by this court in Hammer v. Milling Co., 130 U. S. 291, 299, 9 Sup. Ct. 548, after quoting from Section 2324: 'These provisions, as appears on their face, are designed to secure a definite description—one so plain that the claim can be readily ascertained. A reference to some natural object or permanent monument is named for that purpose. Of course the section means, when such reference can be made. Mining lode claims are frequently found where there are no permanent monuments or natural objects other than rocks or neighboring hills. Stakes driven into the ground are in such cases the most certain means of identification.' ''   Bennett v. Harkrader, 15 S. C. R. 863, 158 U. S. 441.

The most important act in the locating of a mining claim is the marking of its boundaries on the ground, as the location is governed by the boundaries as marked, rather than by the certificate of location.[25]

Directions for Marking.—The following directions will comply with the laws of the United States, the regulations of the Interior Department, and with any miners' rules likely to be adopted:[25]

1. The boundaries should be marked before the location certificate is filed.

2. A "discovery shaft" should be sunk or a drift or tunnel run, until it uncovers the vein in place, and in any event the shaft should be ten feet deep, the tunnel ten feet below the surface where it intersects the vein, and the drift or adit should be ten feet along the vein.

3. The boundaries should be marked in the form of a parallelogram so that the vein will intersect both end lines.

4. A "location stake" should be set within the claim, upon which should be posted a description of the location.

5. Stakes should be set at each corner of the claim, in the middle of the side lines, and on the end lines where they intersect the middle of the vein, hewed on the *in* side or sides, and numbered.

---

[25] Meydenbáuer v. Stevens, 78 F. 787; Book v. Justice M. Co., 58 F. 106; Walrath v. Champion M. Co., 63 F. 552, 72 F. 978.

6. A location notice should be posted on the "location stake," stating the date of discovery, the name of the lode, the point of discovery, the number of feet claimed on each side of that point, and the direction of the strike. FORM 2.

7. The lines may be further indicated, also, by blazing trees, clearing off the underbrush if any, or by staking, piling stones or marking thereon in any way so as to make them perceptible to ordinary observation. FORM 3.

8. If the character of the ground is such that stakes cannot be driven they may be set in piles of stone; and if they cannot be set at their proper places they may be fixed at the nearest points thereto, having distinctly marked thereon the course and distance from their proper locations.

The Location of a Claim.—By discovery and demarkation as above suggested, the location of a claim is completed, unless the law or Miners' Rules require a record of the location to be made. It is always best to complete the record of the claim as soon as possible, even where not absolutely necessary, and in Alaska the record should be made, unless the claim is being continuously worked, as elsewhere stated, within thirty days after the discovery. In the sense in which the word "location" is used in mining law, it means the necessary acts of appropriation, while the word "claim" means the land appropriated, and may include several locations.

Location carries with it the right of possession, which is in law a property right and may be the subject of sale and transfer. While the title to a claim of value should be perfected and a patent obtained, the locator is not required to do so, and comparatively few avail themselves of that advantage.[26] · FORM 4.

RECORDING OF CLAIMS.

PROVISION OF U. S. STATUTES.

Records of Claims, Shall Contain What.—All records of mining claims hereafter made shall contain the name or names of the locators, the date of the location, and such a description of the claim or claims located by reference to some natural object or permanent monument as will identify the claim. § 2324, Id.

LAND OFFICE REGULATIONS.

Care Required.—Locators cannot exercise too much care in defining their locations at the outset, inasmuch as the law requires that all records of mining locations made subsequent to May 10, 1872, shall contain the name or names of the locators, the date of the location and such a *description of the claim or claims* located, by reference to some natural object or permanent monument, as will identify the claim. § 9, circular, Dec. 15, 1897.

Local Laws or Rules Control.—The location notice must be filed for record in all respects as re-

---

[26] Carroll v. Price, 81 F. 187; Meydenbauer v. Stevens, 78 F. 787; North N. M. Co. v. Orient M. Co., 1 F. 522, 11 F. 125; Aurora H. Co. v. 85 M. Co., 34 F. 515; Moyle v. Bullene, 44 P. 69, Col.; Moore v. Hamerslay, 41 P. 805, Cal.; Gleson v. Martin White M. Co., 13 Nev. 442; Poire v. Wells, 6 Col. 406; Mt. Diablo M. & M. Co. v. Callison, 5 Sawy. 439, 5 Land D. 199; St. Louis S. Co. v. Kemp, 104 U. S. 636; McFetters v. Pierson, 15 Col. 201, Golden Terra; M. Co. v. Smith, 2 Dak. 377; Forbes v. Gracey, 94 U. S. 762.

quired by the State or Territorial laws and local rules and regulations, if there be any. § 13, Id.

Same Rule Applies to Placers.—The regulations hereinbefore given as to the manner of marking locations on the ground, and placing the same on record, must be observed in the case of placer locations so far as the same are applicable, the law requiring, however, that where placer claims are upon *surveyed* public lands the locations must hereafter be made to conform to legal subdivisions thereof as near as practicable. § 36, Id.

Survey and Plat to Be Filed in Land Office.—The survey and plat of mineral claims required to be filed in the proper land office with application for patent must be made subsequent to the recording of the location of the mine. § 40, Id.

LAW OF ALASKA.

Claim Shall Be Recorded.—To establish a valid claim, the discoverer or person wishing to establish a claim shall post a notice on the lead or vein, with the name or names attached, which shall protect the claim or claims for thirty days, and before the expiration of said thirty days he or they shall cause the claim or claims to be recorded as hereinafter provided, and describing as near as may be the claim or claims, and their location, but continuous working of said claim or claims shall obviate the necessity of such record. If any claim shall not be worked for twelve consecutive months, it shall be forfeited and considered liable to location by any person or persons, unless the owner or owners be absent on account of sickness or in the service of their country in time of war. Laws of Oregon, Oct. 24, 1864, § 3828, H. A. L. O. 1887,

CERTIFICATES OF MINING LOCATIONS, WHERE RECORDED.

Clerk of Court, Keeper of Public Records.—He (the clerk of the U. S. District Court for Alaska) shall be ex-officio recorder of deeds and mortgages and *certificates of location of mining claims* and other contracts relating to real estate and register of wills for said district, and shall establish secure offices in the towns of Sitka and Wrangel, in said district, for the safekeeping of all his official records, and of records concerning the reformation and establishment of the present status of titles to lands, as hereinafter directed. § 4, 23 S. L. 24, Vol. I Supp. 430.

Court May Establish Separate Recording Offices to Be in Charge of Commissioners.—Provided, That the district court hereby created may direct, if it shall deem it expedient, the establishment of separate offices at the settlements of Wrangel. Oonalashka and Juneau City (and Kadiak), respectively, for the recording of such instruments as may pertain to the several natural divisions of said district most convenient to said settlements, the limits of which shall, in the event of such direction, be defined by said court; and said offices shall be in charge of the commissioners respectively as hereinafter provided. § 4, .Id.

Nine Commissioners to Be Appointed.—That there shall be appointed by the President (nine) commissioners in and for the said district who shall have the jurisdiction and powers of commissioners of the United States Circuit Courts in any part of said district, but who shall reside, one at Sitka, one at Wrangel, one at Oonalashka, one at Juneau City (and one at Kadiad), and four at points to be designated by the President.   § 5, Id., as amended.

Requirements as to Alaska Defined.—The effect of the foregoing legislation is to require, as to Alaska, that the certificate of location be recorded, unless the claim is being continuously worked, and that, otherwise, within thirty days of the time of discovery such certificates shall be recorded with the commissioners for the district in which the claim is located, he being *ex-officio* clerk of the U. S. District Court for that district. [27]

Exception as to Occupant.—While the claimant is occupying his claim, personally or by agent or employe, and is engaged daily in the work of development, no record is necessary, provided it is duly marked out on the ground and has posted thereon a description of the claim.

Not Subject to Local Legislation.—The law as thus defined is not subject to change by local law or miners' rules, but only by act of Congress, notwithstanding that, generally speaking, "Section 2324, of the Revised Statutes, makes the manner of locating mining claims and recording them subject to the laws of the State or Territory, and the regulations of each mining district, when they are not in conflict with the laws of the United States."   Kendall

[27] Haws v. Victoria C. M. Co., 16 S. C. R. 282, 160 U. S. 308; Meydenbauer v. Stevens, 78 F. 787; Preston v. Hunter, 67 F. 996; Fuller v. Harris, 29 F. 814; Jupiter M. Co. v. Bodie C. M. Co., 11 F. 666.

v. San Juan S. M. Co., 12 S. C. R. 779, 144 U. S. 658.

Trespasser Can Acquire No Rights.—"In an action to recover possession of mining claims, it appeared that one of defendants, while employed by plaintiff in working these claims, of which the latter was in actual possession, conceived the intention of taking possession thereof for his own benefit; that he procured the assistance of another defendant in making a pretended location on the same ground; that shortly thereafter the former defendant in the night time ousted plaintiff, and that the illegal dispossession thus accomplished was thereafter maintained by force. Held, that defendants, being mere intruders or trespassers, without even color of title, could not allege the insufficiency or illegality of plaintiff's title by way of defense to the action." Haws v. Victoria C. M. Co., 16 S. C. R. 282, 160 U. S. 303.

Location on Reserved Land.—"Where a party was in possession of a mining claim on the withdrawal of a reservation caused by a treaty with the Indians, with the requisite discovery, with surface boundaries sufficiently marked, with a notice of location posted, and with a disclosed vein of ore, he could, by adopting what had been done, and causing a proper record to be made, and performing the amount of labor or making the improvements necessary to hold the claim, date his rights from that day. * * * As they failed to comply with the law in making a record of the location certificate of their lode, it does not lie with them to insist that their wrongful entry upon the premises during the existence of the Indian reservation operated in their favor against parties who went upon the premises after they had become a part of the public domain, and made a proper location certificate and record thereof, and complied in other particulars with the requirements of the law." Kendall v. San Juan S. M. Co., 12 S. C. R. 779, 144 U. S. 658.

Location Certificate.—The location is not regarded as complete until the location certificate is filed for record in the proper office. The essentials of such a certificate are:

1. The name of the locator.

2. The date of location.

3. A description of the claim by reference to natural objects or permanent monuments, sufficient to identify it.[28] FORM 4.

Date of Discovery in Location Certificate.—It should also contain the date of discovery, as that is the time of the inception of the locator's rights, and to which his title will relate, when he obtains it.

Ties.—The only difficulty in preparing the certificate of location is in describing the claim. The certificate should simply describe the boundaries as marked on the ground, giving the course and distance from the discovery shaft and at least one corner stake each, or from each of at least two corner stakes, to at least two natural points or objects, or

---

[28] Preston v. Hunter. 67 F. 996; Gird v. California O. Co., 60 F. 531; Book v. Justice M. Co., 58 F. 106; First N. B. v. Bissell, 4 F. 694; Gleeson v. Martin White M. Co., 13 Nev. 442; Book v. Justice M. Co., 58 F. 106; Jupiter M. Co. v. Bodie C. M. Co , 11 F. 666.

established monuments, sufficiently prominent and permanent to be easily identified, and from which the *locus* of the claim may be ascertained at any time.

CLAIMS FORFEITED UNLESS WORK PERFORMED OR IMPROVEMENTS MADE THEREON.

PROVISION OF U. S. STATUTES.

Labor Required Annually.—On each claim located after the tenth day of May, eighteen hundred and seventy-two, and until a patent has been issued therefor, not less than one hundred dollars' worth of labor shall be performed or improvements made during each year. On all claims located prior to the tenth day of May, eighteen hundred and seventy-two, ten dollars' worth of labor shall be performed or improvements made by the tenth day of June, eighteen hundred and seventy-four, and each year thereafter, for each one hundred feet in length along the vein until a patent has been issued therefor; but where such claims are held in common, such expenditure may be made upon any one claim; § 2324, Id.

Tunnels, Cost of—How Treated. Labor on Tunnel Is Labor on Claim.—That Section 2324, of the Revised Statutes, be, and the same is hereby, amended so that where a person or company has or may run a tunnel for the purposes of developing a lode or lodes, owned by said person or company, the money so expended in said tunnel shall be taken and considered as expended on said lode or lodes, whether located prior to or since the passage of said act; and such person or company shall not be required to perform work on the surface of said lode or lodes in order to hold the same as required by said act. § 2324, Id.

On Unpatented Claims Year's Work Required by Law, to Commence January 1, After Location.— "Provided, That the period within which the work required to be done annually on all unpatented mineral claims shall commence on the first day of January succeeding the date of location of such claim, and this section shall apply to all claims located since the tenth day of May, Anno Domini, eighteen hundred and seventy-two." 21 Stat. L. 61, I Supp. 276.

LAND OFFICE REGULATIONS.

Prior to May 10, 1872.—In order to hold the possessory title to a mining claim located prior to May 10, 1872, and for which a patent has not been issued, the law requires that *ten dollars* shall be expended annually in labor or improvements on each claim of *one hundred feet* on the course of the vein or lode until a patent shall have been issued therefor; but where a number of such claims are held in common upon the same vein or lode, the aggregate expenditure that would be necessary to hold all the claims, at the rate of ten dollars per hundred feet, may be made upon any one claim. The first annual expenditure upon claims of this class should have been performed subsequent to May 10, 1872, and prior to January 1, 1875. From and after January 1, 1875, the required amount must be expended *annually* until patent issues. § 14, Id, circular, Dec. 15, 1897.

Since May 10, 1872.—In order to hold the possessory right to a location made since May 10, 1872, not less than one hundred dollars' worth of labor must be performed or improvements made thereon annually until entry shall have been made. Under the provisions of the act of Congress, approved January 22, 1880, the first annual expenditure becomes due and must be performed during the calendar year succeeding that in which the location was made. Expenditure made or labor performed prior to the first day of January succeeding the date of location will not be considered as a part of or applied upon the first annual expenditure required by law. § 15, Id.

Forfeiture.—Failure to make the expenditure or perform the labor required upon a location made before or since May 10, 1872, will subject a claim to relocation, unless the original locator, his heirs, assigns or legal representatives have resumed work after such failure and before relocation. § 16, Id.

Certificate of Entry Equivalent to Patent.—Annual expenditure is not required subsequent to entry, the date of issuing the patent certificate being the date contemplated by statute. § 17, Id.

LAW OF ALASKA.

Not Worked for Twelve Months.—If any claim shall not be worked for twelve consecutive months, it shall be forfeited, and considered liable to location by any person or persons, unless the owner or owners be absent on account of sickness or in the service of their country in time of war. Laws of Oregon, Oct. 24, 1864, § 3828, H. A. L. O. 1887.

Superseded by U. S. Statutes.—Every person or company of persons, after establishing such claim or claims, shall, within one year after recording or taking such claim or claims, work or cause to be worked such claim to the amount of fifty dollars for each and every claim.

Owner of Several Claims May Work on One.— Provided, That any person or company, either joint or incorporate, owning claims on any lead or vein, shall be allowed to work upon any one claim the whole amount required as above for all the claims, and thereby be exempted from working on the rest of his or their claims in said lead or vein.

Record Proof of Compliance With Law.—Provided further, That when the individual, company or corporation owning any quartz claim or claims shall file the affidavit of said owner or one of the members of the company or corporation with the county clerk of the county in which said claims are situated, to the effect that the amount of work required by this act has been performed on such claim (or if there be more than one claim then on each of them), together with the affidavit of two disinterested persons to the same effect, with the addition, "that they are not interested directly or indirectly in said claim or claims," and such claims shall thereafter be considered as real estate, and the title therein shall be vested in such person, company or corporation against all others, save the government of the United States; and the improvements, machinery and buildings thereon only shall be taxed as other property. Laws of Oregon, Dec. 19, 1865, § 3830, H. A. L. O. 1887.

Purchase Certificate Dispenses With Requirement of Annual Labor.—"In other words, when the price is paid, the right to a patent immediately arises. * * * There is no conflict in the rulings of this court upon the question. With one voice they affirm that when the right to a patent exists the full equitable title has passed to the purchaser, with all the benefits, immunities and burdens of ownership, and that no third party can acquire from the government interests as against him.'' Benson M. & S. Co. v. Alta M. & S. Co., 12 S. C. R. 877, 145 U.S. 428.

The effect of all the foregoing legislation and regulations as to annual labor on claims is:

1. Extent of Annual Expenditure.—Work or improvements to the extent of at least $100 are required annually, since May 10, 1872, on each claim. [29]

2. First Year.—No work or improvements other than that necessary to make a valid location are required during the year in which the location is made.

3. No Date Fixed.—The required work may be done or improvements made at any time during the year, for instance, on the first day of one year and the last day of the next.

4. Character of Work.—Any work done or improvements made, to the extent of $100 annually, with reference to the development of the lode, will comply with the law, whether such development is by means of tunnel, shaft, drift, adit or surface excavation. It is not necessary that the expenditure be made on the claim, if it be for the purpose of its development; and the character of the work or im-

---

[29] Book v. Justice M. Co., 58 F. 106; Gird v. California O. Co., 160 F. 531; Axiom M. Co. v. White et al., 72 N. W. 462, S. D.; Hirschler v. McKindricks, 40 P. 290, Mont.

provements is immaterial, if they contribute to that result. [30]

5. How Long Required.—The annual labor or improvements are required "until a patent has been issued" whether or not the aggregate exceeds $500, but when patent has been duly applied for, the land paid for, and entry made, the "purchase certificate" issued by the register and receiver of the local land office is equivalent to a patent. [31]

6. Record proof of the annual labor or improvements is not required as it should be, but the law of Alaska (Oregon) permits that course to be pursued, and the privilege should certainly be taken advantage of by all claimants to thus secure stability and authoritativeness of title. [32]

7. $500 Expenditure.—Upon March 14, 1898, rule 53 of the circular of December 15, 1897, was amended so as to require an aggregate of $500 worth of labor or improvements for each location, no matter how many locations may be included in a "claim," to entitle a claimant to a patent.

The old rule, that it was a sufficient compliance with the law to prove $500 worth of labor or improvements on the "claim" regardless of the number of locations it might include, is still applied to cases in which "applications for patent were made and passed to entry before July 1, 1898, or which are by

---

[30] Gird v. California O. Co., 60 F. 531; St. Louis S. & R. Co. v. Kemp, 11 F. 94; U. S. v. Iron S. M. Co., 24 F. 568; Altoona Q. M. Co. v. Untegral Q. M. Co., 45 P. 1047, Cal.

[31] Aurora H. C. M. Co. v. 85 M. Co., 34 F. 515.

[32] Book v. Justice M. Co., 58 F. 106.

protests or adverse claims prevented from being passed to entry before that time.''

` **8. $500—How Computed.**—If the applicant can show that the aggregate of his expenditure for labor or improvements on his claim since he located or acquired the same, no matter how many years may have elapsed in the interim in which he was completely in default, his proof will be sufficient as to that requirement of law. [33]

9. Personal Requirement.—Improvements on a purchased claim cannot be availed of so as to dispense with the requirement of annual labor. [34]

RELOCATION OF CLAIMS.

PROVISION OF U. S. STATUTES.

Forfeited Claims May be Relocated.—And upon a failure to comply with these conditions, the claim or mine upon which such failure occurred shall be open to relocation in the same manner as if no location of the same had ever been made, provided that the original locators, their heirs, assigns or legal representatives, have not resumed work upon the claim after failure and before such location. § 2324, Id.

LAND OFFICE REGULATIONS.

Default Subjects Claim to Relocation.—Failure to make the expenditure or perform the labor required upon a location made before or since May 10,

[33] Royston v. Miller, 76 F. 50; Eberle v. Carmichael, 42 P. 95, N. M., Lincoln Placer, 7 L. D. 81.
[34] Noonan v. Caledonia G. M. Co., 7 S. C. R. 911, 121 U. S. 393.

1872, will subject a claim to relocation, unless the original locator, his heirs, assigns or legal representatives have resumed work after such failure and before relocation.   § 16, circular, Dec. 15, 1897.

Conveyance Equivalent to Abandonment.—"We are of opinion, therefore, that by the conveyance of Mrs. Black's husband to his grantee of all his interest as locator in the mining claim in question, he abandoned all his right and interest in the claim to his grantee, and that interest which thus passed to his grantee was not subject to any possible incumbrance of the wife by way of dower in the premises. The interest granted by the United States was of such a nature that a conveyance of Black's right to the possession terminated it to the same extent as if it had been forfeited by non-performance of the conditions provided for in the statute, and hence the wife has no claim for dower in the premises." Black v. Elkhorn M. Co., 16 S. C. R. 1101, 163 U. S. 445.

Forfeiture Must Be Clearly Established.—"A forfeiture cannot be established except upon clear and convincing proof of the failure of the former owner to have work performed or improvements made to the amount required by law." Hammer v. Garfield M. & M. Co., 9 S. C. R. 548, 130 U. S. 291.

From the foregoing legislation in reference to the forfeiture and relocation of claims, considered in connection with the discussion of the preceding parts of § 2324, the following deductions are made:

1. For What Causes Forfeited.—Claims not properly marked on the ground, not recorded when recording is required, or upon which the required annual expenditure has not been made, are subject to forfeiture; but forfeiture may in all such cases be obviated by compliance with the law on the part of the locator, at any time before adverse rights have accrued. [85]

2. Annual Labor.—Where the right to relocate is claimed for failure to perform the annual labor or make the required improvements, the original claimant may cure the default by resuming work on his claim at any time before the relocation is completed. [86]

3. Defaults Cured, Immaterial.—The claimant applying for a patent is entitled thereto if the aggregate of his expenditures on his claim, since location, equals $500, and it is immaterial that during that time there were any number of years in which no labor was performed or improvements made thereon. [86]

4. Default Excused.—Forfeiture cannot be predicated against one who has been wrongfully excluded from the premises during the time of the alleged default. [87]

[85] Book v. Justice M. Co., 58 F. 106; Harkrader v. Carroll, 76 P. 474; Preston v. Hunter, 67 F. 996; Justice M. Co. v. Barclay, 82 F. 554; Slavonian M. Co. v. Perasich, 7 F. 321; Bishop v. Baisley, 31 P. 936, Or.; McCormick v. Baldwin, 37 P. 903, Ca·.

[86] Axiom M. Co. v. White, et al., 72 N. W. 462, S. D.; Dibble v. Castle C. G. M. Co., 70 N. W. 1055, S. D.; Lockhart v. Wills, 50 P. 318. N. M.; Strasburger v. Beecher, 49 P. 740, Mont.; Lakin v. Sierra B. G. M. Co., 25 F. 337; Chambers v. Harrington, 4 S. C. R. 428; 111 U. S., 350; Jackson v. Roby, 3 S. C. R., 306; 109 U. S., 440; Jupiter M. Co. v. Bodie C. M. Co., 11 F. 666; St. Louis S. R. Co. v. Kemp, 11 F. 94.

[87] Haws v. Victoria C. M. Co., 16 S. C. R. 282, 160 U. S. 303; Slavonian M. Co. v. Perasich, 7 F. 321; Trevaskis v. Peard, 44 P. 246, Cal.

5. Annual Labor, Personal Requirement.—One relocating a forfeited or abandoned claim may, for the purpose of perfecting his location, avail himself of the improvements thereon, and may adopt the same boundaries, marking, ties, etc., as the original locator had, but the annual labor or improvements must be his own contribution.

FORFEITURE BY CO-OWNER.
PROVISION OF U. S. STATUTES.

Rights of Co-Owners.—Upon the failure of any one of several co-owners to contribute his proportion of the expenditures required hereby, the co-owners who have performed the labor or made the improvements may, at the expiration of the year, give such delinquent co-owner personal notice in writing or notice by publication in the newspaper published nearest the claim, for at least once a week for ninety days, and if at the expiration of ninety days after such notice in writing or by publication such delinquent should fail or refuse to contribute his proportion of the expenditure required by this section, his interest in the claim shall become the property of his co-owners who have made the required expenditures. § 2324, Id.

LAND OFFICE REGULATIONS.

Proceedings Against Delinquent Co-Owner.—Upon the failure of any one of several co-owners of a vein, lode or ledge, which has not been entered, to contribute his proportion of the expenditures necessary to hold the claim or claims so held in ownership in common, the co-owners, who have performed the labor or made the improvements as required by said Revised Statutes, may, at the expiration of the year, give such delinquent co-owner personal notice in writing, or notice by publication in the newspaper published nearest the claim for at least once a week for ninety days; and if upon the expiration of ninety days after such notice in writing, or upon the expiration of one hundred and eighty days after the first newspaper publication of notice, the delinquent co-owner shall have failed to contribute his proportion to meet such expenditures or improvements, his interest in the claim by law passes to his co-owners who have made the expenditures or improvements as aforesaid. § 18, circular, Dec. 15, 1897.

Proof of Notice and Default Required.—Where a claimant alleges ownership of a forfeited interest under the foregoing provision, the sworn statement of the publisher as to the facts of publication, giving dates and a printed copy of the notice published, should be furnished, and the claimant must swear that the delinquent co-owner failed to contribute his proper proportion within the period fixed by the statute. § 18, Id.

The theory of the foregoing enactment is that the government is the owner of the land, that it may impose such conditions as it sees fit upon the privilege of entering and mining thereon, that those availing themselves of that privilege consent to the conditions, and that upon failure to comply therewith they may be excluded from the land in pursuance of the provisions and conditions. [88]

Service Personal or by Publication.—While it is

always the better practice to serve personally any notice which is to become the basis of property rights, yet it was the evident purpose of Congress, in passing the law quoted, to give to the party seeking the remedy in question the option to make the service personal or by publication regardless of the whereabouts of the party in default, and in that view the statute has been upheld in the late case of Elder v. Horseshoe M. & M. Co., 70 N. W. 1160, S. D.

Only Co-Owner in the Year in Which Labor Is Performed Can Assert Forfeiture.—"The right to acquire by forfeiture, under Rev. St., § 2324, the part interest of one who fails to pay his proportion of the expenditure for annual labor, exists only in favor of one who is a co-owner in the year for which such labor is performed." Turner v. Sawyer, 14 S. C. R. 192, 150 U. S. 578.

Lien Claimant Not a Co-Owner.—"One is not a 'co-owner,' within the meaning of the statute, who merely holds a sheriff's certificate of purchase at an execution sale of a part interest; for title does not pass until he receives a deed thereunder." Turner v. Sawyer, 14 S. C. R. 192, 150 U. S. 578.

Fiduciary Relation Between Co-Owners.—"The owner of a part interest in a mining claim is a co-tenant with the other owners; and if, without their knowledge, he procures a patent in his own name, he becomes a trustee for them, and equity will enforce

88 Royston v. Miller, 76 F. 50; Riste v. Morton, 49 P. 656, Mont.; Bissell v. Foss, 5 S. C. R. 851, 114 U. S. 252; Johnston v. Robinson, 16 F. 903; Continental D. M. I. Co. v. Bliley, 46 P. 633, Col.; Union C. M. Co. v. Taylor, 100 U. S. 42; Hunt v. Patchin, 35 F. 816.

the trust in their favor." Turner v. Sawyer, 14 S. C. R. 192, 150 U. S. 578.

Co-Owner Need Not Adverse.—"The provision of Rev. St., §§ 2325, 2326, for filing adverse claims before the register, does not apply when there is no dispute as to location or boundaries, and the controversy only arises upon the claim of one party to have acquired the interest of the other by legal proceedings." Turner v. Sawyer, 14 S. C. R. 192, 150 U. S. 578.

ABSOLUTE TITLE TO MINERAL LAND MAY BE ACQUIRED BY PATENT.

PROVISION OF U. S. STATUTES.

Patents For Mineral Lands—How Obtained.—A patent for any land claimed and located for valuable deposits may be obtained in the following manner: § 2325, Id.

Application, Plat, Affidavit.—Any person, association or corporation authorized to locate a claim under this chapter, having claimed and located a piece of land for such purposes, who has, or have, complied with the terms of this chapter, may file in the proper land office an application for a patent, under oath, showing such compliance, together with a plat and field notes of the claim or claims in common, made by or under the direction of the United States Surveyor General, showing accurately the boundaries of the claim or claims, which shall be distinctly marked by monuments on the ground, and shall post a copy of such plat, together with a notice of such application for a patent in a conspicuous place on the land embraced in such plat previous to the filing of the application for a patent, and shall file an affidavit of at least two persons that such notice has been duly posted, and shall file a copy of the notice in such land office, and shall thereupon be entitled to a patent for the land, in the manner following: § 2325, Id.

LAND OFFICE REGULATIONS.

Claims in Controversy.—Before receiving and filing a mineral application for patent, local officers will be particular to see that it includes no land which is embraced in a prior or pending application for patent or entry, or for any lands embraced in a railroad selection, or for which publication is pending or has been made by any other claimants, and if, in their opinion, after investigation, it should appear that a mineral application should not, for these or other reasons, be accepted and filed, they should formally reject the same, giving the reasons therefor, and allow the applicant thirty days for appeal to this office under the Rules of Practice. § 49, circular, Dec. 15, 1897.

Survey First Steps.—The claimant is required, in the first place, to have a correct survey of his claim made under authority of the surveyor general of the State or Territory in which the claim lies, such survey to show with accuracy the exterior surface boundaries of the claim, which boundaries are required to be distinctly marked by monuments on the ground. Four plats and one copy of the original field notes in each case will be prepared by the surveyor general; one plat and the original field notes to be retained in the office of the surveyor general, one copy of the plat to be given the claimant for posting upon the claim, one plat and a copy of the field notes to be given the claimant for filing with the proper register, to be finally transmitted by that officer, with other papers in the case, to this office, and one plat tó be sent by the surveyor general to the register of the proper land district, to be retained on his files for future reference. As there is no resident surveyor general for the State of Arkansas, applications for the survey of mineral claims in said State should be made to the commissioner of this office, who, under the law, is *ex-officio* the U. S. surveyor general. § 39, Id.

Location Must Be Recorded.—The survey and plat of mineral claims required to be filed in the proper land office with application for patent must be made subsequent to the recording of the location of the mine; and when the original location is made by survey of a United States deputy surveyor such location survey cannot be substituted for that required by the statute, as above indicated. § 40, Id.

Accuracy Required.—The notices so published and posted must be as full and complete as possible, and embrace all the *data* given in the notice posted upon the claim. Too much care cannot be exercised in the preparation of these notices, inasmuch as upon their accuracy and completeness will depend, in a great measure, the regularity and validity of the whole proceeding. § 51, Id.

Present Possessory Right.—Accompanying the field notes so filed must be the sworn statement of the claimant that he has the possessory right to the premises therein described, in virtue of a compliance by himself (and by his grantors, if he claims by purchase) with the mining rules, regulations and customs of the mining district, State or Territory

77

in which the claim lies, and with the mining laws of Congress; such sworn statement to narrate briefly, but as clearly as possible, the facts constituting such compliance, the origin of his possession, and the basis of his claim to a patent. § 46, Id.

Copy of Location Notice.—This sworn statement must be supported by a copy of the location notice, certified by the officer in charge of the records where the same is recorded, and where the applicant for patent claims the interests of others associated with him in making the location or only as purchaser, in addition to the copy of the location notice must be furnished a complete abstract of title as shown by the record in the office where the transfers are by law required to be recorded, certified to by the officer in charge of the record, under his official seal. The officer should also certify that no conveyances affecting the title to the claim in question appear of record other than those set forth in the abstract, which abstract shall be brought down to the date of the application for patent. Where the applicant claims as sole locator, his affidavit should be furnished to the effect that he has disposed of no interest in the land located. § 47, Id.

Lost Records.—In the event of the mining records in any case having been destroyed by fire or otherwise lost, affidavit of the fact should be made, and secondary evidence of possessory title will be received, which may consist of the affidavit of the claimant, supported by those of any other parties cognizant of the facts relative to his location, occupancy, possession, improvements, etc.; and in such case of lost records, any deeds, certificates of location or purchase, or other evidence which may be in the claimant's possession and tend to establish his claim, should be filed. § 48, Id.

The requirements, under the portion of the U. S.

statutes above quoted, on the part of an applicant for a patent are:

1. That the location certificate should be recorded in the proper recording office.

2. That a survey of the claim should be made by the U. S. Surveyor General, and a copy of his plat and field notes filed in the proper land office.

3. That a copy of the plat, with a notice that the claimant intends to apply for a patent for the platted claim, thereon described, be posted on the claim.

4. That a copy of the notice thus posted, with the affidavit of two witnesses that the same has been duly posted, be filed in the land office.

5. That the affidavit of two or more witnesses be filed proving that the claimant has complied with the law during the year when the application is made and that the claim is not subject to relocation.

6. That the formal application be filed, showing the claimant's compliance with the law and his right to possession and patent, to which should be added a certified copy of the certificate of location, an abstract of title and proof of citizenship.

The proceedings to procure a survey require:

1. An application to the surveyor general for an estimate of the total cost of the work.

2. The deposit of the required sum in a U. S. depository or treasury, and the procuring of triplicate certificates of deposit, one to be retained, one forwarded to the Secretary of the Treasury at Washington, D. C., and one to be attached to the application for survey.

3. An application to the surveyor general of the district for the survey of the claim, to which should be attached a copy of the certificate of deposit and a duly certified copy of the certificate of location, suggesting the name of some authorized deputy surveyor to whom the order for the survey should be sent.

4. The actual survey of the claim as located by a deputy surveyor and the making of a plat and field notes by him, with a detailed statement of the labor done or improvements made thereon, and the value of the same.

5. The preparation by the surveyor general of the official plat of said claim and the approved field notes duly certified to.

Skill and Experience Required in Patent Proceedings.—As the land office does not furnish blanks or forms, except those to be used by its own officers, the applicant must prepare all other papers required in the case, and in doing so should invariably avail himself of the assistance of an experienced mining lawyer, who should supervise the preparation of even the official papers.

PUBLICATION.

PROVISION OF U. S. STATUTES.

Publication of Notice.—The register of the land office, upon the filing of such application, plat, field notes, notices and affidavits, shall publish a notice that such application has been made, for the period of sixty days, in a newspaper, to be by him designated as published nearest to such claim; and he shall also post such notice in his office for the same period. § 2325, Id.

LAND OFFICE REGULATIONS.

Requirements.—Upon the receipt of these papers, if no reason appears for rejecting the application, the register will, at the expense of the claimant (who must furnish the agreement of the publisher to hold applicant for patent alone responsible for charges of publication), publish a notice of such application for the period of sixty days in a newspaper published nearest to the claim, and will post a copy of such notice in his office for the same period. When the notice is published in a *weekly* newspaper, ten consecutive insertions are necessary; when in a *daily* newspaper, the notice must appear in each issue for sixty-one consecutive issues, the first day of issue being excluded in estimating the period of sixty days. § 50, circular, Dec. 15, 1897.

Established Newspaper.—The register shall publish the notice of application for patent in a paper of established character and general circulation, to be by him designated as being the newspaper published nearest the land. § 52, Id.

Proof.—After the sixty days' period of newspaper publication has expired, the claimant will furnish from the office of publication a sworn statement that the notice was published for the statutory period, giving the first and last day of such publication, and his own affidavit showing that the plat and notice aforesaid remained conspicuously posted upon the claim sought to be patented during said sixty days' publication, giving the dates. § 56, Id.

Essentials of Publication.—The requirements above made are:[39]

---

[39] Wight v. Dubois, 21 F. 693.

1. That a copy of the publisher's receipt of payment, or agreement to absolve the Government from responsibility, for the publication, be filed; and

2. That proof of publication be filed when the period has expired.

PROOF OF IMPROVEMENTS.

PROVISION OF U. S. STATUTES.

Certificate of $500' Worth Of Labor Or Improvements.—The claimant at the time of filing this application or at any time thereafter, within the sixty days of publication, shall file with the register a certificate of the United States Surveyor-General that five hundred dollars' worth of labor has been expended or improvements made upon the claim by himself or grantors; that the plat is correct, with such further description by such reference to natural objects or permanent monuments as shall identify the claim, and furnish an accurate description, to be incorporated in the patent. § 2325, Id.

LAND OFFICE REGULATIONS.

Labor for Current Year.—As a condition for the making of application for patent according to Section 2325, there must be a preliminary showing of work or expenditure upon each location, either by showing the full amount sufficient to the maintenance of possession under Section 2324 for the pending year; or, if there has been failure, it should be shown that work has been resumed so as to prevent relocation by adverse parties after abandonment.

The "pending year" means the calendar year in which application is made, and has no reference to a showing of work at date of the final entry. § 37, circular, Dec. 15, 1897.

Proved by Two Witnesses.—This preliminary showing may, where the matter is unquestioned, consist of the affidavit of two or more witnesses familiar with the facts. § 38, Id.

$500 Expenditure Required on Each Location.— The claimant at the time of filing the application for patent, or at any time within the sixty days of publication, is required to file with the register, a certificate of the surveyor general that not less than five hundred dollars' worth of labor has been expended or improvements made, by the applicant or his grantors, upon each location embraced in the application, or if the application embraces several locations held in common, that an amount equal to $500 dollars for each location, has been so expended upon, and for the benefit of, the entire group; that the plat filed by the claimant is correct; that the field notes of the survey, as filed, furnish such an accurate description of the claim as will if incorporated in a patent serve to fully identify the premises and that such reference is made therein to natural objects or permanent monuments as will perpetuate and fix the locus thereof. *Provided*, That as to all applications for patent made and passed to entry before July 1, 1898, or which are by protests or adverse claims prevented from being passed to entry before that time, where the application embraces several locations held in common, proof of an expenditure of $500 upon the group will be sufficient and an expenditure of that amount need not be shown to have been made upon, or for the benefit of, each location embraced in the application. § 53, circular, Dec. 15, 1897, as amended March 14, 1898.

Basis of Information.—The surveyor general should derive his information upon which to base his certificate as to the value of labor expended or improvements made from his deputy who makes the actual survey and examination upon the premises, and such deputy should specify with particularity and full detail the character and extent of such improvements. § 54, Id.

Duplicate Certificate.—It will be the more convenient way to have this certificate indorsed by the surveyor general, both upon the plat and field notes of survey filed by the claimant as aforesaid. § 55, Id.

Duplicate Certificate.—It is the usual practice, and undoubtedly more convenient, to have the certificate above required filed at the time the application for patent is made, as it can then be made part of the plat and field notes. The plat here referred to is that prepared under the direction of the surveyor general from the one furnished by the deputy surveyor.

The land office has adopted the practice of requiring two such certificates, one on the plat and the other on the approved field notes.

What Justifies Certificate.—Since the amendment of land office rule No. 53, above quoted, made March 14, 1898, the certificate above required will be issued only upon proof of labor having been done or improvements made to the extent of $500 on or for each location included in the claim.

The rule in the department has been, however, in pursuance of the supposed authority of the Supreme Court, that it was sufficient to show labor or improvements to the extent of $500 on the "claim" for which a patent was sought, regardless of the number of locations it might include.

The old rule is still applied to those cases in which "applications for patent were made and passed to entry before July 1, 1898, or which are by protests or adverse claims prevented from being passed to entry before that time."[40]

POSTING.

PROVISION OF U. S. STATUTES.

Affidavit of Posting.—At the expiration of the sixty days of publication the claimant shall file his affidavit, showing that the plat and notice have been posted in a conspicuous place on the claim during such period of publication. § 2325, Id.

LAND OFFICE REGULATIONS.

Posting on Claim.—The claimant is then required to post a copy of the plat of such survey in a conspicuous place upon the claim, together with notice of his intention to apply for a patent therefor, which notice will give the date of posting, the name of the claimant, the name of the claim; the mining district and county; whether or not the location is of record, and, if so, where the record may be found, giving the book and page thereof; the number of feet claimed along the vein and the presumed direction thereof; the number of feet claimed on the lode in each direction from the point of discovery or other well defined place on the claim; the names of

---

40 Haws v. Vistoria C. M. Co., 16 S. C. R. 282, 160 U. S. 303.

all adjoining and conflicting claims, or, if none exist, the notice should so state. § 44, circular, Dec. 15, 1897.

Proof of Posting.—After posting the said plat and notice upon the premises, the claimant will file with the proper register and receiver a copy of such plat and the field notes of survey of the claim, accompanied by the affidavit of at least two credible witnesses that such plat and notice are posted conspicuously upon the claim, giving the date and place of such posting; a copy of the *notice* so posted to be attached to and form a part of said affidavit. § 45, Id.

Plat.—The plat forwarded as part of the proof should not be *folded,* but *rolled,* so as to prevent creasing, and either transmitted in a separate package or so inclosed with the other papers that it may pass through the mails without creasing or mutilation. If forwarded separately, the letter transmitting the papers should state the fact. § 45, Id.

Proof of Continuous Posting.—This is the second affidavit in reference to posting. The first was as to the fact that the notice was duly posted, which must be proved by two witnesses.

This affidavit is made by the claimant alone, and is in proof of the fact that during the time of publication the plat and notice remained posted in a conspicuous place on the claim.

ADVERSE CLAIM OR PROTEST MUST BE IN-TERPOSED BEFORE PATENT.

PROVISIONS OF U. S. STATUTES.

Adverse Claims Cut Off By Patent.—If no adverse claim shall have been filed with the register and the receiver of the proper land office at the expiration of the sixty days of publication, it shall be assumed that the applicant is entitled to a patent, upon the payment to the proper officer of five dollars per acre, and that no adverse claim exists; and thereafter no objection from third parties to the issuance of a patent shall be heard, except it be shown that the applicant has failed to comply with the terms of this chapter. § 2325, Id.

LAND OFFICE REGULATIONS.

Payment Required.—Upon the filing of this affidavit (Rule 56) the register will, if no adverse claim was filed in his office during the period of publication, permit the claimant to pay for the land according to the area given in the plat and field notes of survey aforesaid, at the rate of $5 for each acre and $5 for each fractional part of an acre, except as otherwise provided by law, the receiver issuing the usual duplicate receipt therefor. The claimant will also make a sworn statement of all charges and fees paid by him for publication and surveys, together with all fees and money paid the register and receiver of the land office, after which the complete record will be forwarded to the Commissioner of the General Land Office and a patent issued thereon if found regular. § 57, circular, Dec. 15, 1897.

Protest.—At any time prior to the issuance of patent, protest may be filed against the patenting of the claim as applied for, upon any ground tending to show that the applicant has failed to comply with the law in a matter which would avoid the claim. Such protest cannot, however, be made the means of preserving a surface conflict lost by failure to adverse or lost by the judgment of the court in an adverse suit. One holding a present joint interest in a mineral location included in an application for patent who is excluded from the application, so that his interest would not be protected by the issue of patent thereon, may protest against the issuance of a patent as applied for, setting forth in such protest the nature and extent of his interest in such location, and such a protestant will be deemed a party in interest entitled to appeal. This results from the holding that a co-owner excluded from an application for patent does not have an "adverse" claim within the meaning of Sections 2325 and 2326 of the Revised Statutes. See Turner v. Sawyer, 150 U. S. 578-586. § 58, Id.

Trustee.—Any party applying to make entry as *trustee* must disclose fully the nature of the trust and the name of the *cestui que trust;* and such trustee, as well as the beneficiaries, must furnish satisfactory proof of citizenship; and the names of beneficiaries, as well as that of the trustee, must be inserted in the final certificate of entry. § 59, Id.

Register's Certificate.—In sending up the papers in the case the register must not omit certifying to the fact that the notice was posted in his office for the full period of sixty days, such certificate to state distinctly when such posting was done and how long continued. § 73.

Register Must Be Satisfied of Sufficiency of Proofs.—No entry will be allowed until the register has satisfied himself, by a careful examination, that proper proofs have been filed upon all the points indicated in official regulations in force, and that they show a sufficient *bona fide* compliance with the laws and such regulations. § 74, Id.

Entries—How Numbered.—The consecutive series of numbers of mineral entries must be continued, whether the same are of lode or placer claims or mill sites. § 75, Id.

What Adverse Claims Cut Off.—It is only adverse claims arising from "interferences," that is, disputes as to locations or boundaries that are. determined by the failure to adverse.　Questions of title arising otherwise are for the courts. [41]

Res Adjudicata. in Trial by "Protest."—The above provision of statute is discussed under "Adverse Claims."

Rule 58 of the land office is an attempt to avoid the effect of the decision mentioned therein by providing another way for settling questions of title to claims in the Department of the Interior.　No one need try the question of title by "protest," but if the parties do adopt that course, and, after hearing them on the merits, a patent is issued to one of them, it is probable that the decision would be regarded in the courts, as well as in the department, as *res adjudicata* and final.

The foregoing final provisions contemplate:

1. That proof, by affidavit, of due publication shall be filed.

2. That the register or receiver shall certify to the fact that the notice of application was, during the required period, posted conspicuously in his office.

3. That payment shall be made to the receiver at the rate of $5 per acre for the land, and $10 land office fees.

4. That an affidavit shall be filed showing payment of the disbursements hereinbefore mentioned.

---

[41] New Dunderberg M. Co. v. Old, 79 F. 598; Golden Reward M. Co. v. Buxton M. Co , 29 F. 868.

5. That the claimant shall then make and file the formal application for purchase.

6. That the register shall issue to him the final certificate of entry, which entitles him to a patent, and is, in the meantime, its equivalent for all practical purposes;[42] and

7. That a patent shall issue from the United States to the applicant, conveying to him the fee title to the premises.[43]

SURVEYS—HOW MADE.

PROVISIONS OF U. S. STATUTES.

Description of Vein-Claims on Surveyed and Unsurveyed Lands.—The description of vein or lode claims, upon surveyed lands, shall designate the location of the claim with reference to the lines of the public surveys, but need not conform therewith; but where a patent shall be issued for claims upon unsurveyed lands, the surveyor general, in extending the surveys, shall adjust the same to the boundaries of such patented claim, according to the plat or description thereof, but so as in no case to interfere with or change the location of any such patented claim. § 2327, Id.

---

42 Black v. Elkhorn M. Co., 49 F. 198; American M. Co. v. Hopper, 46 F. 47; Wilson v. Fine, 40 F. 52; Aurora H. C. M. Co. v. 85 M. Co., 34 F. 515; Hamilton v. Southern N. G. & S. M. Co., 33 F. 562.

43 Wis. C. R. Co. v. Forsythe, 15 S. C. R. 1020, 159 U. S. 47; Dahl v. Raunheim, 10 S. C. R. 74, 132 U. S. 260; Iron S. M. Co. v. Campbell, 10 S. C. R. 765, 135 U. S. 286; Parley's P. S. M. Co. v. Kerr, 9 S. C. R. 511, 130 U. S. 256; Garrard v. Silver P. M., 82 F. 578; Northern P. R. Co. v. McCormick, 72 F. 736; Savage v. Worsham, 72 F. 601; U. S. v. Winona & S. P. R. Co., 67 F. 948; Murray v. Polglase, 43 P. 505, Mont.

LAND OFFICE REGULATIONS.

Claims—How Described.—The surveyors general should designate all surveyed mineral claims by a progressive series of numbers, beginning with survey No. 37, irrespective as to whether they are situated on surveyed or unsurveyed lands, the claim to be so designated at date of issuing the order therefor, in addition to the local designation of the claim; it being required in all cases that the plat and field notes of the survey of a claim must, in addition to the reference to permanent objects in the neighborhood, describe the locus of the claim, with reference to the lines of public surveys, by a line connecting a corner of the claim with the nearest public corner of the United States surveys, unless such claim be on unsurveyed lands at a distance of more than two miles from such public corner, in which latter case it should be connected with a United States mineral monument. Such connecting line must not be more than *two miles* in length and should be measured on the ground direct between the points, or calculated from actually surveyed traverse lines if the nature of the country should not permit direct measurement. If a regularly established survey corner is within two miles of a claim situated on unsurveyed lands the connection should be made with such corner in preference to a connection with a United States mineral monument. The connecting line must be surveyed by the deputy mineral surveyor at the time of his making the particular survey and be made a part thereof. § 41, Id.

Record of Fractions.—Upon the approval of the survey of a mining claim made upon surveyed lands the surveyor general will prepare and transmit to the local land office and to this office a diagram tracing showing the portions of legal forty-acre subdivisions made fractional by reason of the mineral survey, designating each of such portions by the proper lot number, beginning with No. 1 in each section, and giving the area of each lot. § 42, Id.

Requirements of Survey.—The following particulars should be observed in the survey of every mining claim:

(1) The exterior boundaries of the claim should be represented on the plat of survey and in the field notes.

(2) The intersection of the lines of the survey with the lines of conflicting prior surveys should be noted in the field notes and represented upon the plat.

(3) Conflicts with unsurveyed claims, where the applicant for survey does not claim the area in conflict, should be shown by actual survey.

(4) The total area of the claim embraced by the exterior boundaries should be stated, and also the area in conflict with each intersecting survey, substantially as follows:

	Acres.
Total area of claim	10.50
Area in conflict with survey No. 302	1.56
Area in conflict with survey No. 948	2.33
Area in conflict with Mountain Maid lode mining claim, unsurveyed	1.48

§ 43, Id.

Application Should Specify Excluded Portion.— It does not follow that because mining surveys are required to exhibit all conflicts with prior surveys the areas of conflict are to be excluded. The field notes and plat are made a part of the application for patent, and care should be taken that the description does not inadvertently exclude portions intended to be retained. It is better that the application for patent should state the portions to be excluded in express terms. § 43, Id.

APPLICATION MAY BE MADE PERSONALLY OR BY AGENT.

PROVISIONS OF U. S. STATUTES.

Of Applicants for Mineral Lands.—That applicants for mineral patents, if residing beyond the limits of the district wherein the claim is situated, may make any oath or affidavit required for proof of citizenship before the clerk of any court of record or before any notary public of any State or Territory. 22 S. L., 49, I Supp. 338.

Applications for Patents for Mineral Lands, Etc., May Be Made By Agent When Claimant Resides Out of District.—"Provided, That where the claimant for a patent is not a resident of or within the land district wherein the vein, lode, ledge or deposit sought to be patented is located, the application for patent and the affidavits required to be made in this section by the claimant for such patent may be made by his, her, or its authorized agent, where said agent is conversant with the facts sought to be established by said affidavits pending cases. And provided, That this section shall apply to all applications now pending for patents to mineral lands." 21 Stat. L. 61, I Supp. 276.

Pending Applications; Existing Rights.—Applications for patents for mining claims under former laws now pending may be prosecuted to a final decision in the General Land Office; but in such cases where adverse rights are not affected thereby,

·patents may issue in pursuance of the provisions of this chapter; and all patents for mining claims upon veins or lodes heretofore issued shall convey all the rights and privileges conferred by this chapter where no adverse rights existed on the tenth day of May, eighteen hundred and seventy-two. § 2328, Id.

Placer Claims also Subject to Foregoing Provisions.—Claims usually called "placer"   *   * shall be subject to entry and patent, under like circumstances and conditions, and upon similar proceedings, as are provided for vein or lode claims. § 2329, Id.

When an agent, in behalf of his principal, makes the application for a patent, the following requirements should be complied with:

1. He should file a duly executed and acknowledged power of attorney specially authorizing him to perform for his principal and in his behalf, all the acts necessary or requisite to obtain the desired patent.

2. He should state in all affidavits and papers executed by him for his principal that the latter "is not a resident of or within the land district" where the proceedings are pending; and

3. He should show in such affidavits and papers that he is personally "conversant with the facts sought to be established" by him.

MILL SITES MAY BE ACQUIRED BY MINERS.

PROVISIONS OF U. S. STATUTES.

Patents for Non-Mineral Lands, Etc.—Where non-mineral land, not contiguous to the vein or lode is used, or occupied by the proprietor of such vein or lode for mining or milling purposes, such non-adjacent surface ground may be embraced and included in an application for a patent for such vein or lode, and the same may be patented therewith, subject to the same preliminary requirements as to survey and notice as are applicable to veins or lodes; but no location hereafter made of such non-adjacent land shall exceed five acres, and payment for the same must be made at the same rate as fixed by this chapter for the superficies of the lode. The owner of a quartz mill or reduction works, not owning a mine in connection therewith, may also receive a patent for his mill site, as provided in this section. § 2337, Id.

LAND OFFICE REGULATIONS.

Mill Sites Auxiliary to Claim.—Mill sites are not mineral entries. On the contrary, the land entered must be shown to be non-mineral. They are simply auxiliary to the working of mineral claims, but as the section granting the right of entry is embraced in the chapter of the Revised Statutes relating to mineral lands, they are therefore included in this circular. § 63, circular, Dec. 15, 1897.

Both Included in Same Application.—To avail themselves of this provision of law parties holding the possessory right to a vein or lode, and to a piece of non-mineral land not contiguous thereto, for min-

95

ing or milling purposes, not exceeding the quantity allowed for such purpose by Section 2337, United States Revised Statutes, or prior laws, under which the land was appropriated, the proprietors of such vein or lode may file in the proper land office their application for a patent, under oath, in manner already set forth herein, which application, together with the plat and field notes, may include, embrace and describe, in addition to the vein or lode, such non-contiguous mill site, and after due proceedings as to notice, etc., a patent will be issued conveying the same as one claim. § 64, Id.

Mill Site Only.—The owner of a patented lode may, by an independent application, secure a mill site if good faith is manifest in its use or occupation in connection with the lode and no adverse claim exists. § 64, Id.

Survey.—Where the original survey includes a lode claim and also a mill site the lode claim should be described in the plat and field notes as "Sur. No. 37, A," and the mill site as "Sur. No. 37, B," or whatever may be its appropriate numerical designation; the course and distance from a corner of the mill site to a corner of the lode claim to be invariably given in such plat and field notes, and a copy of the plat and notice of application for patent must be conspicuously posted upon the mill site as well as upon the vein or lode for the statutory period of sixty days. In making the entry no separate receipt or certificate need be issued for the mill site, but the whole area of both lode and mill site will be embraced in one entry, the price being $5 for each acre and fractional part of an acre embraced by such lode and mill site claim. § 65, Id.

Patent for Mill Site Only.—In case the owner of a quartz mill or reduction works is not the owner or claimant of a vein or lode the law permits him to make application therefor in the same manner pre-scribed herein for mining claims, and after due no-tice and proceedings, in the absence of a valid ad-verse filing, to enter and receive a patent for his mill site at said price per acre. § 66, Id.

Non-Mineral Character of Land.—In every case there must be satisfactory proof that the land claimed as a mill site is not mineral in character, which proof may, where the matter is unques-tioned, consist of the sworn statement of two or more persons capable, from acquaintance with the land, to testify understandingly. § 67, Id.

The above provisions of law in reference to mill sites contemplate:[44]

1. Area of Site.—That the owner of a lode may appropriate and obtain a patent for not to exceed five acres of non-mineral land, as a site for mining or milling works, in connection with that particular lode; or

2. The owner of a quartz mill or reduction works, who owns no mine, may obtain a patent for his mill site, if it is on non-mineral land.

3. One Patent for Mine and Mill Site.—In the first case mentioned, the application for survey and patent for the mill site may be included in the ap-plication for the survey and patent of the lode; and

4. Same Proceedings as in Application for Lode Patents.—In either case like proceedings shall be followed in obtaining a patent as in procuring patents to lodes.

Valuable Lode Requires Mill Site.—Where the lode is of sufficient value to justify an application for a patent, a mill site should always be included.

---

[44] Hartman v. Smith, 7 Mont. 19.

7

PLACER AND LODE LOCATIONS GOVERNED BY THE SAME GENERAL PROVISIONS.

PROVISIONS OF U. S. STATUTES.

Conformity of Placer Claims to Surveys, Limit of.—Claims usually called "placers," including all forms of deposit, excepting veins of quartz, or other rock in place, shall be subject to entry and patent, under like circumstances and conditions, and upon similar proceedings, as are provided for vein or lode claims; but where the lands have been previously surveyed by the United States, the entry in its exterior limits shall conform to the legal subdivisions of the public lands. § 2329, Id.

LAND OFFICE REGULATIONS.

One Discovery on Each Location.—But one discovery of mineral is required to support a placer location, whether it be of twenty acres by an individual, or of 160 acres or less by an association of persons. § 25, circular, Dec. 15, 1897.

Marking and Recording.—The regulations hereinbefore given as to the manner of marking locations on the ground, and placing the same on record, must be observed in the case of placer locations so far as the same are applicable, the law requiring, however, that where placer claims are upon *surveyed* public lands the locations must hereafter be made to conform to legal subdivisions thereof as near as practicable. § 36, Id.

LAW OF ALASKA.

Placers are Personal Property.—All interests in mining claims, known as placer or surface diggings, may be granted, sold and conveyed by bill of sale and delivery of possession, as in cases of the sale of personal property. Provided, further, that the bills of sale or conveyances executed on the sale of any placer or surface mining claim shall be recorded within thirty days after the date of such sale, in the office of the county clerk of the county in which such sale is made, in a book to be kept by the county clerk for that purpose, to be called the record of conveyances of mining claims. Laws of Oregon, Oct. 24, 1864, § 3834, H. A. L. O. 1887.

Chattel Mortgages.—Mortgages of interests in placer or surface mining claims shall be executed, acknowledged, recorded and foreclosed as mortgages of chattels. Laws of Oregon, Oct. 24, 1864, § 3835, H. A. L. O. 1887.

Placer Defined.—The statutory definition of the word "placer" is as good as can be suggested. A "placer" does not mean "veins of quartz or other rock in place," and whether the "other rock" is in the form of veins or of a deposit, it is not placer, so long as it is "in place."

Title—How Acquired.—The same directions as hereinbefore applied to lode claims, are applicable also to the acquisition of placer claims.

Discovery.—There must be, as in cases of lode claims, a discovery of the mineral deposit before there can be a location. [4][5]

Location.—The discoverer is limited to thirty days in which to make his location, and should pro-

---

[4][5] Gregory v. Persbaker, 73 Cal. 109, 14 P. 401.

tect himself in the meantime, if delay is necessary, by posting conspicuously on the ground, as in lode discoveries, a notice of his discovery and intention to locate a claim at that place. The claim should be distinctly marked out on the ground, and a location notice, properly dated, specifying the date of discovery, the name of the claim, the description thereof, and the name of the locator, should be posted on the claim.[46] FORMS 6, 7.

Recording.—The same recording law applies to both lode and placer claims, and unless the claimant expects to work his claim continuously, he should file his location certificate within thirty days from the date of discovery.

If the location is on surveyed land the description of the claim in the location certificate will be simple, but if on unsurveyed land the claim should be described as in cases of lode claims, the *locus* being established by reference to natural objects or permanent monuments.

Placers Personal Property.—Under the law of Alaska (Oregon) placers are regarded, for the purpose of sale and transfer, as personal property and may be conveyed by bill of sale, which must be recorded in the proper recording office.

---

[46] Fitzpatrick v. Montgomery, 50 P. 416.

PLACER LOCATIONS CAN NEVER EXCEED 160 ACRES.

PROVISIONS OF U. S. STATUTES.

Subdivisions of Ten-Acre Tracts; Maximum of Placer Locations.—Legal subdivisions of forty acres may be subdivided into ten-acre tracts; and two or more persons, or associations of persons, having contiguous claims of any size, although such claims may be less than ten acres each, may make joint entry thereof; but no location of a placer claim, made after the ninth day of July, eighteen hundred and seventy, shall exceed one hundred and sixty acres for any one person or association of persons, which location shall conform with the United States surveys; and nothing in this section contained shall defeat or impair any bona fide pre-emption or homestead claim upon agricultural lands, or authorize the sale of the improvements of any bona fide settler to any purchaser. § 2330, Id.

LAND OFFICE REGULATIONS.

Subdivisions of Ten-Acre Lots.—By Section 2330 authority is given for the subdivision of forty-acre legal subdivisions into *ten-acre* lots, which is intended for the greater convenience of miners in segregating their claims both from one another and from intervening agricultural lands. § 28, circular, Dec. 15, 1897.

Legal Subdivisions.—It is held, therefore, that under a proper construction of the law these ten-acre lots in mining districts should be considered and dealt with, to all intents and purposes, as legal subdivisions, and that an applicant having a legal claim which conforms to one or more of these ten-acre lots, either adjoining or cornering, may make entry thereof, after the usual proceedings, without further survey or plat. § 29, Id.

Dimensions Should Be Stated.—In cases of this kind, however, the notice given of the application must be very specific and accurate in description, and as the forty-acre tracts may be subdivided into ten-acre lots, either in the form of squares of ten by ten chains, or, if parallelograms, five by twenty chains, so long as the lines are parallel and at right angles with the lines of the public surveys, it will be necessary that the notice and application state specifically what ten-acre lots are sought to be patented in addition to the other data required in the notice. § 30, Id.

Description.—Where the ten-acre subdivision is in the form of a square it may be described, for instance as the "SE. ¼ of the SW. ¼ of NW. ¼," or, if in the form of a parallelogram as aforesaid, it may be described as the "W. ½ of the W. ½ of the SW. ¼ of the NW. ¼ (or the N. ½ of the S. ½ of the NE. ¼ of the SE. ¼) of section——, township ——, range ——," as the case may be; but, in addition to this description of the land, the notice must give all the other *data* that is required in a mineral application, by which parties may be put on inquiry as to the premises sought to be patented. The proofs submitted with applications for claims of this kind must show clearly the character and the extent of the improvements upon the premises. § 31, Id.

Proof of Improvements.—The proof of improvements must show their value to be not less than *five hundred dollars* and that they were made by the applicant for patent or his grantors. The annual expenditure to the amount of $100, required by Section 2324, Revised Statutes, must be made upon placer claims as well as lode claims. § 31, Id.

Joint Entries.—By virtue of the foregoing provisions of statute any number of persons may by combining their claims make a joint application for patent, and jointly enter the lands, notwithstanding the area involved. [47]

Inconsistency of Provisions.—The statute provides, however, that no association of persons can locate more than 160 acres; that is, if, for instance, twenty persons were to form an association for the entry of placer lands, they could by reason of such association enter only 160 acres, while as individuals they could enter 400 acres. The inconsistency of the provisions of this section with those of the next is due to the fact that it was part of the law of 1870, while the next section was enacted in 1872, both being incorporated in the Revised Statutes of 1878.

LOCATIONS MUST CONFORM WITH PUBLIC SURVEYS.

PROVISIONS OF U. S. STATUTES.

Conformity of Placer Claims to Surveys, Limitation of Claims.—Where placer claims are upon surveyed lands, and conform to legal subdivisions, no further survey or plat shall be required, and all placer mining claims located after the tenth day of May, eighteen hundred and seventy-two, shall

---

[47] Erhardt v. Boaro, 5 S. C. R. 565, 113 U. S. 527.

conform as near as practicable with the United States system of public land surveys, and the rectangular subdivision of such surveys, and no such location shall include more than twenty acres for each individual claimant; but where placer claims cannot be conformed to legal subdivisions, survey and plat shall be made as on unsurveyed lands; and where by the segregation of mineral lands in any legal subdivision a quantity of agricultural land less than forty acres remains, such fractional portion of agricultural land may be entered by any party qualified by law, for homestead or pre-emption purposes. § 2331, Id.

LAND OFFICE REGULATIONS.

Maximum for Association.—By Section 2330 it is declared that no location of a placer claim, made after July 9, 1870, shall exceed 160 acres for any one person or association of persons, which location shall conform to the United States surveys. § 33, circular, Dec. 15, 1897.

Maximum for Individual.—Section 2331 provides that all placer mining claims located after May 10, 1872, shall conform as nearly as practicable with the United States systems of public surveys and the subdivisions of such surveys, and no such locations shall include more than twenty acres for each individual claimant. § 34, Id.

Provisions Explained.—The foregoing provisions of law are construed to mean that after the 9th day of July, 1870, no location of a placer claim can be made to exceed 160 acres, whatever may be the number of locators associated together, or whatever the local regulations of the district may allow; and that from and after May 10, 1872, no location can exceed twenty acres for each individual participating therein; that is, a location by two persons cannot exceed forty acres, and one by three persons cannot exceed sixty acres. § 35, Id.

Limitation of Area.—The statute above quoted limits the right of placer location to one claim not exceeding twenty acres in area, for each individual.

The apparent meaning of the limitation is that but one claim of twenty acres can be located by an individual in any one gulch or upon any particular placer ground, but it does not prevent him from making similar locations elsewhere.[48]

Purchases Not Limited.—There is no limit, however, to the number of placer claims which one may purchase, nor to the number which he may combine in one entry or patent. In the laws of Oregon, applied by act of Congress to Alaska, there is a provision that the number of claims which one person may acquire by purchase on any lode or vein may be limited by Miners' Rules. Such a limitation, though contrary to the former policy of federal legislation, would undoubtedly be valid, if properly adopted and published by the Miners' Rules of a district. They would, of course, have no application outside of the district in which they are operative, and would not apply to placers.[49]

[48] Gird v. California D. Co., 60 F. 531; Book v. Justice M. Co., 58 F. 106; English v. Johnson, 17, Cal. 106; Prosser v. Parks, 18 Cal. 48; Table M. T. Co. v. Stranahan, 20 Cal. 209; Patterson v. Keystone M. Co., 28 Cal. 576; Hess v. Winder, 30 Cal. 355.

[49] Carson C. G. & S. M. Co. v. North S. M. Co., 78 F. 597.

LODE MAY OR MAY NOT BE INCLUDED IN PATENT FOR PLACER CLAIM.

PROVISIONS OF U. S. STATUTES.

Proceedings for Patent for Placer Claim, Etc.— Where the same person, association or corporation is in possession of a placer claim, and also a vein or lode included within the boundaries thereof, application shall be made for a patent for the placer claim, with the statement that it includes such vein or lode, and in such case a patent shall issue for the placer claim, subject to the provisions of this chapter, including such vein or lode, upon the payment of five dollars per acre for such vein or lode claim, and twenty-five feet of surface on each side thereof. The remainder of the placer claim, or any placer claim not embracing any vein or lode claim, shall be paid for at the rate of two dollars and fifty cents per acre, together with all costs of proceedings. § 2333, Id.

Known Veins.—And where a vein or lode, such as is described in Section 2320, is known to exist within the boundaries of a placer claim, an application for a patent for such placer claim which does not include an application for the vein or lode claim shall be construed as a conclusive declaration that the claimant of the placer claim has no right of possession of the vein or lode claim; but where the existence of a vein or lode in a placer claim is not known, a patent for the placer claim shall convey all valuable mineral and other deposits within the boundaries thereof.   § 2333, Id.

LAND OFFICE REGULATIONS.

Known Lode Must Be Surveyed.—Applicants for patent to a placer claim, who are also in possession of a known vein or lode included therein, must state in their application that the placer includes such vein or lode. The published and posted notices must also include such statement. If veins or lodes lying within a placer location are owned by other parties, the fact should be distinctly stated in the application for patent, and in all the notices. But in all cases whether the lode is claimed or excluded, it must be surveyed and marked upon the plat; the field notes and plat giving the area of the lode-claim or claims and the area of the placer separately. It should be remembered that an application which omits to include an application for a known vein or lode therein, must be construed as a conclusive declaration that the applicant has no right of possession to the vein or lode. Where there is no known lode or vein, the fact must appear by the affidavit of two or more witnesses. § 32, circular, Dec. 15, 1897.

What Veins or Lodes Excepted.--"A vein or lode may be known to exist so as to except it from the grant, though it has not been located according to law." Sullivan v. Iron S. M. Co., 12 S. C. R. 555, 143 U. S. 431.

Existence of Excluded Lode Must Be Matter of Actual Knowledge.—"The existence of the vein or lode must be a matter of actual knowledge at the time of the application for the patent, and it cannot be excluded from the grant by evidence of subsequent discoveries, or of mere speculation or belief, based upon the fact that a number of shafts sunk in adjacent lands disclosed the existence of certain horizontal deposits which, it was argued, might extend under the tract in question." Sullivan v. Iron S. M. Co., 12 S. C. R. 555, 143 U. S. 431.

Whether Exploration Justified by Quantity of Mineral in Lode, Question of Fact.—"It is, after all, a question of fact for a jury. It cannot be said, as a matter of law in advance, how much of gold or silver must be found in a vein before it will justify exploitation and be properly called a 'known' vein. The amount of the ore, the facility for reaching and working it, as well as the product per ton, are all to be considered in determining whether the vein is one which justified exploitation and working." Iron S. M. Co. v. Mike & S. G. & S. M. Co., 12 S. C. R. 543, 143 U. S. 394, 430.

"Known" Means, Known to the Placer Applicant.—"The knowledge must be that of the applicant for the placer patent, but he is chargeable with knowledge of what is known generally in the community, or what would be disclosed by a reasonable and fair inspection of the premises for the purpose of obtaining title from the government." Iron S. M. Co. v. Mike & S. G. & S. M. Co., 12 S. C. R. 543, 143 U. S. 394, 430.

PATENT FOR PLACER CLAIMS—HOW OBTAINED.

PROVISIONS OF U. S. STATUTES.

Patents.—Claims usually called "placers," including all forms of deposit, excepting veins of quartz, or other rock in place, shall be subject to entry and patent, under like circumstances and conditions, and upon similar proceedings, as are provided for vein or lode claims. § 2329, Id.

LAND OFFICE REGULATIONS.

Same as Lode Claims.—The proceedings to obtain patents for claims usually called placers, including all forms of deposit, excepting veins of quartz or other rock in place, are similar to the proceedings prescribed for obtaining patents for vein or lode claims; but where said placer claim shall be upon surveyed lands, and conforms to legal subdivisions, no further survey or plat will be required; and all placer mining claims located after May 10, 1872, shall conform as nearly as practicable with the United States system of public land surveys and the rectangular subdivisions of such surveys, and no such location shall include more than twenty acres for each individual claimant; but where placer claims cannot be conformed to legal subdivisions, survey and plat shall be made as on unsurveyed lands. But where such claims are located previous to the public surveys, and do not conform to legal subdivisions, survey, plat and entry thereof may be made according to the boundaries thereof, provided the location is in all respects legal. § 60, circular, Dec. 15, 1897.

Former Directions Sufficient.—The proceedings for obtaining patents for veins or lodes having already been fully given, it will not be necessary to repeat them here, it being thought that careful attention thereto by applicants and the local officers will enable them to act understandingly in the matter and make such slight modifications in the notice, or otherwise, as may be necessary in view of the different nature of the two classes of claims;

placer claims being fixed, however, at $2.50 per acre, or fractional part of an acre. § 61, Id.

Character of Land.—The first care in recognizing an application for patent upon a placer claim must be exercised in determining the exact classification of the lands. To this end the clearest evidence of which the case is capable should be presented. § 62, Id.

Placer or Mixed.—If the claim be all placer ground, that fact must be stated in the application and corroborated by accompanying proofs; if of mixed placers and lodes, it should be so set out, with a description of all known lodes situated within the boundaries of the claim. A specific declaration, such as is required by Section 2333, Revised Statutes, must be furnished as to each lode intended to be claimed. All other known lodes are, by the silence of the applicant, excluded by law from all claim by him, of whatsoever nature, possessory or otherwise. § 62, Id.

Field Notes.—Deputy surveyors shall, at the expense of the parties, make full examination of all placer claims surveyed by them, and duly note the facts as specified in the law, stating the quality and composition of the soil, the kind and amount of timber and other vegetation, the locus and size of streams, and such other matters as may appear upon the surface of the claim. This examination should include the character and extent of all surface and underground workings, whether placer or lode, for mining purposes. § 62, Id.

Adaptability to Mining.—In addition to these data, which the law requires to be shown in all cases, the deputy should report with reference to the proximity of centers of trade or residence; also of well known systems of lode deposit or of individual lodes. He should also report as to the use or adaptability of the claim for placer mining; whether water has been brought upon it in sufficient quantity to mine the same, or whether it can be procured for that purpose; and, finally, what works or expenditures have been made by the claimant or his grantors for the development of the claim, and their situation and location with respect to the same as applied for. § 62, Id.

Report of Deputy Surveyor.—This examination should be reported by the deputy under oath to the surveyor general, and duly corroborated; and a copy of the same should be furnished with the application for patent to the claim, constituting a part thereof, and included in the oath of the applicant. § 62, Id.

Prior Applications.—Applications awaiting entry, whether published or not, must be made to conform to these regulations, with respect to examination as to the character of the land. Entries already made will be suspended for such additional proofs as may be deemed necessary in each case. § 62, Id.

The directions hereinbefore given in reference to the procuring of patents for lode claims will be found a sufficient guide in proceedings for obtaining patents of placers.

The Survey.—Where the placer claim contains known veins or lodes a survey thereof should be procured before the application for patent is filed. The application for the placer patent should describe the lodes therein, whether included or excluded, according to the field notes of the survey, and such lodes should be indicated on the plat.[50]

Character of Land.—Precise information is required by the land department as to the character of the land—that it is neither "rock in place" nor agricultural land. This and all the other data required in cases of lode claims are included in the field notes of the deputy surveyor, as well as in the application of the claimant for patent.

LANDS VALUABLE FOR BUILDING STONE SUBJECT TO ENTRY.

PROVISIONS OF U. S. STATUTES.

Entry of Lands Chiefly Valuable For Building Stone Under the Placer-Mining Laws.—Any person authorized to enter lands under the mining laws of the United States may enter lands that are chiefly valuable for building stone under the provisions of the law in relation to placer mineral claims: Provided, That lands reserved for the benefit of the public schools or donated to any State shall not be subject to entry under this act. 27 S. L. 348, II Supp. 65.

LAND OFFICE REGULATIONS.

This act extends the mineral land laws so as to bring lands chiefly valuable for building stone with-

---

50 Senior v. Anderson, 47 P. 454, Col., McDonald v. Lannen, 47 P. 648 Mont.; Sloan v. Glaney, 47 P. 344, Mont.; Faulkner v. Roudoni, 37 P. 883 Cal.; Nevada D. Co. v. Bennett, 45 P. 472, Or.; Creek v. Bozeman, W. W. Co., 38 P. 459, Mont.; Simmons v. Winters, 27 P. 7, 21 O. 42; Barnes v. Sabron, 10 Nev. 243; Iron S. M. Co. v. M. S. G. S. M. Co., 12 S. C. R. 543, 143 U. S. 431; Dahl v. Raunheim, 10 S. C. R. 74, 132 U. S. 260; Iron S. M. Co. v. Campbell, 10 S. C. R. 765, 135 U. S. 286; U. S. v. Iron S. M. Co., 9 S. C. R. 195, 128 U. S. 673; Iron S. M. Co. v. Reynolds, 9 S. C. R. 598, 124 U. S. 374; Noyes v. Mantle, 9 S. C. R. 1132, 127 U. S. 348; Diffeback v. Hawke, 6 S. C. R. 95, 115 U. S. 352; Reynolds v. Iron S. M. Co., 6 S. C. R. 601, 116 U. S. 687; Migeon v. Montana, 77 F. 249, 68 F. 811; Casey v. Thieviege, 48 P. 398, Mont.; Butte M. Co. v. Sloan, 40 P. 217, Mont.; Jones v. Prospect M. T. Co., 21 Nev. 339; Beadville M. Co. v. Fitzgerald, 4 Nor. M. R. 380; Gilpin v. Sierra N. C. M. Co., 2 Idaho 662; Bell v. Skillicorn, 28 P. R. 768; Apple Blossom P. V. Cara L. L. 21 L. D. 438.

in the provisions of said law by authorizing a placer entry of such lands. It does not operate, however, to withdraw lands chiefly valuable for building stone from entry under any existing law applicable thereto. Registers and receivers should therefore make a reference to said act on the entry papers in the case of all placer entries made for lands containing stone chiefly valuable for building purposes. It will be noted that lands reserved for the benefit of public schools or donated to any State are not subject to entry under said act. § 26, circular, Dec. 15, 1897.

LANDS CONTAINING MINERAL OILS SUBJECT TO ENTRY.

PROVISIONS OF U. S. STATUTES.

Entry and Patenting of Lands Containing Petroleum and Other Mineral Oils Under the Placer Mining Laws.—Any person authorized to enter lands under the mining laws of the United States may enter and obtain patent to lands containing petroleum or other mineral oils, and chiefly valuable therefor, under the provisions of the laws relating to placer mineral claims: Provided, That lands containing such petroleum or other mineral oils which have heretofore been filed upon, claimed, or improved as mineral, but not yet patented, may be held and patented under the provisions of this act the same as if such filing, claim or improvement were, subsequent to the date of the passage hereof. 29 S. L. 526, III Supp.

LAND OFFICE REGULATIONS.

Placer Law Extended.—It is to be observed that the provisions of the mineral laws relating to placers are by said act extended so as to allow the location and entry thereunder of public lands chiefly valuable for petroleum or other mineral oils, and entries of that nature made prior to the passage of said act are to be considered as though made thereunder. § 27, circular, Dec. 15, 1897.[51]

WATER RIGHTS MAY BE ACQUIRED BY LAW.

PROVISIONS OF U. S. STATUTES.

Vested Rights to Use Water for Mining, Etc.; Right of Way for Canals.—Whenever, by priority of possession, rights to the use of water for mining, agricultural, manufacturing or other purposes, have vested and accrued, and the same are recognized and acknowledged by the local customs, laws, and the decisions of courts, the possessors and owners of such vested rights shall be maintained and protected in the same; and the right of way for the construction of ditches and canals for the purposes herein specified, is acknowledged and confirmed: but whenever any person, in the construction of any ditch or canal, injures or damages the possession of any settler on the public domain, the party committing such injury or damage shall be liable to the party injured for such injury or damage. § 2339, Id.

---

[51] Gird v. California O. Co., 60 F. 531.

VESTED WATER RIGHTS NOT IMPAIRED.

PROVISIONS OF U. S. STATUTES.

Patents, Pre-emptions, and Homesteads Subject to Vested and Accrued Water Rights.—All patents granted, or pre-emption or homesteads allowed, shall be subject to any vested and accrued water rights, or rights to ditches and reservoirs used in connection with such water rights, as may have been acquired under or recognized by the preceding section. § 2340, Id.

CONDITIONS AS TO EASEMENTS FOR DITCHES, DRAINS, ETC., MAY BE PROVIDED BY LOCAL LEGISLATION.

PROVISIONS OF U. S. STATUTES.

What Conditions of Sale May be Made by Local Legislature.—As a condition of sale, in the absence of necessary legislation by Congress, the local legislature of any State or Territory may provide rules for working mines, involving easements, drainage, and other necessary means to their complete development; and those conditions shall be fully expressed in the patent. § 2338, Id.

LAW OF ALASKA.

Flumes and Ditches are Real Estate.—Ditches used for mining purposes and mining flumes, permanently affixed to the soil, be and the same are hereby declared real estate during the time the same shall be used for that purpose. Laws of Oregon, Oct. 29, 1870, § 3833, H. A. L. O. 1887.

Abandonment for One Year.—Provided, That

whenever any person, company or corporation, being the owner or proprietor of any such ditch, flume or water right, have or shall abandon the same, and who shall for one year thereafter cease to exercise ownership over such water right, ditch or flume, and every company, corporation or person who shall remove from this State, with the intent or purpose to change his or their residence, and shall remain absent one year without using or exercising ownership over such water right, ditch or flume by a legally authorized agent, shall be deemed to have lost all title, claim or interest therein. Laws of Oregon, Oct. 29, 1870, § 3833, H. A. L. O. 1887.

Authority of Miners.—Miners shall be empowered to make local laws in relation to the possession of water rights, the possession and working of placer claims, and the survey and sale of town lots in mining camps, subject to the laws of the United States. Laws of Oregon, Oct. 24, 1864, § 3832, H. A. L. O. 1887.

Liens.—The laws relative to the sale and transfer of real estate and the application of the liens of mechanics and laborers therein, be and they are hereby made applicable to said ditches and flumes. Id, Oct. 24, 1864, § 3834, H. A. L. O. 1887.

Abandonment.—After one year of abandonment by the owner, ditches, flumes or water rights are subject to appropriation by others. Mere disuse is not sufficient to deprive the owner of such property, but, besides that, the actual intent to abandon must be proved as a fact by one seeking to appropriate the same on that ground.

Change of Residence.—By the law applicable to Alaska, if the owner of a ditch or flume depart from the territory with the intention of residing elsewhere, and does not, for one year, by agent or employe, or otherwise, care for, protect or use such ditch or flume, his right thereto ceases. The question of the intent to establish a residence elsewhere, is, like in the case of abandonment, a question of fact to be proved as any other essential fact in a case.

Interpretation of the Law.—The subject of the foregoing legislation is one of the most important in mining law. The provisions of the Mining act, from which the above extracts are quoted, considered as a whole, in reference to water rights, lead to these conclusions:

1. **Water Subject to Appropriation.**—Miners are free to appropriate from neighboring streams, lakes or reservoirs on the public domain by tapping or diverting the same in flumes, ditches or canals, water for mining purposes.[52]   FORM 8.

2. **Priority of possession** gives priority of right.[53]

3. **Supply Limited.**—Where the quantity of water, on the public lands, available for mining purposes in a particular locality is limited, and only in such

---

[52] Sturr v. Beck, 10 S. C. R. 350, 133 U. S. 541; Integral Q. M. Co. v. Altoona Q. M. Co., 75 F. 379; Montana Co. v. Gehring. 75 F. 384; Smith v. Corbit, 48 P. 725, Cal.; Cardoza v. Calkins, 48 P. 1010, Cal.; Suffolk G. M. & M. Co. v. San M. C. M. & M. Co., 48 P. 829, Wy.; Bruening v. Dorr, 47 P. 290, Col.; Santa P. W. v. Peralta, 45 P. 168 Cal.; Gassert v. Noyes, 44 P. 959, Mont.; Moyer v. Preston, 44 P. 845, Wy.; Gould v. Eaton, 44 P. 319, Cal.; Austin v. Chandler, 42 P. 483, Ariz.; Becker v. Marble C. I. Co.; 49 P. 892, U.; Smyth v. Neal, 49 P. 893, U.; Wells v. Kryenhagen, 49 P. 128, Cal.; Smith v. Green, 41 P. 1022, Cal.; Moss v. Rose, 41 P. 666, Or.. Jensen v. Hunter, 41 P. 14, Cal.; Hargrave v. Cook, 41 P. 18, Cal.; Sullivan v. Northern S. M. Co., 40 P. 709, U.; Missouri P. R. Co. v. Keyes, 40 P. 275, Kan.

[53] Broder v. Water Co., 101 U S. 274; Basey v. Gallagher, 87 U. S. 670; Atchinson v. Peterson, 87 U. S. 507; Montrose C. Co. v. Loutsenhizer 48 P. 532, Col.; Parker v. City, 48 P. 631, Kan.; San L. W. Co. v. Estrada, 48 P. 1075, Cal.; Smith v. Hope M. Co., 45 P. 682, Mont.; Murray v. Tingley, 50 P. 723, Mont..

cases, the quantity to which each person may be entitled is subject to regulation by those requiring its use; provided, however, that a miner in the actual possession and use of a quantity of water only sufficient for his own purposes cannot be deprived thereof by miners' rules or regulations subsequently adopted, to which he has not given his consent, but he may be deprived of the surplus over his requirements. [54]

4. Right of Way Condition of Entry.—All mining locations and entries are subject to right of way for flumes and ditches located prior thereto necessary for mining purposes on neighboring claims, and the owners of mining claims, patented or unpatented, can claim no compensation for such prior right of way, that being a condition to the right to locate mineral land. [55]

5. Appropriation.—A valid appropriation of water rights may be made solely for the purpose of selling it to those engaged in agricultural, manufacturing, mining or other pursuits requiring the use of water, though the appropriator has no personal interest in any such enterprise, as recently decided by the Supreme Court of Oregon, although the common understanding among miners has been that one who had no ownership in a mining claim, and did not require water for agricultural, manufacturing or other pur-

---

[54] Jennison v. Kirk, 98 U. S. 453.

[55] Ellinghouse v. Taylor, 48 P. 757, Mont.; Jacob v. Day, 44 P. 243, Cal.; Bear L. R. W. I. Co. v. Garland, 17 S. C. R. 7, 164 U. S. 1; Bybee v. Oregon C. R. Co., 11 S. C. R. 641, 139 U. S. 663; Wilson v. Higbee, 62 F. 723; Contra, Consolidated C. Co. v. C. P. R. Co., 51 Cal. 269; People v. Pittsburg R. Co., 53 Cal. 694; Shall v. German C. Co., 118 Ill. 427; Lorenz v. Jacob, 63 Cal. 73; Amador M. Co. v. Dewitt, 73 Cal. 482.

poses, could not appropriate water rights, so as to deprive the miners thereof or to exact tribute from them therefor, but that they might, by the adoption of regulations, take possession of such water rights for the common use in mining operations, or they might by the same means recognize and authorize the appropriation of such a one, and provide for compensation to him for supplying water to those requiring it for such purposes. [56]

6. Compensation to Settlers.—There is no right of way, except by compensation for the injury done, over lands duly appropriated by others; but where ditches or flumes were constructed across such lands, or water rights acquired thereon, while the same were part of the public domain, subsequent owners cannot claim compensation for the construction or presence of such ditches or flumes and cannot interfere with the vested water rights thereon. [57]

Subject to Local Legislation.—By Section 2338, R. S. U. S., local laws may be passed regulating the subject of easements for ditches, flumes, etc. This provision has, however, no application to Alaska.

NOTICE OF ADVERSE CLAIM MUST BE GIVEN BEFORE PATENT ISSUED.

PROVISIONS OF U. S. STATUTES.

Adverse Claims Cut Off by Patent.—If no adverse claim shall have been filed with the regis-

56 Nevada D. Co. v. Burnett, 45 P. 472.

57 Montana Co. v. Gehring, 75 F. 384; Nippel v. Forker, 47 P. 766, Col.; Hall v. Lincoln, 50 P. 1047, Col.

ter and the receiver of the proper land office at the expiration of the sixty days of publication, it shall be assumed that the applicant is entitled to a patent, upon the payment to the proper officer of five dollars per acre, and that no adverse claim exists; and thereafter no objection from third parties to the issuance of a patent shall be heard, except it be shown that the applicant has failed to comply with the terms of this chapter. § 2325, Id.

LAND OFFICE REGULATIONS.

Protest Against Patent Issuing.—At any time prior to the issuance of patent, protest may be filed against the patenting of the claim as applied for, upon any ground tending to show that the applicant has failed to comply with the law in a matter which would avoid the claim. Such protest cannot, however, be made the means of preserving a surface conflict lost by failure to adverse or lost by the judgment of the court in an adverse suit. One holding a present joint interest in a mineral location included in an application for patent who is excluded from the application, so that his interest would not be protected by the issue of patent thereon, may protest against the issuance of a patent as applied for, setting forth in such protest the nature and extent of his interest in such location, and such a protestant will be deemed a party in interest entitled to appeal. This results from the holding that a co-owner excluded from an application for patent does not have an "adverse" claim within the meaning of Sections 2325 and 2326, of the Revised Statutes. See Turner v. Sawyer, 150 U. S. 578-586 § 58, circular, Dec. 15, 1897.

Protest Not Obligatory.—There is no obligation

upon a rival claimant to "protest" against the issuance of a patent, where he would not be required to file an adverse claim, but if he does so and submits the controversy to the land department, its decision may be conclusive. As stated in St. Louis S. Co. v. Kemp, 104 U. S. 636.

"So, also, according to the doctrine in the cases cited, if the patent be issued without authority, it may be collaterally impeached in a court of law. This exception is subject to the qualification, that when the authority depends upon the existence of particular facts or upon the performance of certain antecedent acts, and it is the duty of the land department to ascertain whether the facts exist or the facts have been performed, its determination is as conclusive of the existence of the authority against any collateral attack, as is its determination upon any other matter properly submitted to its decision."[58]

Question of Superiority of Title May Be Tried in Courts.—"Where each party has a patent from the Government, and the question is as to the superiority of the title under those patents, if this depends upon extrinsic facts not shown by the patents themselves, we think it is competent, in any judicial proceeding where this question of superiority of title arises, to establish it by proof of these facts." Iron Silver M. Co. v. Campbell, 10 S. C. R. 765, 135 U. S. 286.

Foregoing Provisions Apply Only to Disputes as

---

[58] Durango L. & C. Co. v. Evans, 80 F. 425.

to Boundaries and Locations.—"The provision of Rev. St., Sections 2325 and 2326, for filing adverse claims before the register, does not apply when there is no dispute as to location or boundaries, and the controversy only arises upon the claim of one party to have acquired the interest of the other by legal proceedings." Turner v. Sawyer, 14 S. C. R. 192, 150 U. S. 578.[59]

Defrauded Party May Seek Redress in Courts.— " 'The general rule is,' says Mr. Justice Catron, 'that where several parties set up conflicting claims to property, with which a special tribunal may deal, as between one party and the Government, regardless of the rights of others, the latter may come into the ordinary courts of justice and litigate the conflicting claim.' * * * Nor do the regulations of the commissioner of the general land office, whereby a party may be held to prove his better claim to enter, oust the jurisdiction of the courts of justice. We announce this to be the settled doctrine of this court." Turner v. Sawyer, 14 S. C. R. 192, 150 U. S. 578.

Purpose of Above Statutory Provisions.—"The purpose of the statute seems to be that, where there are two claimants to the same mine, neither of whom has yet acquired the title from the Government, they shall bring their respective claims to the

[59] Enterprise M. Co. v. Rico Aspen C. M. Co., 17 S. C. R. 762, 167 U. S. 108; Northern P. R. Co. v. McCormick, 72 F. 736; U. S. v. Des Moines V. R. Co., 70 F. 435; Enterprise M. Co. v. Rico Aspen C. M. Co., 53 P. 321, 66 F. 200, 167 U. S. 108, 17 S. C. R. 762; Girard v. Carson, 44 P. 508, Col.; New Dunderberg M. Co. v. Old, 79 F. 598; Golden Reward M. Co. v. Buxton M. Co., 29 F. 868; Northern P. R. Co. v. Saunders, 47 F. 604; Hunt v. Patchin, 35 F. 816; Wight v. Dubois, 21 F. 693; Northern P. R. Co. v. Cannon, 54 F. 252; U. S. v. Iron S. M. Co., 24 F. 568.

same property, in the manner prescribed in the statute, before some judicial tribunal located in the
neighborhood where the property is, and that the
result of this judicial investigation shall govern the
action of the officers of the land department in determining which of these claimants shall have the
patent—the final evidence of title—from the Government." Iron Silver M. Co. v. Campbell, 10 S.
C. R. 765, 135 U. S. 286.

Prior Patentee Not Affected Thereby.—"For
these reasons, we do not believe that these sections,
2325 and 2326, are intended to apply to the case of
a party who has a prior patent for the land." Iron
Silver M. Co. v. Campbell, 10 S. C. R. 765, 135 U.
S. 286.

**After Patent, Government Has No Control Over
Land.**—"We have more than once held that, when
the Government has issued and delivered its patent
for lands of the United States, the control of the
department over the title to such land has ceased,
and the only way in which the title can be impeached
is by a bill in chancery; and we do not believe that,
as a general rule, the man who has obtained a patent
from the Government can be called to answer in regard to that patent before the officers of the land
department of the Government." Iron Silver M.
Co. v. Campbell, 10 S. C. R. 765, 135 U. S. 286.

PROCEEDING STAYED UPON FILING OF ADVERSE CLAIM.

PROVISIONS OF U. S. STATUTES.

Adverse Claim, Proceedings on.—Where an adverse claim is filed during the period of publication, it shall be upon oath of the person or persons making the same, and shall show the nature, boundaries and extent of such adverse claim; and all proceedings, except the publication of notice and making and filing of the affidavit thereof, shall be stayed until the controversy shall have been settled or decided by a court of competent jurisdiction, or the adverse claim waived. § 2326, Id.

LAND OFFICE REGULATIONS.

How Filed.—An adverse mining claim must be filed with the register and receiver of the land office where the application for patent was filed, or with the register and receiver of the district in which the land is situated at the time of filing the adverse claim. It must be on the oath of the adverse claimant, or it may be verified by the oath of any duly authorized agent or attorney in fact of the adverse claimant cognizant of the facts stated. § 80, circular, Dec. 15, 1897.[60]

Contents.—The adverse notice must fully set forth the nature and extent of the interference or conflict; whether the adverse party claims as a purchaser for valuable consideration or as a locator; if the former, a certified copy of the original location, the original conveyance, a duly certified copy thereof, or an abstract of title from the office of the proper recorder should be furnished, or if the trans-

---

[60] Anchor v. How, 50 F. 366; Hamilton v. Southern N. G. & S. M. Co., 33 F. 562.

action was a merely verbal one he will narrate the circumstances attending the purchase, the date thereof, and the amount paid, which facts should be supported by the affidavit of one or more witnesses, if any were present at the time, and if he claims as a locator he must file a duly certified copy of the location from the office of the proper recorder. § 83, Id.

Plat Required.—In order that the *"boundaries"* and *"extent"* of the claim may be shown, it will be incumbent upon the adverse claimant to file a plat showing his entire claim, its relative situation or position with the one against which he claims, and the extent of the conflict. This plat must be made from an actual survey by a United States Deputy Surveyor, who will officially certify thereon to its correctness; and in addition there must be attached to such plat of survey a certificate or sworn statement by the surveyor as to the approximate value of the labor performed or improvements made upon the claim by the adverse party or his predecessors in interest, and the plat must indicate the position of any shafts, tunnels or other improvements, if any such exist, upon the claim of the party opposing the application, and by which party said improvements were made. § 84, Id.

Plat Dispensed With.—*Provided, however,* That if the application for patent describes the claim by legal subdivisions, the adverse claimant, if also claiming by legal subdivisions, may describe his adverse claim in the same manner without further survey or plat. § 84, Id.

Notice to Parties.—Upon the foregoing being filed within the sixty days' publication, the register, or in his absence the receiver, will give notice in writing to *both parties* to the contest that such adverse claim has been filed, informing them that the party who filed the adverse claim will be required within thirty days from the date of such filing to commence proceedings in a court of competent jurisdiction to determine the question of right of possession, and to prosecute the same with reasonable diligence to final judgment, and that, should such adverse claimant fail to do so, his adverse claim will be considered waived, and the application for patent be allowed to proceed upon its merits. § 85, Id.

Proceedings Stayed.—When an adverse claim is filed as aforesaid, the register or receiver will indorse upon the same the precise date of filing, and preserve a record of the date of notifications issued thereon; and thereafter all proceedings on the application for patent will be suspended, with the exception of the completion of the publication and posting of notices and plat, and the filing of the necessary proof thereof, until the controversy shall have been adjudicated in court, or the adverse claim waived or withdrawn. § 86, Id.

AGENT MAY VERIFY CLAIM IN THE DISTRICT; CLAIMANT MAY MAKE VERIFICATION WHERE HE RESIDES.

PROVISIONS OF U. S. STATUTES.

Adverse Claim May be Verified by Agent.— The adverse claim required by Section twenty-three hundred and twenty-six, of the Revised Statutes, may be verified by the oath of any duly authorized agent or attorney in fact of the adverse claimant cognizant of the facts stated; and the adverse claimant, if residing, or at the time being beyond the limits of the district wherein the claim is situated, may make oath to the adverse claim before the clerk of any court of record of the United States, or the State or Territory where the adverse claimant may then be, or before any notary public of such State or Territory. 22 S. L. 49, I Supp. 338.

LAND OFFICE REGULATIONS.

Agency Proved.—Where an agent or attorney in fact verifies the adverse claim, he must distinctly swear that he is such agent or attorney, and accompany his affidavit by proof thereof. § 81, circular, Dec. 15, 1897.

Within District.—The agent or attorney in fact must make the affidavit in verification of the adverse claim within the land district where the claim is situated. § 82, Id.

LIMITATION OF TIME.

PROVISIONS OF U. S. STATUTES.

Adverse Claimant Must Commence Proceedings When.—It shall be the duty of the adverse claimant, within thirty days after filing his claim, to commence proceedings in a court of competent jurisdiction, to determine the question of the right of possession, and prosecute the same with reasonable diligence to final judgment; and a failure so to do shall be a waiver of his adverse claim. § 2326, Id.

LAND OFFICE REGULATIONS.

Dismissal.—Where such suit has been dismissed, a certificate of the clerk of the court to that effect or a certified copy of the order of dismissal will be sufficient. § 88, circular, Dec. 15, 1897.

Relinquishment Not Accepted.—After an adverse claim has been filed and suit commenced, a relinquishment or other evidence of abandonment will not be accepted, but the case must be terminated and proof thereof furnished as required by the last two paragraphs. § 89, Id.

Laches of Adverse Claimant.—Where an adverse claim has been filed, but no suit commenced against the applicant for patent within the statutory period, a certificate to that effect by the clerk of the State court having jurisdiction in the case, and also by the clerk of the Circuit Court of the United States for the district in which the claim is situated, will be required. § 90, Id.

Tribunal.—In Alaska such actions must be conducted in the U. S. District Court for that district.

Form of Proceedings.—The form of the actions contemplated is not regulated by any law, and will follow the usual practice in law or equity, as the circumstances require, as was said in Perego v. Dodge, 16 S. C. R. 971, 163 U. S. 160:

"Thus, the determination of the right of possession as between the parties is referred to a court of competent jurisdiction, in aid of the land office, but the form of action is not provided for by the statute; and, apparently, an action of law or a suit in equity would lie, as either might be appropriate under the particular circumstances—an action to recover possession when plaintiff is out of possession, and a suit to quiet title when he is in possession."[61]

---

[61] Hammer v. Garfield M. M. Co., 9 S. C. R. 548, 130 U. S. 291; Walverton v. Nichols, 7 S. C. R. 289, 119 U. S. 485; Rutter v. Shoshone M. Co., 75 F. 37; Inez M. Co. v. Kinney, 46 F. 882; Burke v. Bunker H. M. & C. Co., 46 F. 644; Doe v. Waterloo M. Co., 43 F. 219; McEvoy v. Hyman, 25 F. 1539; Shultz v. Allyn, 48 P. 960, Ariz.; Iba v. Central A., 42 P. 20, Wy.

Jury Trial May Be Waived.—"Indeed, if the case were treated as an action of law, the trial by jury might have been waived, and we think was waived in this instance." Perego v. Dodge, 16 S. C. R. 971, 163 U. S. 160.

Jury Trial Not Imperative.—"The whole proceeding is merely in aid of the land department, and the object of the amendment was to secure that aid as much in cases where both parties failed to establish title as where judgment was rendered in favor of either; and, while the finding by a jury is referred to, we think that where the adverse claimant chooses to proceed by bill to quiet title, and, as between him and the applicant for the patent, neither is found entitled to relief, the court can render a decree to that effect, just as it would render judgment on a verdict if the action were at law. If Congress had intended to provide that litigation of this sort must be at law, or must invariably be tried by a jury, it would have said so." Perego v. Dodge, 16 S. C. R. 971, 163 U. S. 160.

Extent of Improvements Material.—"In an action by the locator of a mining claim to recover its possession from one who has illegally ousted it therefrom, plaintiff may, to show its good faith in working the claim, introduce evidence that it expended several thousand dollars in so doing between the time it took possession and such ouster." Haws v. Victoria C. M. Co., 16 S. C. R. 282, 160 U. S. 303.

Court May Order Inspection.—"Ought a court

of equity, in a mining case, when it has been convinced of the importance thereof for the purposes of the trial, to compel an inspection and survey of the works of the parties, and admittance thereto, by means of the appliances in use at the mine? All the analogies of equity jurisprudence favor the affirmative of this proposition." Montana Co. v. St. Louis M. & M. Co., 14 S. C. R. 507, 152 U. S. 160.

PATENT TO CONFORM TO COURT'S DE-CISION.

PROVISIONS OF U. S. STATUTES.

Patent Issued According to Judgment.—After such judgment shall have been rendered, the party entitled to the possession of the claim, or any portion thereof, may, without giving further notice, file a certified copy of the judgment roll with the register of the land office, together with the certificate of the surveyor general, that the requisite amount of labor has been expended, or improvements made thereon, and the description required in other cases; and shall pay to the receiver five dollars per acre for his claim, together with the proper fees, whereupon the whole proceedings, and the judgment roll, shall be certified by the register to the Commissioner of the General Land Office, and a patent shall issue thereon for the claim, or such portion thereof as the applicant shall appear, from the decision of the court, to rightly possess. § 2326, Id.

DIVERSE INTERESTS INVOLVED.

Interest of Several Parties—How Protected.—If it appears from the decision of the court that several parties are entitled to separate and different portions of the claim, each party may pay for his portion of the claim with the proper fees, and file the certificate and description by the surveyor general, whereupon the register shall certify the proceedings and judgment roll to the Commissioner of the General Land Office, as in the preceding case, and patents shall issue to the several parties according to their respective rights. § 2326, Id.

LAND OFFICE REGULATIONS.

Copy of Judgment to Be Filed.—Where an adverse claim has been filed and suit thereon commenced within the statutory period, and final judgment determining the right of possession rendered in favor of the applicant, it will not be sufficient for him to file with the register a certificate of the clerk of the court, setting forth the facts as to such judgment, but he must, before he is allowed to make entry, file a certified copy of the judgment, together with the other evidence required by Section 2326, Revised Statutes. § 87, circular, Dec. 15, 1897.

MUTUAL FAILURE OF PROOF.

In Suits on Mining Claims, if Neither Party Proves Title, Jury to so Find, Etc.—In any action brought pursuant to Section 2326, of the Revised Statutes, title to the ground in controversy shall not be established by either party, the jury shall so find, and judgment shall be entered according to the verdict. [62]

---

[62] Bennett v. Harkrader, 15 S. C. R. 863, 158 U. S. 441; Larkin v. Upton, 12 S. C. R. 614, 144 U. S. 19; Doe v. Waterloo M. Co., 70 F. 455; Bay S. S. M. Co. v. Brown, 21 F. 167; Moyle v. Bullene, 44 P. 69, Col.; Girard v. Carson, 44 P. 508, Col.; Currency M. Co. v. Bently, 50 P. 920.

No Costs Allowed.—In such case costs shall not be allowed to either party, and the claimant shall not proceed in the land office or be entitled to a patent for the ground in controversy until he shall have perfected his title. 21 S. L. 505, I Supp. 324.

Jurisdiction of State and Federal Courts.—"A suit in a State court to try the right of possession of a mining claim and the right to a patent therefor, although it is brought in accordance with Rev. St., Section 2326, does not necessarily involve a federal question, so as to give a right of appeal to the United States Supreme Court." Bushnell v. Crooke M. & S. Co., 13 S. C. R. 771, 148 U. S. 682.

ACTIONS FOR POSSESSION OR DAMAGES.

PROVISIONS OF U. S. STATUTES.

Possessory Actions for Recovery of Mining Titles.—No possessory action between persons, in any court of the United States, for the recovery of any mining title, or for damages to any such title, shall be affected by the fact that the paramount title to the land, in which such mines lie, is in the United States; but each case shall be adjudged by the law of possession. § 910, Id.

LAW OF ALASKA.

United States District Court of Alaska; Exclusive Jurisdiction of Questions of Mining Rights.—But the said District Court (for the District of Alaska) shall have exclusive jurisdiction in all cases in equity or those involving a question of title to land, or *mining rights*, or the constitutionality of a law, and in all criminal offenses which are capital. 23 S. L. 24, I Supp. 430.

Pleadings.—The pleadings in such action must be in writing, and the complaint set forth the facts constituting the plaintiff's right of possession, together with such a description of the mining claim as can be conveniently given, and sufficient to identify it, and that the defendant wrongfully withholds the possession thereof from the plaintiff. Laws of Oregon, Oct. 21, 1864, § 2176, H. A. L. O. 1887.

Answer.—The answer of the defendant must contain a specific denial of each material allegation of the complaint controverted by him, or of any knowledge or information thereof sufficient to form a belief, and a statement of any new matter constituting a defense to the action. Laws of Oregon, Oct. 21, 1864, § 2177, H. A. L. O. 1887.

Patent Immaterial.—The locator of a mining claim is invested with the same protection in his title and right as if he were the fee owner of it, and, where necessary, may pursue the same remedies of law, regardless of the fact that the legal title remains in the government.[63]

Forum for Trial of Questions of Mining Rights. —The Organic act of Alaska gives the U. S. District Court for the District of Alaska exclusive jurisdiction of such actions, and the provision of the laws of Oregon, applied to Alaska, giving justices of the peace jurisdiction of actions for the recovery of the possession of mining claims, is void, being in conflict with that act of Congress.

Form of Actions.—The form of action to obtain possession provided by the law of Alaska (Oregon) adds or changes nothing. The same form would be adopted in such an action, in the absence of the stat-

---

[63] Sparks v. Pierce, 6 S. C. R. 102, 115 U. S. 408; Meydenbauer v. Stevens, 78 F. 787.

ute, and in mining litigation generally the same rules as to practice and forms of action apply as to similar litigation in regard to other classes of property. [64]

Adverse Possession.—In order to be available against a claimant prior in time, the year of adverse possession must be computed from the expiration of his rights. [65]

Customs, Etc.—Miners' customs, usages and regulations are all of equal authority as evidence, and it may be shown that written regulations formally adopted by the miners of a district have been superseded by custom or usage on the part of the same miners. Harvey v. Ryan, 48 Col. 626.

Statute of Limitation.—One year's adverse possession of a mining claim, immediately preceding the commencement of an action therefor, by the defendant or those under whom he holds, if pleaded, is a bar to the action for the possession thereof. Laws of Oregon, Oct. 21, 1864, § 2178, H. A. L. O. 1887.

Miners' Rules and Customs.—On the trial of an action to recover the possession of a mining claim, the customs, usages, or regulations established and in force in the mining district or diggings in which such claim is situated not in conflict with any law of the United States or of this State, so far as they may be pertinent and applicable to the issue to be tried, may be proven as facts, and when so proven shall be deemed the law governing the rights of the parties thereto. Laws of Oregon, Oct. 21, 1864, § 2181, H. A. L. O. 1887.

---

[64] Cheesman v. Shreeve, 40 F. 787; Aurora H. C. M. Co. v. 85 M. Co., 34 F. 515; Fuller v. Harris, 29 F. 814; Shultz v. Allyn, 48 P. 960, Ariz.; MaKay v. McDougal, 48 P. 988, Mont.; Bishop v. Baisley, 41 P. 936, Or.; Skym v. Weske C. Co., 47 P. 466, Col.
[65] Reynolds v. Iron S. M. Co., 6 S. C. R. 610, 116 U. S. 687; Altoona Q. M. Co. v. Integral Q. M. Co., 45 P. 1047, Cal.

Form of Judgment for Plaintiff.—If, on the trial of the action, judgment be given for the plaintiff, it must be to the effect that the plaintiff recover the possession of the mining claim mentioned in the complaint, or such part thereof as he may be found entitled to, together with the costs and disbursements of the action, and thereafter the plaintiff is entitled to have such judgment enforced by a writ of restitution, which writ shall be deemed an execution against property so far as such costs and disbursements are concerned. Laws of Oregon, Oct. 21, 1864, § 2179, H. A. L. O. 1887.

Form of Judgment for Defendant.—If judgment be given for the defendant, it must be to the effect that the plaintiff is not entitled to the possession of the mining claim mentioned in the complaint, or any part thereof, and that the defendant recover of the plaintiff the costs and disbursements of the action. Laws of Oregon, Oct. 21, 1864, § 2180, H. A. L. O. 1887.

AGRICULTURAL AND MINERAL LANDS DISTINGUISHED.

PROVISIONS OF U. S. STATUTES.

Lands Subject to Pre-emption.—All lands belonging to the United States, to which the Indian title has been or may hereafter be extinguished, shall be subject to the right of pre-emption, under the conditions, restrictions and stipulations provided by law. § 2257, Id.

Lands Not Subject to Pre-emption.—The following classes of lands, unless otherwise specially provided for by law, shall not be subject to the rights of pre-emption, to-wit: * * * * * Lands on which are situated any known salines or mines. § 2258, Id.

Mineral Lands Not Subject to Homestead Entry. —Nor shall any mineral lands be liable to entry and settlement under its provisions. (Chap. V. on Homesteads.) § 2302, Id.

Mineral Lands Reserved.—In all cases lands valuable for minerals shall be reserved from sale, except as otherwise expressly directed by law. § 2318, Id.

LAND OFFICE REGULATIONS.

Mineral Character Determined.—The Rules of Practice in cases before the United States district land offices, the General Land Office, and the Department of the Interior will, so far as applicable, govern in all cases and proceedings arising in contests and hearings to determine the mineral character of lands. § 101, circular, Dec. 15, 1897.

Public Land Reserved as Mineral.—No public land shall be withheld from entry as agricultural land on account of its mineral character except such as is returned by the surveyor general as mineral; and the presumption arising from such a return may be overcome by testimony taken in the manner hereinafter described. § 102, Id.

Hearings.—Hearings to determine the character of lands are practically of two kinds, as follows:

Alleged to Be Agricultural.—(1) Lands returned as mineral by the surveyor general.[66]

When such lands are sought to be entered as agricultural under laws which require the submission of final proof after due notice by publication and posting, the filing of the proper non-mineral

---

[66] Johnson v. Morris, 72 F. 890; U. S. v. Culver, 52 F. 81; Winters v. Bliss, 14 L. D. 59.

affidavit in the absence of allegations that the land is mineral will be deemed sufficient as a preliminary requirement. A satisfactory showing as to character of land must be made when final proof is submitted.

In case of application to enter, locate or select such lands as agricultural, under laws in which the submission of final proof after due .publication and posting is *not* required, notice thereof must first be given by publication for sixty days and posting in the local office during the same period, and affirmative proof as to the character of the land submitted. In the absence of allegations that the land is mineral, and upon compliance with this requirement, the entry, location or selection will be allowed, if otherwise regular.

Claimed as Mineral.—(2) Lands returned as agricultural and alleged to be mineral in character. [67]

Where as against the claimed right to enter such lands as agricultural it is alleged that the same are mineral, or are applied for as mineral lands, the proceedings in this class of cases will be in the nature of a contest, and the practice will be governed by the rules in force in contest cases. § 103, Id.

SETTLERS MAY ACQUIRE TITLE TO AGRICULTURAL LANDS IN MINING DISTRICTS.

PROVISIONS OF U. S. STATUTES.

Mineral Lands, in which no Valuable Mines are Discovered, Open to Homesteads.—Wherever, upon the lands heretofore designated as mineral lands, which have been excluded from survey and sale,

[67] U. S. v. Reed, 28 F. 482.

there have been homesteads made by citizens of the United States, or persons who have declared their intention to become citizens, which homesteads have been made, improved, and used for agricultural purposes, and upon which there have been no valuable mines of gold, silver, cinnabar or copper discovered, and which are properly agricultural lands, the settlers or owners of such homesteads shall have a right of pre-emption thereto, and shall be entitled to purchase the same at the price of one dollar and twenty-five cents per acre, and in quantity not to exceed one hundred and sixty acres; or they may avail themselves of the provisions of Chapter V. of this title, relating to "Homesteads." § 2341, Id.

LAND OFFICE REGULATIONS.

Hearings.—At the hearings under either of the aforesaid classes, the claimants and witnesses will be thoroughly examined with regard to the character of the land; whether the same has been thoroughly prospected; whether or not there exists within the tract or tracts claimed any lode or vein of quartz or other rock in place, bearing gold, silver, cinnabar, lead, tin or copper, or other valuable deposit which has ever been claimed, located, recorded or worked; whether such work is entirely abandoned or whether occasionally resumed; if such lode does exist, by whom claimed, under what designation, and in which subdivision of the land it lies; whether any placer mine or mines exist upon the land; if so, what is the character thereof—whether of the shallow surface description or of the deep cement, blue lead or gravel deposits; to what extent mining is carried on when water can be obtained, and what the facilities are for obtaining water for mining purposes; upon what particular ten-acre subdivisions mining has been done, and at what time the land was abandoned for mining purposes, if abandoned at all. § 106, circular, Dec. 15, 1897.

Agricultural Capacities.—The testimony should also show the agricultural capacities of the land, what kind of crops are raised thereon, and the value thereof; the number of acres actually cultivated for crops of cereals or vegetables, and within which particular ten-acre subdivision such crops are raised; also which of these subdivisions embrace the improvements, giving in detail the extent and value of the improvements, such as house, barn, vineyard, orchard, fencing, etc., and mining improvements. § 107, Id.

Existence of Mineral.[68]—The testimony should be as full and complete as possible; and in addition to the leading points indicated above, where an attempt is made to prove the mineral character of lands which have been entered under the agricultural laws, it should show at what date, if at all, valuable deposits of mineral were first known to exist on the lands. § 108, Id.

SURVEY TO DIVIDE AGRICULTURAL AND MINERAL LANDS.

PROVISION OF U. S. STATUTES.

Mineral Lands How Set Apart as Agricultural Lands.—Upon the survey of the lands described in the preceding section, the Secretary of the Interior may designate and set apart such portions

---

[68] German I. Do. v. Hayden, 40 P. 453, Col.

of the same as are clearly agricultural lands, which lands shall thereafter be subject to pre-emption and sale as other public lands, and be subject to all the laws and regulations applicable to the same. § 2342, Id.

LAND OFFICE REGULATIONS.

Survey at Applicant's Expense.—When the case comes before this office such decision will be made as the law and the facts may justify; in cases where a survey is necessary to set apart the mineral from the agricultural land, the proper party *at his own expense* will be required to have the work done, at his option, either by United States deputy, county or other local surveyor; application therefor must be made to the register and receiver, accompanied by a description of the land to be segregated, and the evidence of service upon the opposite party of notice of his intention to have such segregation made; the register and receiver will forward the same to this office, when the necessary instructions for the survey will be given. The survey in such case, where the claims to be segregated are vein or lode claims, must be executed in such manner as will conform to the requirements in Section 2320, United States Revised Statutes, as to length and width and parallel end lines. § 109, circular, Dec. 15, 1897.

Verification of Survey.—Such survey when executed must be properly sworn to by the surveyor, either before a notary public, officer of a court of record or before the register or receiver, the deponent's character and credibility to be properly certified to by the officer administering the oath. § 110, Id.

Report to Surveyor General.—Upon the filing of

the plat and field notes of such survey with the register and receiver, duly sworn to as aforesaid, they will transmit the same to the surveyor gèneral for his verification and approval; who, if he finds the work correctly performed, will properly mark out the same upon the original township plat in his office, and furnish authenticated copies of such plat and description both to the proper local land office and to this office, to be affixed to the duplicate and triplicate township plats respectively. § 111, Id.

Plat.—With the copy of plat and description furnished the local office and this office, must be a diagram tracing, verified by the surveyor general, showing the claim or claims segregated, and designating the separate fractional agricultural tracts in each forty-acre legal subdivision by the proper lot number, beginning with No. 1 in each section, and giving the area in each lot, the same as provided in paragraph 45, in the survey of mining claims on surveyed lands. § 112, Id.

Mineral Land.—The fact that a certain tract of land is decided upon testimony to be mineral in character is by no means equivalent to an award of the land to a miner. In order to secure a patent for such land he must proceed as in other cases, in accordance with the foregoing regulations.

Blank forms for proofs in mineral cases are not furnished by the General Land Office. § 113, Id.

TESTIMONY MAY BE GIVEN BEFORE ANY AUTHORIZED OFFICER OF THE DISTRICT.

PROVISIONS OF U. S. STATUTES.

Proofs—How Taken in Contests.—In cases of contest, as to the mineral or agricultural character of land, the testimony and proofs may be taken as herein provided, on personal notice of at least ten days to the opposing party; or if such party cannot be found, then by publication of at least once a week for thirty days in a newspaper, to be designated by the register of the land office as published nearest to the location of such land; and the register shall require proof that such notice has been given. § 2335, Id.

Testimony by Deposition.—Such depositions may be taken before "any officer authorized to administer oaths within the land district," in the manner above stated, but it is usually better to present the testimony orally before the deciding officers, if it can be done.

MINERAL LANDS RESERVED FROM GRANTS.

PROVISIONS OF U. S. STATUTES.

Grants of Lands to States or Corporations Not to Include Mineral Lands.—No act passed at the first session of the Thirty-eighth Congress, granting lands to States or corporations to aid in the construction of roads, or for other purposes, or to extend the time of grants made prior to the thirtieth day of January, eighteen hundred and sixty-five, shall be so construed as to embrace mineral lands, which in all cases are reserved exclusively to the United States, unless otherwise specially provided in the act or acts making the grant. § 2346, Id.

LAND OFFICE REGULATIONS.

Railroad Selections.—Where a railroad company

seeks to select lands not returned as mineral, but within six miles of any mining location, claim or entry, or where in the case of a selection by a State, the lands sought to be selected are within a township in which there is a mining location, claim or entry, publication must be made of the lands selected at the expense of the railroad company or State for a period of sixty days, with posting for the same period in the land office for the district in which the lands are situated, during which period of publication the local land officers will receive protests or contests for any of said tracts or subdivisions of lands claimed to be more valuable for mining than for agricultural purposes. § 104, circular, Dec. 15, 1897.

Report to Commissioner.—At the expiration of the period of publication the register and receiver will forward to the Commissioner of the General Land Office the published list, noting thereon any protests or contests or suggestions as to the mineral character of any such lands, together with any information they may have received as to the mineral character of any of the lands mentioned in said list, when a hearing may be ordered. § 105, Id.

CITIZENSHIP—HOW ESTABLISHED.

PROVISIONS OF U. S. STATUTES,

Mineral Lands Open to Purchase by Citizens.— All valuable mineral deposits in lands belonging to the United States, both surveyed and unsurveyed, are hereby declared to be free and open to exploration and purchase; and the lands in which they are found to occupation and purchase by citizens of the United States, and those who have declared their intention to become such. § 2319, Id.

Proof of Citizenship.—Proof of citizenship, under this chapter, may consist, in the case of an individual, of his own affidavit thereof; in the case of an association of persons unincorporated, of the affidavit of their authorized agent, made on his own knowledge, or upon information and belief; and in the case of a corporation, organized under the laws of the United States, or of any State or Territory thereof, by the filing of a certified copy of their charter, or certificate of incorporation. § 2321, Id.

Of Applicants for Mineral Lands.—Applicants for mineral patents, if residing beyond the limits of the district wherein the claim is situated, may make any oath or affidavit required for proof of citizenship before the clerk of any court of record, or before any notary public of any State or Territory. 22 S. L. 49, I Supp. 338.

LAND OFFICE REGULATIONS.

Manner of Proof of Citizenship.—The proof necessary to establish the citizenship of applicants for mining patents must be made in the following manner: In case of an incorporated company, a certified copy of their charter or certificate of incorporation must be filed. In case of an association of persons unincorporated, the affidavit of their duly authorized agent, made upon his own knowledge or upon information and belief, setting forth the residence of each person forming such association, must be submitted. This affidavit must be accompanied by a power of attorney from the parties forming such association, authorizing the person who makes the affidavit of citizenship to act for them in the matter of their application for patent. § 68, circular, Dec. 15, 1897.

Proof by Agent.—In case of an individual or an association of individuals who do not appear by their duly authorized agent, you will require the affidavit of each applicant, showing whether he is a native or naturalized citizen, when and where born, and his residence. § 69, Id.

Citizenship Only Restriction on Right of Entry. —The foregoing provisions of law as to citizenship is the only restriction upon the right to enter mineral lands on the public domain, the privilege being otherwise open to all, regardless of age or sex.[69]

Naturalized Citizen.—In case an applicant has declared his intention to become a citizen or has been naturalized, his affidavit must show the date, place and the court before which he declared his intention, or from which his certificate of citizenship issued, and present residence. § 70, Id.

Affidavit—Where Made.—The affidavit of the claimant as to his citizenship may be taken before the register or receiver or any other officer authorized to administer oaths within the land district; or, if the claimant is residing beyond the limits of the district, the affidavit may be taken before the clerk of any court of record or before any notary public of any State or Territory. § 71, Id.

Any Place or Officer.—If citizenship is established by the testimony of disinterested persons, such testimony may be taken at any place before

---

[69] Harris v. Kellog, 49 P. 708, Cal.; Thompson v. Spray 72 Cal., 528, 14 I. 182.

any person authorized to administer oaths, and whose official character is duly verified. § 72, Id.

Proof by Affidavit Sufficient.—"At all events, in view of the practical difficulties in making the proofs, or for some other reason, the statute has modified the rule of evidence in this instance, and made such affidavits not only competent, but sufficient proof of citizenship; for it requires no other. * * * and in my judgment the provisions apply to all the purposes of the act—to the litigation of all claims arising under the act, whether in the department, or in the ordinary courts of the country." North N. M. Co. v. Orient M. Co., 11 Fed. 125.[70]

Alien Locator's Entry Made Valid by Naturalization.—"Mr. Justice Lamar, when Secretary of the Interior, ruled that, an alien having made homestead entry, and subsequently filed his intention to become a citizen, the alienage at time of entry, in the absence of an adverse claim, would not defeat the right of purchase. Jackson v. Beach, 1 Johns. Cas. 399; Governeur v. Robertson, 11 Wheat. 332, and Osterman v. Baldwin, 6 Wall. 116, were cited to the point that naturalization has a retroactive effect, so as to be deemed a waiver of all liability to forfeiture, and a confirmation of title. This seems to have long been the settled rule in the land department." Manuel v. Wulff, 14 S. C. R. 651, 152 U. S. 505.

Alien Grantee Made Competent by Naturaliza-

---

[70] North N. M. Co. v. Orient M. Co., 11 F. 125; Shultz v. Allyn, 48 P. 960, Ariz.

tion.—"The alien grantee of a qualified locator of a mining claim takes by virtue of the conveyance, and not by operation of law. His incapacity to take and hold, by reason of alienage, is open to question by the Government only; and the infirmity is removed by naturalization before judgment rendered in proceedings on adverse claim to a patent." Manuel v. Wulff, 14 S. C. R. 651, 152 U. S. 505.

Corporation May Locate Mining Claim.[71]—"A corporation, all of whose members are citizens of the United States, is competent to locate a mining claim." McKinley v. Wheeler, 9 S. C. R. 638, 130 U. S. 630.

Corporation Claimant Treated as One Person.— "There may be some question raised as to the extent of a claim which a corporation may be permitted to locate as an original discoverer. It may, perhaps, be treated as one person, and entitled to locate only to the extent permitted to a single individual." McKinley v. Wheeler, 9 S. C. R. 638, 130 U. S. 630.

ALIENS MAY ACQUIRE TITLE TO MINERAL LANDS.

PROVISIONS OF U. S. STATUTES.

Transfers Not Restricted.—Nothing herein contained shall be construed to prevent the alienation of a title conveyed by a patent for a mining claim to any person whatever. § 2326, Id.

[71] McKinley v. Wheeler, 9 S. C. R. 638, 130 U. S. 630; Doe v. Waterloo M. Co., 70 F. 455; Thomas v. Chisholm, 13 Col. 105, 21 P. 1019; North Noonday M. Co. v. Orient M. Co., 1 F. 522.

Alien Land Ownership in Territories Prohibited.
—No alien or person who is not a citizen of the
United States, or who has not declared his intention to become a citizen of the United States in the
manner provided by law, shall acquire title to or
own any land in any of the Territories of the United
States except as hereinafter provided.

In Cities, Mines, Etc.—This act shall not be construed to prevent any persons not citizens of the
United States from acquiring or holding lots or par-
cels of lands in any incorporated or platted city,
town or village, or in any mine or mining claim, in
any of the Territories of the United States.

Public Lands Not Affected.[72]—Nor to authorize
aliens to acquire title from the United States to any
of the public lands of the United States or to in any
manner affect or change the laws regulating the disposal of the public lands of the United States. 29
S. L. 618, II Supp. 573.

FEES ESTABLISHED BY LAW.
PROVISIONS OF U. S. STATUTES.

Fees and Commissions of Register and Receiver.
—Registers and receivers, in addition to their sal-
aries, shall be allowed each the following fees and
commissions, namely: * * * * A fee of five dollars for filing and acting upon each application
for patent or adverse claim filed for mineral lands,
to be paid by the respective parties. § 2238, Id.

72 Billings v. Aspen M. & S. Co. 51 F. 338, 52 F. 250; Lone Jack M. Co.
v. Megginson, 82 F. 89; Wood v. Aspen M. & S. Co., 36 F. 25; Croesus M.
Co. v. Colorado Co., 19 F. 78; Santa P. W. v. Peralta, 45 P. 168, Cal.

LAND OFFICE REGULATIONS.

Patent Applications.—The fees payable to the register and receiver for filing and acting upon applications for mineral land patents are $5 to. each officer, to be paid by the applicant for patent at the time of filing, and the like sum of $5 is payable to each officer by an adverse claimant at the time of filing his adverse claim. § 97, circular, Dec. 15, 1897.

Receiver's Receipt.—At the time of payment of fee for mining application or adverse claim the receiver will issue his receipt therefor in duplicate, one to be given the applicant or adverse claimant, as the case may be, and one to be forwarded to the Commissioner of the General Land Office *on the day of issue.* The receipt for mining application should have attached the certificate of the register that the lands included in the application are vacant lands subject to such appropriation. § 98, Id.

Report to Commissioner.—The register and receiver will, at the close of each month, forward to this office an abstract of mining applications filed, and a register of receipts, accompanied with an abstract of mineral lands sold, and an abstract of adverse claims filed. § 99, Id.

Fees Credited of U. S.—The fees and purchase money received by registers and receivers must be placed to the credit of the United States in the receiver's monthly and quarterly account, charging up in the disbursing account the sums to which the register and receiver may be respectively entitled as fees and commissions, with limitations in regard to the legal maximum. § 100, Id.

FEES SUBJECT TO REGULATION BY COMMISSIONER OF U. S. LAND OFFICE.

PROVISIONS OF U. S. STATUTES.

Surveyor General to Appoint Surveyors of Mining Claims, Etc.—The Surveyor General of the United States may appoint, in each land district containing mineral lands, as many competent surveyors as shall apply for appointment to survey mining claims. § 2334, Id.

Fees of Surveyor, Etc., to be Paid by Claimant.—The expenses of the survey of vein or lode claims, and the survey and subdivision of placer claims into smaller quantities than one hundred and sixty acres, together with the cost of publication of notices, shall be paid by the applicants, and they shall be at liberty to obtain the same at the most reasonable rates, and they shall also be at liberty to employ any United States deputy surveyor to make the survey. § 2334, Id.

Maximum Charges Fixed by Commissioner.—The Commissioner of the General Land Office shall also have power to establish the maximum charges for surveys and publication of notices under this chapter; and, in case of excessive charges for publication, he may designate any newspaper published in a land district where mines are situated, for the publication of mining notices in such district, and fix the rates to be charged by such paper. § 2334. Id.

Affidavit of Charges and Fees Filed with Final Proof.—And, to the end that the Commissioner

may be fully informed on the subject, each applicant shall file with the register a sworn statement
of all charges and fees paid by such applicant for
publication and surveys, together with all fees and
money paid the register and the receiver of the
land office, which statement shall be transmitted,
with the other papers in the case, to the Commissioner of the General Land Office. § 2334, Id.

LAND OFFICE REGULATIONS.

Publication Fees.—Under this authority of law
the following rates have been established as the
maximum charges for newspaper publications in
mining cases:

(1) Where ·a daily newspaper is designated the
charge shall not exceed $7 for each ten lines of
space occupied, and where a weekly newspaper is
designated as the medium of publication $5 for the
same space will be allowed. Such charge shall be
accepted as full payment for publication in each
issue of the newspaper for the entire period required by law.

It is expected that these notices shall not be so
abbreviated as to curtail the description essential to
a perfect notice, and the said rates established upon
the understanding that they are to be in the usual
body type used for advertisements.

(2) For the publication of citations in contests or
hearings involving the character of lands the charges
shall not exceed $8 for five publications in weekly
newspapers or $10 for publications in daily news-
papers for thirty days. § 91, circular, Dec. 15, 1897.

Deputy Surveyors.—The surveyors general of the
several districts will, in pursuance of said law, appoint in each land district as many *competent* deputies

for the survey of mining claims as may seek such appointment, it being distinctly understood that all expenses of these notices and surveys are to be borne by the mining claimants and not by the United States. The claimant may employ *any* deputy surveyor within such district to do his work in the field. § 92, Id.

Must Give Bond.—Each deputy mineral surveyor before entering upon the duties of his office or appointment shall be required to enter into such bond for the faithful performance of his duties as may be prescribed by the regulations of the Land Department in force at that time. § 92, Id.

Fees for Office Work.—With regard to the *platting* of the claim and other *office work* in the surveyor general's office, that officer will make an estimate of the cost thereof, which amount the claimant will deposit with any assistant United States treasurer or designated depository in favor of the United States Treasurer, to be passed to the credit of the fund created by "individual depositors for surveys of the public lands," and file with the surveyor general duplicate certificates of such deposit in the usual manner. § 93, Id.

At Least One Deputy in Each District.—The surveyors general will endeavor to appoint mineral deputy surveyors, so that one or more may be located in each mining district for the greater convenience of miners. § 94, Id.

Verified Report of Deputy.—The usual oaths will be required of these deputies and their assistants as to the correctness of each survey executed by them.

The duty of the deputy mineral surveyor ceases when he has executed the survey and returned the field notes and preliminary plat thereof with his report to the surveyor general.

Deputy Cannot Act as Attorney.—He will not be allowed to prepare for the mining claimant the papers in support of an application for patent or otherwise perform the duties of an attorney before the land office in connection with a mining claim. § 95, Id.

Exhorbitant Fees.—Should it appear that excessive or exorbitant charges have been made by any surveyor or any publisher, prompt action will be taken with the view of correcting the abuse. § 96, Id.

TITLE TO LODE OR PLACER CLAIMS MAY BE ACQUIRED BY VIRTUE OF LOCAL STATUTES OF LIMITATION.

PROVISIONS OF U. S. STATUTES.

What Evidence of Possession, Etc., to Establish a Right to a Patent.—Where such person or association, they and their grantors, have held and worked their claims for a period equal to the time prescribed by the statute of limitations for mining claims of the State or Territory where the same may be situated, evidence of such possession, and working of the claims for such period, shall be sufficient to establish a right to a patent thereto under this chapter, in the absence of any adverse claim. § 2332, Id.

LAND OFFICE REGULATIONS.

Convenient Provision.—This provision of law will greatly lessen the burden of proof, more especially in the case of old claims located many years since, the records of which, in many cases, have been destroyed by fire, or lost in other ways during the lapse of time, but concerning the possessory right to which all controversy or litigation has long been settled. § 76, circular, Dec. 15, 1897.

Proof of Statute.—When an applicant desires to make his proof of possessory right in accordance with this provision of law, he will not be required to produce evidence of location, copies of conveyances or abstracts of title, as in other cases, but will be required to furnish a duly certified copy of the statute of limitation of mining claims for the State or Territory, together with his sworn statement giving a clear and succinct narration of the facts as to the origin of his title, and likewise as to the continuation of his possession of the mining ground covered by his application; the area thereof; the nature and extent of the mining that has been done thereon; whether there has been any opposition to his possession, or litigation with regard to his claim and, if so, when the same ceased; whether such cessation was caused by compromise or by judicial decree, and any additional facts within the claimant's knowledge having a direct bearing upon his possession and bona fides which he may desire to submit in support of his claim. § 77, Id.

Non-Pendency of Litigation.—There should likewise be filed a certificate, under seal of the court having jurisdiction of mining cases within the judicial district embracing the claim, that no suit or action of any character whatever involving the right of possession to any portion of the claim applied for is pending, and that there has been no litigation before said court affecting the title to said claim or any part thereof for a period equal to the time fixed by the statute of limitations for mining claims in the State or Territory as aforesaid, other than that which has been finally decided in favor of the claimant. § 78, Id.

Corroborative Evidence.—The claimant should support his narrative of facts relative to his possession, occupancy and improvements by corroborative testimony of any disinterested person or persons of credibility who may be cognizant of the facts in the case and are capable of testifying understandingly in the premises. § 79, Id.

LAW OF ALASKA.

Statute of Limitation—One Year.—One year's adverse possession of a mining claim, immediately preceding the commencement of an action therefor, by the defendant or those under whom he holds, if pleaded, is a bar to the action for the possession thereof. Laws of Oregon, Oct. 21, 1864, § 2178, H. A. L. O. 1887.

Forfeiture After One Year.—If any claim shall not be worked for twelve consecutive months, it shall be forfeited, and considered liable to location by any person or persons, unless the owner or owners be absent on account of sickness or in the service of their country in time of war. Laws of Oregon, Oct. 24, 1864, § 3828, H. A. L. O. 1887.

One Year's Adverse Possession of Claims in Alaska.—The year of adverse possession which shall constitute a bar to an action for the possession of a claim applies only to unpatented claims and cannot commence to run until the claimant against whom the fact is urged has been in default in complying with the requirements of law, if the plea be made by a subsequent, against a prior, locator. It would be possible for one to be unlawfully in possession, for more than a year, of the claim of another who had fully complied with the law, but the trespasser could thereby acquire no rights.[78]

Possession or Location Impossible on a Claim Not in Default.—The law (Section 2322, R. S.), in express terms, guarantees to the locator complying therewith exclusive possession and enjoyment of his claim, and it is therefore impossible that an intruder, acting in defiance of its provisions, could secure title or rights which the government would recognize. As said in Belk v. Meagher, 104 U. S. 279, "Locations can only be made where the law allows it to be done. Any attempt to go beyond that will be of no avail. Hence, a relocation on lands actually covered at the time by another valid and subsisting location is void; and this not only against the prior locator, but all the world, because the law allows no such thing to be done. * * * The right to the possession comes only from a valid location. Consequently, if there is no location there can be no possession under it. Location does not, necessarily, follow from possession, but possession from location."

Forfeiture.—Likewise the law of Alaska (Oregon) providing for a forfeiture after one year's failure to work, means one year after the rights of the claimant have expired. It is practically the same as the federal statute on the subject (Section 2324), but is void in respect to the exception therein made

---

[78] Hamilton v. Southern N. G. & S. M. Co., 33 F. 562; Harris v. Equator M. S. Co., 8 F. 863; Altoona Q. M. Co. v. Integral Q. M. Co., 45 P. 1047, Cal.

"unless the owner or owners be absent on account of sickness or in the service of their country in time of war," the same being to that extent in conflict with the provisions of the U. S. statutes.

RIGHT OF LIEN PRESERVED.
PROVISIONS OF U. S. STATUTES.

Liens Not Impaired by Patent.—But nothing in this chapter shall be deemed to impair any lien which may have attached in any way whatever to any mining claim, or property thereto attached prior to the issuance of a patent. § 2332, Id.

As there was no law in force in Oregon on May 17, 1884, in reference to liens on mines, there is no statutory lien of that kind available in that Territory. [74]

Mechanic's liens upon ditches and flumes may be enfored under the following statute:

"The laws relative to the sale and transfer of real estate and the application of the liens of mechanics and laborers therein, be and they are hereby made applicable to said ditches and flumes." Laws of Oregon, Oct. 24, 1864, § 3834, H. A. L. O. 1887.

AFFIDAVITS MAY BE VERIFIED AND PROOF TAKEN BEFORE ANY AUTHORIZED OFFICER IN THE LAND DISTRICT.
PROVISIONS OF U. S. STATUTES. -

Verification of Affidavits, Etc.—All affidavits required to be made under this chapter may be veri-

---

[74] Bear L. R. W. I. Co. v. Garland, 17 S. C. R. 7, 104 U. S. 1.

fied before any officer authorized to administer oaths within the land district where the claims may be situated, and all testimony and proofs may be taken before any such officer; and, when duly certified by the officer taking the same, shall have the same force and effect as if taken before the register and receiver of the land office. § 2335, Id.

COMPLETE DEVELOPMENT OF MINES MAY BE REQUIRED BY LOCAL LEGISLATION.

PROVISIONS OF U. S. STATUTES.

What Conditions of Sale May be Made by Local Legislature.—As a condition of sale, in the absence of necessary legislation by Congress, the local legislature of any State or Territory may provide rules for working mines, involving easements, drainage, and other necessary means to their complete development; and those conditions shall be fully expressed in the patent. § 2338, Id.

Local Legislation Is Congressional Legislation. —The only legislation of the kind mentioned in the foregoing provision of statute possible for Alaska must come from Congress, and, consequently, such law is a nullity as to that Territory.

PRESIDENT GIVEN AUTHORITY TO PRO-VIDE NECESSARY OFFICERS IN MINING DISTRICTS.

PROVISIONS OF U. S. STATUTES.

Additional Land Districts and Officers, Power

of the President to Provide.—The President is authorized to establish additional land districts, and to appoint the necessary officers under existing laws, wherever he may deem the same necessary for the public convenience in executing the provisions of this chapter. § 2343, Id.

EXISTING RIGHTS PROTECTED.

PROVISIONS OF U. S. STATUTES.

Provisions of this Chapter Not to Affect Certain Rights.—Nothing contained in this chapter shall be construed to impair in any way, rights or interests in mining property acquired under existing laws; nor to affect the provisions of the act entitled "An act granting to A. Sutro the right of way and other privileges to aid in the construction of a draining and exploring tunnel to the Comstock lode, in the State of Nevada," approved July twenty-five, eighteen hundred and sixty-six. § 2344, Id.

STATES NOT SUBJECT TO MINING LAWS.

PROVISIONS OF U. S. STATUTES.

Mineral Lands in Certain States Excepted.—The provisions of the preceding sections of this chapter shall not apply to the mineral lands situated in the States of Michigan, Wisconsin, and Minnesota, which are declared free and open to exploration and purchase, according to legal subdivisions, in like manner as before the tenth day of May, eighteen hundred and seventy-two. And any bona fide entries of such lands within the

States named since the tenth of May, eighteen hundred and seventy-two, may be patented without reference to any of the foregoing provisions of this chapter. Such lands shall be offered for public sale in the same manner, at the same minimum price, and under the same rights of pre-emption as other public lands. § 2345, Id.

TOWNSITE ENTRIES IN ALASKA AUTHORIZED, BUT MINERAL RESERVED.

PROVISIONS OF U. S. STATUTES.

Alaska — Town Sites; How Entered.—That until otherwise ordered by Congress lands in Alaska may be entered for town site purposes, for the several use and benefit of the occupants of such town sites, by such trustee or trustees as may be named by the Secretary of the Interior for that purpose, such entries to be made under the provisions of section twenty-three hundred and eighty-seven of the Revised Statutes as near as may be. § 11, 26 S. L. 1095, I Supp. 940.

Survey and Division of Lots.—And when such entries shall have been made the Secretary of the Interior shall provide by regulation for the proper execution of the trust in favor of the inhabitants of the town site, including the survey of the land into lots, according to the spirit and intent of said Section 2387, of the Revised Statutes, whereby the same results would be reached as though the entry had been made by a county judge and the disposal of the lots in such town site and the proceeds of the sale thereby had been prescribed by the legislative authority of a State or Territory. Id.

Limit of Entry.—Provided, That no more than 640 acres shall be embraced in one town site entry. Id.

PRECIOUS METALS RESERVED.

Town Site Entries Not to Include Mining Rights.—That town site entries may be made by incorporated towns and cities on the mineral lands of the United States, but no title shall be acquired by such towns or cities to any vein of gold, silver, cinnabar, copper or lead, or to any valid mining claim or possession held under existing law. 16, Id.

Mining Claims in Incorporated Town Reserved.—When mineral veins are possessed within the limits of an incorporated town or city, and such possession is recognized by local authority or by the laws of the United States, the title to town lots shall be subject to such recognized possession and the necessary use thereof and when entry has been made or patent issued for such town sites to such incorporated town or city, the possessor of such mineral vein may enter and receive patent for such mineral vein, and the surface ground appertaining thereto. Id.

Prior Right of Surface Owner Protected.—Provided, That no entry shall be made by such mineral vein claimant for surface ground where the owner or occupier of the surface ground shall have had possession of the same before the inception of the title of the mineral vein applicant. Id.

LAND CONTAINING COAL OR PRECIOUS METAL RESERVED.

Title to lands in Alaska may, also, be acquired for purposes of "trade and manufactures," under the provisions of §§ 12 and 13 of the above mentioned act of Congress; but it will be observed that by the terms of the following quoted section of the same act, land containing coal, or the precious metals, is excluded from the operation of said act.

What Lands Reserved from Entry Under this Act.—That none of the provisions of the last two preceding sections of this act (concerning sales of land for trade and manufactures) shall be so construed as to warrant the sale of any lands belonging to the United States which shall contain coal or the precious metals. § 14, 26 S. L. 1095, I. Supp. 944.

TOWN SITE AND OTHER RESERVATIONS CONSTRUED.

Patent for Town Site or Trade and Manufactures Excepts Known Mineral.—The following provisions of statute as to town site entries, and entries for purposes of trade and manufacture, are, of course, applicable to unpatented lands only, for when a patent is issued in either case, it conveys to the patentee whatever underlies the surface, the only exception being when at the time of the issuance of the patent the patentee was aware that the entry contained valuable mineral deposits of the kind reserved by the law above quoted.

The rule in such cases is stated in Dower v. Richards, 14 S. C. R. 452, 151 U. S. 658, as follows:

"It is established by former decisions of this court that, under the acts of Congress which govern this case, in order to except mines or mineral lands from the operation of a town site patent, it is not sufficient that the lands do in fact contain minerals, or even valuable minerals, when the town site patent takes effect, but they must, at that time, be known to contain minerals of such extent and value as to justify expenditures for the purpose of extracting them; and, if the lands are not known at that time to be so valuable for mining purposes, the fact that they have once been valuable, or are afterwards discovered to be still valuable, for such purposes, does not defeat or impair the title of persons claiming under the town site patent."[75]

Town Site Lands Outside of Patented Portion.— "Valuable mineral deposits in such lands outside of the patent are equally open to exploration and purchase as those in lands outside of the town site. It was in reference to mines in unoccupied public lands in unpatented town sites that the language in Steel v. Smelting Co. was used, and to them and to mines in public lands in patented town sites outside of the limits of the patent it is only applicable." Davis v. Wiebbold, 11 S. C. R. 628, 139 U. S. 507.

---

[75] Deffeback v. Hawke, 6 S. C. R. 95, 115 U. S. 352; Steel v. St. L. R. Co., 1 S. C. R. 389, 106 U. S. 447; Carter v. Thompson, 65 F. 329; Bonner v. Meikle, 82 F. 697; Martin v. Browner, 11 Col. 12; Hartman v. Smith. 7 Mont. 19; Butte City S. H. L. C., 6 Mont 397, 12 P. 858; Silver Bow M. & M. Co. v. Clark, 5 Mont. 378, 5 P. 574; Talbot v. King, 6 Mont. 76, 9 P. 434; Poire v. Wells, 6 Col. 406.

MINERAL ENTRIES IN FOREST RESERVATIONS.

PROVISIONS OF U. S. STATUTES.

The following is an extract from circular entitled "Rules and Regulations Governing Forest Reservations," established under section 24 of the act of March 3, 1891 (26 Stat. L. 1095). Approved June 30, 1897. (24 L. D. 589-593-594.)

LOCATION AND ENTRY OF MINERAL LANDS.

Mineral Lands in Forest Reserves.—The law provides that "any mineral lands in any forest reservation which have been or which may be shown to be such, and subject to entry under the existing mining laws of the United States and the rules and regulations applying thereto, shall continue to be subject to such location and entry," notwithstanding the reservation. This makes mineral lands in the forest reserves subject to location and entry under the general mining laws in the usual manner. § 19, circular, Dec. 15, 1897.

Timber on Such Claims.—Owners of valid mining locations made and held in good faith under the mining laws of the United States and the regulations thereunder are authorized and permitted to fell and remove from such mining claims any timber growing thereon, for actual mining purposes in connection with the particular claim from which the timber is felled or removed. (For further use of timber by miners see below, under heading "Free use of timber and stone.") § 20, Id.

FREE USE OF TIMBER AND STONE.

Timber and Stone Free.—The law provides that "The Secretary of the Interior may permit, under regulations to be prescribed by him, the use of timber and stone found upon such reservations, free of charge, by bona fide settlers, miners, residents and prospectors for minerals, for firewood, fencing, buildings, mining, prospecting and other domestic purposes, as may be needed by such persons for such purposes; such timber to be used within the State or Territory, respectively, where such reservations may be located." § 21, Id.

Use Limited to Actual Needs.—This provision is limited to persons resident in forest reservations who have not a sufficient supply of timber or stone on their own claims or lands for the purposes enumerated, or for necessary use in developing the mineral or other natural resources of the lands owned or occupied by them. Such persons, therefore, are permitted to take timber and stone from public lands in the forest reservations under the terms of the law above quoted, strictly for their individual use on their own claims or lands owned or occupied by them, but not for sale or disposal, or use on other lands, or by other persons. Provided, That where the stumpage value exceeds $100, application must be made to and permission given by the department. § 21, Id.

EXTENT TO WHICH COAL LANDS MAY BE ENTERED.

PROVISIONS OF U. S. STATUTES.

Entry of Coal Lands.—Every person above the age of twenty-one years, who is a citizen of the United States, or who has declared his intention to become such, or any association of persons severally qualified as above, shall, upon application to the register of the proper land office, have the right to enter, by legal subdivisions, any quantity of vacant coal lands of the United States not otherwise appropriated or reserved by competent authority, not exceeding one hundred and sixty acres, to such individual person, or three hundred and twenty acres to such association, upon payment to the receiver of not less than ten dollars per acre for such lands, where the same shall be situated more than fifteen miles from any completed railroad, and not less than twenty dollars per acre for such lands as shall be within fifteen miles of such road. § 2347, Id.

Monopoly of Coal Lands Forbidden.—"It is the case of an association seeking to evade an act of Congress by using, for its own benefit, the names of both its members and employes to obtain from the Government vacant coal lands, which it could not legally obtain upon entries made in its own name, and which it was expressly forbidden to enter by reason of some of its members having previously taken the benefit of the statute." United States v. Trinidad C. & C. Co., 11 S. C. R. 57, 137 U. S. 160.

PREFERENCE RIGHT OF ENTRY TO THOSE IN POSSESSION.

PROVISIONS OF U. S. STATUTES.

Pre-emption of Coal Lands.—Any person or association of persons severally qualified, as above provided, who have opened and improved, or shall hereafter open and improve, any coal mine or mines upon the public lands, and shall be in actual possession of the same, shall be entitled to a preference right of entry, under the preceding section, of the mines so opened and improved: Provided, That when any association of not less than four persons, severally qualified as above provided, shall have expended not less than $5,000 in working and improving any such mine or mines such association may enter not exceeding 640 acres, including such mining improvements. § 2348, Id.

TIME WITHIN WHICH CLAIM MUST BE MADE.

PROVISIONS OF U. S. STATUTES.

Pre-emption Claims of Coal Lands to Be Presented Within Sixty Days, Etc.—All claims under the preceding section must be presented to the register of the proper land district within sixty days after the date of actual possession and the commencement of improvements on the land, by the filing of a declaratory statement therefor; but when the township plat is not on file at the date of such improvement, filing must be made within sixty days from the receipt of such plat at the district office; and where the improvements shall have been made prior to the expiration of three months from the third day of March, eighteen hundred and seventy-three, sixty days from the expiration of such three months shall be allowed for the filing of a declaratory statement, and no sale under the provisions of this section shall be allowed until the expiration of six months from the third day of March, eighteen hundred and seventy-three. § 2349, Id.

NUMBER OF ENTRIES AND TIME OF PROOF AND PAYMENT LIMITED.

PROVISIONS OF U. S. STATUTES.

Only One Entry Allowed.—The three preceding sections shall be held to authorize only one entry by the same person or association of persons; and no association of persons any member of which shall have taken the benefit of such sections, either as an individual or as a member of any other association, shall enter or hold any other lands under the provisions thereof; and no member of any association which shall have taken the benefit of such sections shall enter or hold any other lands under their provisions. § 2350, Id.

Forfeiture After One Year.—And all persons claiming under Section 2348 shall be required to prove their respective rights and pay for the lands filed upon within one year from the time prescribed for filing their respective claims; and upon failure to file the proper notice, or to pay for the land within the required period, the same shall be subject to entry by any other qualified applicant. § 2350, Id.

PRIORITY SECURES PREFERENCE.

PROVISIONS OF U. S. STATUTES.

Conflicting Claim.—In case of conflicting claims upon coal lands where the improvements shall be commenced, after the third day of March, eighteen hundred and seventy-three, priority of possession and improvement, followed by proper filing and continued good faith, shall determine the preference right to purchase. And also where improvements have already been made prior to the third day of March, eighteen hundred and seventy-three, division of the land claimed may be made by legal subdivisions, to include, as near as may be, the valuable improvements of the respective parties. The Commissioner of the General Land Office is authorized to issue all needful rules and regulations for carrying into effect the provisions of this and the four preceding sections. § 2351, Id.

LANDS VALUABLE FOR MINES OF GOLD, SILVER OR COPPER NOT SUBJECT TO PRE-EMPTION.

PROVISIONS OF U. S. STATUTES.

Rights Reserved.—Nothing in the five preceding sections shall be construed to destroy or impair any rights which may have attached prior to the third day of March, eighteen hundred and seventy-three, or to authorize the sale of lands valuable for mines of gold, silver or copper. § 2352, Id.

FORM 1.

LODE DISCOVERER'S NOTICE.

Notice is hereby given that as discoverer of this lode, I claim the right to locate two claims thereon, one on each side of this point, each 1,500 feet in length along the strike of the lode.

Dated, May 1, 1898. DISCOVERER.

FORM 2.

LODE LOCATION NOTICE.

(To be posted).

Notice is hereby given that I have this day located the John Brown lode, discovered by me May 1, 1898, and hereby claim 750 feet easterly and 750 feet westerly of this point (or of the discovery shaft) along the strike of said lode.

Dated, May 31, 1898. LOCATOR.

FORM 3.

MARKING ON GROUND.

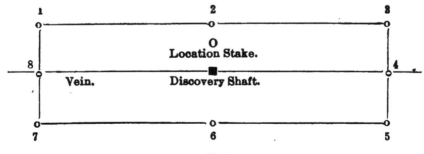

FORM 4.
LODE LOCATION CERTIFICATE.
(To be recorded).

This is to certify that I am a citizen of the United States; that on May 1, 1898, I discovered the John Brown lode in the Circle City Mining District of Alaska, and upon said date duly posted thereon notice of such discovery; that on May 31, 1898, after due exploration, I located the same, duly marked on the ground the boundaries of the same, and duly posted notice of location thereon describing the same as by law required; that said claim is now being and since its said discovery (or location) has been, continuously worked by me; that I hereby claim the exclusive possession and enjoyment of all the surface included within the lines of said location and of all veins, lodes and ledges throughout their entire depth, the top or apex of which lies inside of such surface lines extended downward vertically, although such veins, lodes or ledges may so far depart from a perpendicular in their course downward as to extend outside the vertical side lines of such surface location; that the description of said claim as marked on the ground is as follows:

(Give the technical description of the surveyor, or, if that is not possible, describe it as marked, with reference to permanent objects.)

CLAIMANT OF JOHN BROWN LODE.
Dated, May 31, 1898.

FORM 5.
NOTICE OF LOCATION OF TUNNEL SITE.
(To be posted and recorded).

Notice is hereby given that the site of the Jim

Crow tunnel was located and work commenced thereon May 1, 1898, by me; that since said time work has been continuously and is now being prosecuted thereon by me; that this stake marks the face of said tunnel which runs in a direct line easterly and westerly; that as the proprietor of said tunnel I hereby claim all the veins or lodes, throughout their entire depth, within 3,000 feet from this point on the line thereof in a westerly direction which shall be discovered in said tunnel, to the same extent as if discovered from the surface; said tunnel is more particularly described as follows:

(Give surveyor's description.)

PROPRIETOR OF JIM CROW TUNNEL.
Dated, May 31, 1898.

FORM 6.

NOTICE OF PLACER DISCOVERY.

(To be posted).

Notice is hereby given that I have this day discovered the Washington Placer location at this point and claim the right to locate thereat a claim twenty acres in area.

Dated May 1, 1898.   DISCOVERER.

FORM 7.

PLACER LOCATION CERTIFICATE.

(To be posted and recorded).

Notice is hereby given that on May 1, 1898, I discovered and commenced work on Washington Placer, near the headwaters of Copper river, in the Copper River Mining District, Alaska; that I have ever since continuously worked and am now working the same; that the boundaries of said claim have been duly located and marked on the ground; that a more particular description of said claim, of which I am the owner, is as follows:

(Describe according to U. S. survey, or, if not surveyed, describe by metes and bounds.)

CLAIMANT.

Dated, May 31, 1898.

FORM 8.
NOTICE OF WATER APPROPRIATION.
(To be posted at place of diversion).

Notice is hereby given that I claim 1,000 miners' inches of this stream (or lake) to be diverted at this point and carried thence in ditches and flumes, in a westerly direction, to the Washington Placer, owned by me, near the headwaters of Copper river, in the Copper River Mining District, Alaska, for use thereon in mining operations.

Dated, May 1, 1898.　　　　APPROPRIATOR.

GLOSSARY.

Common Mining Terms Defined.

Amalgam ...... Quicksilver combined with gold and silver.
Apex .... Top.
Assay.......... Chemical test of ores.
Back.......... Roof.
Bank .... Accumulation, or surface, at top of shaft.
Bar Diggings .. River placers subject to overflow.
Bench Diggings. River placers not subject to overflow.
Booming ...... Placer washing.
Brooching ..... Smoothing.
Buddling ...... Washing.
Cap........... Pinch.
Carbonates..... Lead, oxide and carbonic acid.
Cheek .... Wall.
Chloride....... Chlorine united with another element.
Cinnabar....... Mercury and sulphur.
Close Season... When placers cannot be worked.
Collar......... Surface part of shaft timbering.
Contact....... Union of different formations.
Country....... Surrounding formation.
Cribbing....... Projecting above surface.
Cross Cut...... Level across a vein.
Debris........ Waste.
Diggings....... Placer mines.
Dike .... Barren rock.
Deluvian....... Deposit of earth, loose rock, etc.
Dip .... Angle of descent.
Drift.......... Level on a vein.
Dry Diggings.. Placers never subject to overflow.
Exploration.... Development.
Face .... Point of reaching cover.
Feeder........ Offshoot.
Fissure Vein... Lode.
Float .... Detached mineralized rock.
Flume......... Ditch.
Flux.......... Ingredients used in smelting ores.
Foot-wall ..... Wall beneath a vein.
Free Miner..... Licensed miner.
Galena........ Lead.
Gangue........ Matrix.
Gneiss .... Crystalline rock.

Hanging-wall... Wall above a vein.
Hill Diggings.. Placers on hills.
Horse .... A barren obstruction in a vein.
In place....... Not detached.
Lagging ...... Spanning timber.
Lead .... Lode.
Level......... Drift.
Lode .... Vein.
Matrix....... Basic stone of a vein.
Mica .... A transparent mineral.
Millrun........ Output not separated.
Miner's Inch ... Flow of 11¼ gallons per minute.
Pay Rock..... Mineralized rock.
Pay Streak..... Mineralized part of rock.
Pinch......... Contact of walls cutting off vein.
Pitch .... Dip.
Placer .... A deposit not "rock in place."
Pocket .... Detached ore.
Porphyry ..... Rock containing crystals of feldspar.
Pyrites........ Iron and sulphur.
Quartz........ Silex, occurring in crystals.
Quicksilver .... Mercury.
Royalty....... The lessor's percentage.
Segregations... Detached portions of veins in place.
Slickensides.... Smooth places on walls or ore.
Slide......... Loose deposit covering rock.
Sluice......... Box for washing ore.
Smelting ...... Method of extracting precious metals.
Spiling........ Timber to be driven in ground.
Stamp-mill..... Machine for crushing ore.
Stoping....... Pulling down ore in a drift.
Strike .... Course.
Sulphide....... Sulphur and metal.
Sump......... Drainage pit in shaft.
Tailings. ...... Refuse.
Upcast........ Ventilating shaft.
Vug........... Cavity.
Wall .... Rock in contact with vein.

INDEX TO PART I.

MINING LAWS OF THE UNITED STATES.

PART II.

MINING LAWS OF CANADA.

PROVISIONAL DISTRICT OF THE YUKON,
NORTHWEST TERRITORIES.

REGULATIONS

Governing Placer Mining in the Provisional District of the Yukon, Northwest Territories.

(Approved by Order in Council of 18th January, 1898).

"FREE MINER" shall mean a male or female over the age of eighteen but not under that age, or joint stock company, named in, and lawfully possessed of, a valid existing free miner's certificate, and no other.

"LEGAL POST" shall mean a stake standing not less than four feet above the ground and flatted on two sides for at least one foot from the top. Both sides so flatted shall measure at least four inches across the face. It shall also mean any stump or tree cut off and flatted or faced to the above height and size.

"CLOSE SEASON" shall mean the period of the year during which placer mining is generally suspended, the period to be fixed by the Mining Recorder in whose district the claim is situated.

"MINERAL" shall include all minerals whatsoever other than coal.

"JOINT STOCK COMPANY" shall mean any company incorporated for mining purposes under a Canadian charter or licensed by the Government of Canada.

"MINING RECORDER" shall mean the official appointed by the Gold Commissioner to record applications and grant entries for claims in the Mining Divisions into which the Commissioner may divide the Yukon District.

1. EVERY PERSON OVER, BUT NOT UN-
DER EIGHTEEN YEARS OF AGE, and every
joint stock company, shall be entitled to all the
rights and privileges of a free miner, under these
regulations and under the regulations governing
quartz mining, and shall be considered a free miner
upon taking out a free miner's certificate. A free
miner's certificate issued to a joint stock company
shall be issued in its corporate name. A free miner's
certificate shall not be transferable.

2. A FREE MINER'S CERTIFICATE may be
granted for one year to run from the date thereof
or from the expiration of the applicant's then existing certificate, upon the payment therefor of the
sum of $10.00, unless the certificate is to be issued
in favor of a joint stock company, in which case the
fee shall be $50.00 for a company having a nom-
inal capital of $100,000.00 or less, and for a company
having a nominal capital exceeding $100,000.00,
the fee shall be $100.00. Only one person or joint
stock company shall be named in a certificate.

3. A free miner's certificate shall be in the following form:

DOMINION OF CANADA.

FREE MINER'S CERTIFICATE.

(Non-transferable.)

Date....................   No........

Valid for one year only.

This is to certify that............of..........has
paid me this day the sum of.......... , and is entitled to all the rights and privileges of a free miner,

under any mining regulations of the Government of Canada, for one year from the...........day of ....18....

THIS CERTIFICATE SHALL ALSO GRANT TO THE HOLDER THEREOF THE PRIVILEGE OF FISHING AND SHOOTING, subject to the provisions of any Act which has been passed, or which may hereafter be passed for the protection of game and fish; also the privilege of cutting timber for actual necessities, for building houses, boats, and for general mining operations; such timber, however, to be for the exclusive use of the miner himself, but such permission shall not extend to timber which may have been heretofore or which may hereafter be granted to other persons or corporations.

4. FREE MINER'S CERTIFICATES MAY BE OBTAINED by applicants in person at the Department of the Interior, Ottawa, or from the agents of Dominion Lands at Winnipeg, Manitoba; Calgary, Edmonton, Prince Albert, in the Northwest Territories; Kamloops and New Westminster, in the Province of British Columbia; at Dawson City in the Yukon District; also from agents of the Government at Vancouver and Victoria, B. C., and at other places which may from time to time be named by the Minister of the Interior.

5. IF ANY PERSON OR JOINT STOCK COMPANY shall apply for a free miner's certificate at the agent's office during his absence, and shall leave the fee required by these regulations, with the officer or other person in charge of said office, he or it shall be entitled to have such certificate from the date of such application; and any free miner shall at any time be entitled to obtain a free miner's certificate commencing to run from the expiration of his then

existing free miner's certificate, provided that when he applies for such certificate he shall produce to the agent, or in case of his absence shall leave with the officer or other person in charge of the agent's office, such existing certificate.

6. IF ANY FREE MINER'S CERTIFICATE BE ACCIDENTALLY DESTROYED OR LOST, the owner thereof may, on payment of a fee of two dollars, have a true copy of it, signed by the agent, or other person by whom or out of whose office the original was issued. Every such copy shall be marked "Substituted Certificate;" and unless some material irregularity be shown in respect thereof, every original or substituted free miner's certificate shall be evidence of all matters therein contained.

7. NO PERSON OR JOINT STOCK COM-PANY WILL BE RECOGNIZED AS HAVING ANY RIGHT OR INTEREST in or to any placer claim, quartz claim, mining lease, bed-rock flume grant, or any minerals in any ground comprised therein, or in or to any water right, mining ditch, drain, tunnel, or flume, unless he or it and every person in his or its employment shall have a free miner's certificate unexpired. And on the expiration of a free miner's certificate the owner thereof shall absolutely forfeit all his rights and interest in or to any placer claim, mining lease, bed-rock flume grant, and any minerals in any ground com-pirsed therein, and in or to any and every water right, mining ditch, drain, tunnel, or flume, which may be held or claimed by such owner of such ex-pired free miner's certificate, unless such owner shall, on or before the day following the expiration of such certificate, obtain a new free miner's certificate, Provided, nevertheless, that should any co-owner fail to keep up his free miner's certificate, such failure shall not cause a forfeiture or act as an abandonment

of the claim, but the interest of the co-owner who shall fail to keep up his free miner's certificate shall, *ipso facto*, be and become vested in his co-owners, *pro rata* according to their former interests; provided, nevertheless, that a shareholder in a joint stock company need not be a free miner, and, though not a free miner, shall be entitled to buy, sell, hold, or dispose of any shares therein.

8. EVERY FREE MINER shall, during the continuance of his certificate, but not longer, have the right to enter, locate, prospect, and mine for gold and other minerals upon any lands in the Yukon District, whether vested in the Crown or otherwise, except upon Government reservations for town sites, land which is occupied by any building, and any land falling within the curtilage of any dwelling house, and any land lawfully occupied for placer mining purposes, and also Indian reservations.

9. PREVIOUS TO ANY ENTRY being made upon lands lawfully occupied, such free miner shall give adequate security, to the satisfaction of the Mining Recorder, for any loss or damage which may be caused by such entry; and after such entry he shall make full compensation to the occupant or owner of such lands for any loss or damage which may be caused by reason of such entry; such compensation, in case of dispute, to be determined by a court having jurisdiotion in mining disputes, with or without a jury.

10. A CREEK OR GULCH CLAIM SHALL BE 250 FEET LONG measured in the general direction of the creek or gulch. The boundaries of the claim which run in the general direction of the creek or gulch shall be lines along bed or rim rock three feet higher than the rim or edge of the creek,

or the lowest general level of the gulch within the claim, so drawn or marked as to be at every point three feet above the rim or edge of the creek or the lowest general level of the gulch, opposite to it at right angles to the general direction of the claim for its length, but such boundaries shall not in any case exceed 1,000 feet on each side of the center of the stream or gulch.

11. IF THE BOUNDARIES BE LESS THAN ONE HUNDRED FEET APART HORIZON-TALLY, they shall be lines traced along bed or rim rock one hundred feet apart horizontally, following as nearly as practicable the direction of the valley for the length of the claim.

12. A RIVER CLAIM shall be situated only on one side of the river and shall not exceed 250 feet in length, measured in the general direction of the river. The other boundary of the claim which runs in the general direction of the river shall be lines along bed or rim rock three feet higher than the rim or edge of the river within the claim so drawn or marked as to be at every point three feet above the rim or edge of the river opposite to it at right angles to the general direction of the claim for its length, but such boundaries shall not in any case be less than 250 feet, or exceed a distance of 1,000 feet from low water mark of the river.

13. A "HILL CLAIM" shall not exceed 250 feet in length, drawn parallel to the main direction of the stream or ravine on which it fronts. Parallel lines drawn from each end of the base line at right angles thereto, and running to the summit of the hill (provided the distance does not exceed 1,000 feet), shall constitute the end boundaries of the claim.

14. ALL OTHER PLACER CLAIMS shall be 250 feet square.

15. EVERY PLACER CLAIM SHALL BE AS NEARLY AS POSSIBLE RECTANGULAR IN FORM, and marked by two legal posts firmly fixed in the ground in the manner shown in diagram No. 4. The line between the two posts shall be well cut out so that one post may, if the nature of the surface will permit, be seen from the other. The flatted side of each post shall face the claim, and on each post shall be written on the side facing the claim a legible notice stating the name or number of the claim, or both if possible, its length in feet, the date when staked, and the full Christian and surname of the locator.

16. EVERY ALTERNATE TEN CLAIMS shall be reserved by the Government of Canada. That is to say, when a claim is located, the discoverer's claim and nine additional claims adjoining each other and numbered consecutively will be open for registration. Then the next ten claims of 250 feet each will be reserved for the Government, and so on. The alternate group of claims reserved for the Crown shall be disposed of in such manner as may be decided by the Minister of the Interior.

17. THE PENALTY FOR TRESPASSING upon a claim reserved by the Crown, shall be immediate cancellation by the Mining Recorder of any entry or entries which the person trespassing may have obtained, whether by original entry or purchase, for a mining claim, and the refusal by the Mining Recorder of the acceptance of any application which the person trespassing may at any time make for a claim. In addition to such penalty, the Mounted Police, upon a requisition from the Mining Recorder to that effect, shall take the necessary steps to eject the trespasser.

18. IN DEFINING THE SIZE OF CLAIMS,

they shall be measured horizontally irrespective of inequalities on the surface of the ground.

19. IF ANY FREE MINER OR PARTY OF FREE MINERS DISCOVER A NEW MINE, and such discovery shall be established to the satisfaction of the Mining Recorder, creek, river, or hill, claims of the following size shall be allowed, namely:

To one discoverer, one claim, 500 feet in length.

To a party of two discoverers, two claims, amounting together to 1,000 feet in length.

To each member of a party beyond two in number, a claim of the ordinary size only.

20. A NEW STRATUM OF AURIFEROUS EARTH OR GRAVEL situated in a locality where the claims have been abandoned shall for this purpose be deemed a new mine, although the same locality shall have been previously worked at a different level.

21. THE FORMS OF APPLICATION for a grant for placer mining, and the grant of the same, shall be those contained in Forms "H" and "I" in the schedule hereto.

22. A CLAIM SHALL BE RECORDED with the Mining Recorder in whose district it is situated, within ten days after the location thereof, if it is located within ten miles of the Mining Recorder's office. One extra day shall be allowed for every additional ten miles or fraction thereof.

23. IN THE EVENT OF THE CLAIM BEING MORE THAN ONE HUNDRED MILES FROM A RECORDER'S OFFICE, and situated where other claims are being located, the free miners, not less than five in number, are authorized to meet and appoint one of their number a "Free Miner's Recorder," who shall act in that capacity until a

Mining Recorder is appointed by the Gold Commissioner.

24. THE "FREE MINERS' RECORDER" shall, at the earliest possible date after his appointment, notify the nearest Government Mining Recorder thereof, and, upon the arrival of the Government Mining Recorder, he shall deliver to him his records and the fees received for recording the claims. The Government Mining Recorder shall then grant to each free miner whose name appears in the records, an entry for his claim on form "I" of these regulations, provided an application has been made by him in accordance with form "H" thereof, the entry to date from the time the "Free Miners' Recorder" recorded the application.

25. IF THE "FREE MINERS' RECORDER" FAILS within three months to notify the nearest Government Mining Recorder of his appointment, the claims which he may have recorded will be canceled.

26. DURING THE ABSENCE OF THE MINING RECORDER from his office, the entry for a claim may be granted by any person whom he may appoint to perform his duties in his absence.

27. ENTRY shall not be granted for a claim which has not been staked by the applicant in person in the manner specified in these regulations. An affidavit that the claim was staked out by the applicant shall be embodied in form "H" in the schedule hereto.

28. AN ENTRY FEE of fifteen dollars shall be charged the first year, and an annual fee of fifteen dollars for each of the following years. This provision shall apply to claims for entries which have already been granted.

29. A STATEMENT OF THE ENTRIES granted and fees collected shall be rendered by the Mining Recorder to the Gold Commissioner at least every three months, which shall be accompanied by the amount collected.

30. A ROYALTY OF TEN PER CENT on the gold mined shall be levied and collected on the gross output of each claim. The royalty may be paid at banking offices to be established under the auspices of the Government of Canada, or to the Gold Commissioner, or to any Mining Recorder authorized by him. The sum of $2,500.00 shall be deducted from the gross annual output of a claim when estimating the amount upon which royalty is to be calculated, but this exemption shall not be allowed unless the royalty is paid at a banking office or to the Gold Commissioner or Mining Recorder. When the royalty is paid monthly or at longer periods, the deduction shall be made ratable on the basis of $2,500.00 per annum for the claim. If not paid to the bank, Gold Commissioner or Mining Recorder, it shall be collected by the customs officials or police officers when the miner passes the posts established at the boundary of a district. Such royalty to form part of the consolidated revenue, and to be accounted for by the officers who collect the same in due course. The time and manner in which such royalty shall be collected shall be provided for by regulations to be made by the Gold Commissioner.

31. DEFAULT IN PAYMENT OF SUCH ROYALTY, if continued for ten days after notice has been posted on the claim in respect of which it is demanded, or in the vicinity of such claim, by the Gold Commissioner or his agent, shall be followed by cancellation of the claim. Any attempt to defraud the Crown by withholding any part of the revenue thus provided

for, by making false statements of the amount taken out, shall be punished by cancellation of the claim in respect of which fraud or false statements have been committed or made. In respect to the facts as to such fraud or false statements or non-payment of royalty, the decision of the Gold Commissioner shall be final.

32. AFTER THE RECORDING OF A CLAIM the removal of any post by the holder thereof or by any person acting in his behalf for the purpose of changing the boundaries of his claim, shall act as a forfeiture of the claim.

33. THE ENTRY of every holder of a grant for placer mining must be renewed and his receipt relinquished and replaced every year, the entry fee being paid each time.

34. THE HOLDER OF A CREEK, GULCH OR RIVER CLAIM may, within sixty days after staking out the claim, obtain an entry for a hill claim adjoining it, by paying to the Mining Recorder the sum of one hundred dollars. This permission shall also be given to the holder of a creek, gulch or river claim obtained under former regulations, provided that the hill claim is available at the time an application is made therefor.

35. NO MINER SHALL RECEIVE A GRANT OF MORE THAN ONE MINING CLAIM in a mining district, the boundaries of which shall be defined by the Mining Recorder, but the same miner may also hold a hill claim, acquired by him under these regulations in connection with a creek, gulch or river claim, and any number of claims by purchase; and any number of miners may unite to work their claims in common, upon such terms as they may arrange, provided such agreement is registered

with the Mining Recorder and a fee of five dollars paid for each registration.

36. ANY FREE MINER OR MINERS MAY SELL, mortgage or dispose of his or their claims, provided such disposal be registered with, and a fee of two dollars paid to the Mining Recorder, who shall thereupon give the assignee a certificate in the form "J" in the schedule hereto.

37. EVERY FREE MINER shall during the continuance of his grant have the exclusive right of entry upon his own claim for the miner-like working thereof, and the construction of a residence thereon, and shall be entitled exclusively to all the proceeds realized therefrom, upon which, however, the royalty prescribed by these regulations shall be payable; provided that the Mining Recorder may grant to the holders of other claims such right of entry thereon as may be absolutely necessary for the working of their claims, upon such terms as may to him seem reasonable. He may also grant permits to miners to cut timber thereon for their own use.

38. EVERY FREE MINER shall be entitled to the use of so much of the water naturally flowing through or past his claim, and not already lawfully appropriated, as shall, in the opinion of the Mining Recorder, be necessary for the due working thereof, and shall be entitled to drain his own claim free of charge.

39. A CLAIM SHALL BE DEEMED TO BE ABANDONED and open to occupation and entry by any person when the same shall have remained unworked on working days, excepting during the close season, by the grantee thereof, or by some person on his behalf for the space of * seventy-two hours, unless sickness or other reasonable cause be

---

* 72 hours means three consecutive days of 24 hours each.

shown to the satisfaction of the Mining Recorder, or unless the grantee is absent on leave given by the Mining Recorder, and the Mining Recorder, upon obtaining evidence satisfactory to himself, that this provision is not being complied with, may cancel the entry given for a claim.

40. IF ANY CASES ARISE FOR WHICH NO PROVISION IS MADE in these regulations, the provisions of the regulations governing the disposal of mineral lands other than coal lands, approved by His Excellency the Governor in Council on the 9th of November, 1889, or such other regulations as may be substituted therefor, shall apply.

FORM H.—APPLICATION FOR GRANT FOR PLACER MINING, AND AFFIDAVIT OF APPLICANT.

I (or we)..........of............hereby apply, under the Yukon Placer Mining Regulations, for a grant of a claim for placer mining as defined in the said regulations, in (here describe locality) and I (or we) solemnly swear:

1. That from indications I (or we) have observed on the claim applied for, I (or we) have reason to believe that there is therein a deposit of gold.

2. That I (or we) am (or are) to the best of my (or our) knowledge and belief the first to observe such indications, or:

3. That the said claim was previously granted to (here name the last grantee) but has remained unworked by the said grantee for not less than.......
....

4. That I (or we) am (or are) unaware that the land is other than vacant Dominion Lands.

5. That I (or we) did on the...............day of.............mark out on the ground, in accordance in every particular with the provisions of the mining regulations for the Yukon District, the claim for which I (or we) make this application, and in so doing I (or we) did not encroach on any other claim or mining location previously laid out by any other person.

6. That the length of the said claim, as nearly as I (or we) could measure, is.........feet, and that the description of this date hereto attached, signed by me (or us) sets (or set) forth in detail, to the best of my (or our) knowledge and ability, its position.

7. That I (or we) make this application in good faith, to acquire the claim for the sole purpose of mining to be prosecuted by myself (or us) or by myself and associates, or by my (or our) assigns.

Sworn before me⎫
at.............. ⎪
this........day ⎬ (Signature)
of ....18... ⎭

FORM I.—GRANT FOR PLACER MINING.

No..........

Department of the Interior,
                    Agency................18....

In consideration of the payment of the fee of fifteen dollars prescribed by clause 28 of the mining regulations for the Yukon District, by...........(A. B.)........of.............accompanying his (or their) application No. .... dated.........18.., for a mining claim in...............(here insert description of locality).

The Minister of Interior hereby grants to the said ....(A. B.).........for the term of one year from the date hereof, the exclusive right of entry upon the claim...........(here describe in detail the claim granted) for the miner-like working thereof, and the construction of a residence thereon, and the exclusive right to all the proceeds realized thereupon, upon which, however, the royalty prescribed by the regulations shall be paid.

The said...........(A. B.)...........shall be entitled to the use of so much of the water naturally flowing through or past his (or their) claim, and not already lawfully appropriated, as shall be necessary for the due working thereof, and to drain his (or their) claim free of charge.

This grant does not convey to the said......... ....(A. B.) any right of ownership in the soil covered by the said claim, and the said grant shall lapse and be forfeited unless the claim is continuously and in good faith worked by the said....... (A. B.).........or his (or their) associates.

The rights hereby granted are those laid down in the aforesaid mining regulations, and no more, and are subject to all the provisions of the said regulations, whether the same are expressed herein or not.

....
Mining Recorder.

FORM J.—CERTIFICATE OF THE ASSIGNMENT OF A PLACER MINING CLAIM.

No.........

       Department of the Interior,

               Agency....................18....

This is to certify that..........(B. C).........

of....................has (or have) filed an assignment in due form, dated..............18...., and accompanied by a registration fee of two dollars, of the grant to.............(A. B.)............of ....;.of the right to mine in.........(here insert description of claim)...........for one year from the................18....

This certificate entitles the said..........(B. C.) ....to all the rights and privileges of the said.............(A. B.)............in respect to the claim assigned, that is to say, to the exclusive right of entry upon the said claim for the miner-like working thereof and the construction of a residence thereon, and the exclusive right to all the proceeds realized therefrom (upon which, however, the royalty prescribed by the regulations shall be paid), for the remaining portion of the year for which the said claim was granted to the said.............. (A. B.).................that is to say, until the ....day of...........18....

The said...........(B. C.)...........shall be entitled to the use of so much of the water naturally flowing through or past his (or their) claim and not already lawfully appropriated, as shall be necessary for the due working thereof and to drain his claim, free of charge.

This grant does not convey to the said......... (B. C.)..............any right of ownership in the soil covered by the said claim, and the said grant shall lapse and be forfeited unless the claim is continuously and in good faith worked by the said ....(B. C.)..............or his (or their) associates.

The rights hereby granted are those laid down in the Yukon Placer Mining Regulations, and no more, and are subject to all the provisions of the said regulations, whether the same are expressed herein or not.

....

Mining Recorder.

REGULATIONS

Governing the Issue of Leases to Dredge for Minerals in the Beds of Rivers in the Provisional District of Yukon, Northwest Territories.

———

(Approved of by Order in Council No. 125, of the 18th January, 1898.)

———

THE FOLLOWING REGULATIONS ARE ADOPTED FOR THE ISSUE OF LEASES to persons or companies who have obtained a free miner's certificate in accordance with the provisions of the regulations governing placer mining in the Provisional District of Yukon, to dredge for minerals other than coal in the submerged beds or bars of rivers in the Provisional District of Yukon, in the Northwest Territories:

1. THE LESSEE shall be given the exclusive right to subaqueous mining and dredging for all minerals with the exception of coal in and along an unbroken extent of five miles of a river following its sinuosities, to be measured down the middle thereof, and to be described by the lessee in such manner as to be easily traced on the ground; and although the lessee may also obtain as many as five other leases, each for an unbroken extent of five miles of a river, so measured and described, no more than six such leases will be issued in favor of an individual or company, so that the maximum extent of river in and along which any individual or company shall be given the exclusive right above mentioned, shall under no circumstances exceed thirty miles. The lease shall provide for the

survey of the leasehold under instructions from the Surveyor General, and for the filing of the returns of survey in the Department of the Interior within one year from the date of the lease.

2. THE LEASE SHALL BE FOR A TERM OF TWENTY YEARS, at the end of which time all rights vested in, or which may be claimed by the lessee under his lease, are to cease and determine. The lease may be renewable, however, from time to time thereafter in the discretion of the Minister of the Interior.

3. THE LESSEE'S RIGHT of mining and dredging shall be confined to the submerged beds or bars in the river below low water mark, that boundary to be fixed by its position on the first day of August in the year of the date of the lease.

4. THE LEASE SHALL BE SUBJECT TO THE RIGHTS OF ALL PERSONS who have received or who may receive entries for claims under the Placer Mining Regulations.

5. THE LESSEE SHALL HAVE AT LEAST ONE DREDGE in operation upon the five miles of river leased to him, within two seasons from the date of his lease, and if, during one season when operations can be carried on, he fails to efficiently work the same to the satisfaction of the Minister of the Interior, the lease shall become null and void unless the Minister of the Interior shall otherwise decide. Provided that when any company or individual has obtained more than one lease, one dredge for each fifteen miles or portion thereof shall be held to be compliance with this regulation.

6. THE LESSEE SHALL PAY A RENTAL OF $100.00 per annum for each mile of river so leased to him. The lessee shall also pay to the

Crown a royalty of ten per centum on the output in excess of $15,000.00, as shown by sworn returns to be furnished monthly by the lessee to the Gold Commissioner during the period that dredging operations are being carried on; such royalty, if any, to be paid with each return.

6. THE LESSEE WHO IS THE HOLDER OF MORE THAN ONE LEASE shall be entitled to the exemption as to royalty provided for by the next preceding regulation to the extent of $15,000.00 for each five miles of river for which he is the holder of a lease; but the lessee under one lease shall not be entitled to the exemption as to royalty provided by the next two preceding regulations, where the dredge or dredges used by him have been used in dredging by another lessee, or in any case in respect of more than thirty miles.

7. THE LESSEE SHALL BE PERMITTED TO CUT free of all dues, on any land belonging to the Crown, such timber as may be necessary for the purposes of his lease, but such permission shall not extend to timber which may have been heretofore or may hereafter be granted to other persons or corporations.

8. THE LESSEE SHALL NOT INTERFERE in any way with the general right of the public to use the river in which he may be permitted to dredge, for navigation and other purposes; the free navigation of the river shall not be impeded by the deposit of tailings in such manner as to form bars or banks in the channel thereof, and the current or stream shall not be obstructed in any material degree by the accumulation of such deposits.

9. THE LEASE SHALL PROVIDE that any person who has received or who may receive entry under the Placer Mining Regulations shall be enti-

tled to run tailings into the river at any point thereon, and to construct all works which may be necessary for properly operating and working his claim. Provided that it shall not be lawful for such person to construct a wing-dam within one thousand feet from the place where any dredge is being operated, nor to obstruct or interfere in any way with the operation of any dredge.

10. THE LEASE SHALL RESERVE all roads, ways, bridges, drains, and other public works, and all improvements now existing, or which may hereafter be made in, upon or under any part of the river, and the power to enter and construct the same, and shall provide that the lessee shall not damage nor obstruct any public ways, drains, bridges, works and improvements now or hereafter to be made upon, in, over, through, or under the river; and that he will substantially bridge or cover and protect all the cuts, flumes, ditches and sluices, and all pits and dangerous places at all points where they may be crossed by a public highway or frequented path or trail, to the satisfaction of the Minister of the Interior.

11. THAT THE LESSEE, his executors, administrators, or assigns, shall not nor will assign, transfer or sublet the demised premises, or any part thereof, without the consent in writing of the Minister first had and obtained.

PART II.

MINING LAWS OF CANADA.

BRITISH COLUMBIA.

AN ACT RELATING TO GOLD AND OTHER MINERALS EXCEPTING COAL [as amended in 1897].

1896, c. 34. 1897, c. 28.

HER MAJESTY, by and with the advice and consent of the Legislative Assembly of the Province of British Columbia, enacts as follows:

1. SHORT TITLE.—This act may be cited as the "Mineral act, 1896."

2. INTERPRETATION.—In the construction of this act the following expressions shall have the following meanings respectively, unless inconsistent with the context:

"MINE" shall mean any land in which any vein or lode or rock in place, shall be mined for gold or other minerals, precious or base, except coal.

"MINERAL" shall mean all valuable deposits of gold, silver, platinum, iridium or any of the platinum group of metals, mercury, lead, copper, iron, tin, zinc, nickel, aluminum, antimony, arsenic, barium, bismuth, boron, bromine, cadmium, chromium, cobalt, iodine, magnesium, manganese, molybdenum, phosphorus, plumbago, potassium, sodium, strontium, sulphur (or any combination of the aforementioned elements with themselves or with any other elements), asbestos, emery, mica and mineral pigments.

LIMESTONE, MARBLE, CLAY OR ANY BUILDING STONE when mined for building purposes shall not be considered as mineral within the meaning of this act.

"ROCK IN PLACE" shall be deemed to mean and include mineral, not necessarily in a vein or lode; that is, when discovered in the same place or position in which it was originally formed or deposited, as distinguished from loose fragmentary or broken rock or float which, by decomposition or erosion of the rocks, is found in wash, loose earth, gravel or sand.[1]

"VALUABLE DEPOSITS OF MINERAL" shall be deemed to mean and include mineral "in place" in appreciable quantity, having a present or prospective value sufficient to justify exploration.

"VEIN" OR "LODE."—Whenever either of these terms is used in this act, "rock in place" shall be deemed to be included.

"MINERAL CLAIM" shall mean the personal right of property or interest in any mine.

"MINING PROPERTY" shall include every mineral claim, ditch, mill site or water right used for mining purposes, and all other things belonging to a mine or used in the working thereof.

"LEGAL POST" shall mean a stake standing not less than four feet above the ground, and squared or faced on four sides for at least one foot from the top, and each side so squared or faced shall measure at least four inches on its face so far as squared or faced, and any stump or tree cut off and squared or faced to the above height and size. Provided when the survey is made the center of the tree or stump where it enters the ground shall be taken as the point to or from which measurement shall be made.

"LOCATION LINE" shall be the straight line between posts numbers one and two.

"MILL SITE" shall mean a plot of ground located, as defined by this act, for the purpose of erecting thereon any machinery or other works for transporting, crushing, reducing or sampling ores, or for the transmission of power for working mines.

---

1 Nelson et al. v. Jerry et al., 5 B. C. L. R. 896.

"FREE MINER" shall mean a person or joint stock company, or foreign company, named in and lawfully possessed of a valid existing free miner's certificate, and no other.

"RECORD," "REGISTER" AND "REGISTRATION" shall have the same meaning, and shall mean an entry in some official book kept for that purpose.

"FULL INTEREST" shall mean any mineral claim of the full size, or one of several shares into which a mineral claim shall be equally divided.

"CAUSE" shall include any suit or action.

"JUDGMENT" shall include "order" or "decree."

"REAL ESTATE" shall mean any mineral land in fee simple under this or any act relating to gold mines, or to minerals other than coal.

"JOINT STOCK COMPANY" shall mean any company for mining purposes.

(*a*) Incorporated under the "Companies' act, 1897," or any act repealed thereby; or

(*b*) Registered as a foreign company under any act repealed by the "Companies' act, 1897;" or

(*c*) Licensed or registered as an extra-Provincial company under the "Companies' act, 1897;" or

(*d*) Incorporated by any special act. 1897, c. 28, s. 2.

PART I.

Free Miners and Their Privileges.

3. WHO MAY BE A FREE MINER.—Every person over, but not under, eighteen years of age, and every joint stock company, shall be entitled to all the rights and privileges of a free miner, and shall be considered a free miner, upon taking out a

free miner's certificate. A minor who shall become a free miner shall, as regards his mining property and liabilities contracted in connection therewith, be treated as of full age. A free miner's certificate issued to a joint stock company shall be issued in its corporate name. A free miner's certificate shall not be transferable.

3a. LICENSES TO COMPANIES.—Notwithstanding anything to the contrary in Section 4, of the "Mineral act, 1896," or Section 4, of the "Placer Mining act, 1891," or elsewhere in the said acts or other the mining laws of the Province, no free miner's certificate shall be issued to a joint stock company for a longer period than one year, and such certificate shall date from the 30th day of June in each year; and every free miner's certificate held by a joint stock company at the passing of this act shall be valid and existing until and shall expire on the 30th day of June, 1897. Upon applying to renew any such certificate on or before said 30th day of June, the joint stock company shall be entitled to a rebate of a proportionate amount of the fee paid for a certificate heretofore issued according to the further time for which it would, but for this section, have been valid. 1897, c. 2, s. 161.

4. DURATION OF CERTIFICATE.—A free miner's certificate may be granted for one or more years, to run from the date thereof, or from the expiration of the applicant's then existing certificate, upon the payment therefor of the fees set out in the Schedule of Fees to this act. Only one person or one joint stock company shall be named therein.

5. FORM OF CERTIFICATE.—A free miner's certificate shall be in the following form:

BRITISH COLUMBIA.

Free Miner's Certificate.

NOT TRANSFERABLE.

Date,   No.
 Valid for   year only.
 This is to certify that   of
has paid me this day the sum of   , and
is entitled to all the rights and privileges of a free
miner for   year from the   day
of   , 18 .
 (Signature of Gold Commissioner or Mining
 Recorder, as the case may be.)

6. APPLICATION AT RECORDER S OF-
FICE IN HIS ABSENCE.—If any person or joint
stock company shall apply for a free miner's certificate
at the Mining Recorder's office during his absence,
and shall leave the fee required by this act with the
officer or other person in charge of said office, he or
it shall be entitled to have such certificate from the
date of such application; and any free miner shall
at any time be entitled to obtain a free miner's certificate, commencing to run at the expiration of his
then existing free miner's certificate, provided that
when he applies for such certificate he shall produce
to the Mining Recorder, or in case of his absence
shall leave with the officer or other person in charge
of the Mining Recorder's office, such existing certificate.

7. "SUBSTITUTED CERTIFICATE." — If
any free miner's certificate be accidentally destroyed or lost, the owner thereof may, on payment
of the fees set out in the schedule to this act, have
a true copy of it, signed by the Mining Recorder, or
other person by whom or out of whose office the

original was issued. Every such copy shall be marked "substituted certificate," and unless some material irregularity be shown in respect thereof, every original or substituted free miner's certificate shall be evidence of all matters therein contained. [2]

8. PENALTY FOR MINING WITHOUT CERTIFICATE.—Every person and joint stock company engaged in mining for minerals (other than coal) shall take out a free miner's certificate, and every person or joint stock company who mines or works as a miner in any mineral claim, mine held as real estate, or tunnel, or on any flume, drain or ditch, without having taken out and obtained such certificate, shall, on conviction thereof in a summary way, forfeit and pay a penalty not exceeding $25, besides costs. Provided, always, that nothing herein contained shall prejudice the right to collect wages or payment for work done by any person who, through not being a free miner, has rendered himself liable to the above penalty.

9. UNCERTIFICATED PERSON NOT ENTITLED TO INTEREST IN MINING PROPERTY.—Subject to the proviso hereinafter stated, no person or joint stock company shall be recognized as having any right or interest in or to any mineral claim, or any minerals therein, or in or to any water right, mining ditch, drain, tunnel or flume, unless he or it shall have a free miner's certificate unexpired. And on the expiration of a free miner's certificate the owner thereof shall absolutely forfeit all his rights and interests in or to any mineral claim, and all and any minerals therein, and in or to any and every water right, mining ditch, drain, tunnel or flume, which may be held or claimed by such owner of such expired free miner's certificate,

---

2 Wells v. Petty, 5 B. C. L. R. 353; Stussi v. Brown, 5 B. C. L. R. 880.

unless such owner shall on or before the day following the expiration of such certificate, obtain a new free miner's certificate.

INTEREST OF A CO-OWNER FAILING TO KEEP UP HIS LICENSE SHALL VEST IN THE OTHER CO-OWNERS.—Provided, nevertheless, should any co-owner fail to keep up his free miner's certificate, such failure shall not cause a forfeiture or act as an abandonment of the claim; but the interest of the co-owner who shall fail to keep up his free miner's certificate shall, ipso facto, be and become vested in his co-owners pro rata, according to their former interests.

A SHAREHOLDER NEED NOT HAVE SUCH LICENSE.—Provided, nevertheless, that a shareholder in a joint stock company need not be a free miner, and, though not a free miner, shall be entitled to buy, sell, hold or dispose of any shares therein.

NOT TO APPLY WHEN CROWN GRANT ISSUED.—And provided, also, that this section shall not apply to mineral claims for which a Crown grant has been issued.

IN CASE OF PURCHASE OF CLAIM WHERE DEFAULT HAS BEEN MADE IN KEEPING UP CERTIFICATE.—Provided, always, that if any person or company shall acquire, by purchase or otherwise, any mine or mineral claim, or interest therein, and it shall appear that some person or company through whom he or it claims title has neglected to take out or keep up a free miner's certificate, according to the provisions of this act, such person or company so acquiring such mine or mineral claim, or interest therein, may, within one month from the time when he or it shall first acquire knowledge thereof, or if knowledge already acquired within one month after this act becomes law, pay to the Recorder of the Mining Division in which the claim affected is situated the fee or fees which ought to have been paid by such person or company in default as aforesaid, and thereupon the title of such person or company so acquiring the said mine or mineral claim, or interest therein, shall be deemed to be and always to have been as good and effectual as if no such default had occurred, but this last proviso shall not affect litigation pending at the passage of this act. [8]

10. OWNERS AND CONTRACTORS TO PAY LICENSE FOR EMPLOYES.—Every owner of a mine or mineral claim, and every contractor for the performance of any work upon a mine or mineral claim, shall pay the annual fee for a free miner's license for any person in their employment and liable for the fee, and may deduct the amount so paid on account of such person from the amount of salary or wages due or to become due to him from such employer upon production and delivery of the receipt for such tax to such person.

TO FURNISH COLLECTOR WITH LIST OF EMPLOYES.—Every such owner or contractor shall furnish to the Mining Recorder or Collector, when requested by him so to do, from time to time, a list of all persons in his employ, or indirectly employed by him, liable to pay the said license fee; but no such statement shall bind the Recorder or Collector or excuse him from making due inquiry to ascertain its correctness.

11. PENALTY.—If any person fails to pay the said license fee for his employes, or to deliver to the Recorder or Collector the list mentioned in the preceding section when required to do so, or know-

---

[8] Nelson et al. v. Jerry et al., 5 B. C. L. R. 896.

ingly states anything falsely in such list, such person shall be liable to a penalty not exceeding $100, to be recovered, together with the amount of the unpaid license fees, upon summary conviction before one justice of the peace.

12. WHERE FREE MINER MAY MINE, PROSPECT, ETC.—Every free miner shall, during the continuance of his certificate, but not longer, have the right to enter, locate, prospect and mine upon any waste lands of the Crown for all minerals other than coal, and upon all lands the right whereon to so enter upon, prospect and mine all minerals other than coal shall have been, or hereafter shall be, reserved to the Crown and its licensees, and also to enter, locate, prospect and mine for gold and silver upon any lands the right whereon to so enter and mine such gold and silver shall have been, or shall be, reserved to the Crown and its licensees.

OCCUPIED LANDS. —Excepting out of all the above description of lands any land occupied by any building, and any land falling within the curtilage of any dwelling house, and any orchard, and any land for the time being actually under cultivation, and any land lawfully occupied for mining purposes other than placer mining, and also Indian reservations and military or naval reservations.

HYDRAULIC WORKS.—Provided that where any hydraulic mining works, established in accordance with the "Placer Mining act, 1891," have been in operation, the land which may have been uncovered by the operation of such works shall not be located or mined upon by any free miner other than the person or persons carrying on such hydraulic works for a space of six months next after the same shall have been so uncovered. Provided, that in the event of such entry being made upon lands already lawfully occupied for other than mining pur-poses, and not being a portion of lands granted to and held by or for a railway company under any railway subsidy act heretofore or to be hereafter passed, such free miner shall give adequate security to the satisfaction of the Gold Commissioner or Mining Recorder for any loss or damages which may be caused by such entry if requested by the owner or owners of such land, and should he refuse to give such security when so requested his right to such claim or mine shall cease and determine.

COMPENSATION.—Provided, that after such entry he shall make full compensation to the occu-pant or owner of such lands for any loss or damages which may be caused by reason of such entry; such compensation, in case of dispute, to be determined by the court having jurisdiction in mining disputes, with or without a jury.[4] 1897, c. 28, s. 3.

13. RIGHT TO KILL GAME.—Any free miner shall be at liberty, at any period of the year, while actually prospecting or engaged in mining, to kill game for his own use.

14. "PLACER MINING ACT."—A free miner shall have all the rights and privileges granted to free miners by the "Placer Mining act."

15. SIZE AND FORM OF FREE MINER'S CLAIM.—Any free miner desiring to locate a min-eral claim, shall, subject to the provisions of this act with respect to land which may be used for mining, enter upon the same and locate a plot of ground measuring where possible, but not exceeding 1,500 feet in length by 1,500 feet in breadth, in as nearly as possible a rectangular form; that is to say: All angles shall be right angles, except in cases where

[4] Bainbridge v. Esquimalt, 4 B. C. L. R. 181.

a boundary line of a previously surveyed claim is adopted as common to both claims, but the lines need not necessarily be meridional. In defining the size of a mineral claim, it shall be measured horizontally, irrespective of inequalities of the surface of the ground.

16. MODE OF STAKING A CLAIM.—A mineral claim shall be marked by two legal posts, placed as near as possible on the line of the ledge or vein, and the posts shall be numbered 1 and 2, and the distance between posts 1 and 2 shall not exceed 1,500 feet, the line between posts Nos. 1 and 2 to be known as the location line, and upon posts Nos. 1 and 2 shall be written the name given to the mineral claim, the name of the locator, and the date of the location. Upon No. 1 post there shall be written, in addition to the foregoing, "Initial Post," the approximate compass bearing of No. 2 post, and a statement of the number of feet lying to right and to the left of the line from No. 1 to No. 2 post, thus: "Initial post. Direction of post No. 2.   feet of this claim lie on the right, and   feet on the left of the line from No. 1 to No. 2 post."

RECORDING.—All the particulars required to be put on No. 1 and No. 2 posts shall be furnished by the locator to the Mining Recorder, in writing, at the time the claim is recorded, and shall form a part of the record of such claim.

MARKING.—When a claim has been located, the holder shall immediately mark the line between posts Nos. 1 and 2 so that it can be distinctly seen; in a timbered locality, by blazing trees and cutting underbrush, and in a locality where there is neither timber nor underbrush he shall set legal posts or erect monuments of earth or rock not less than two feet high and two feet in diameter at base, so that such line can be distinctly seen.

DISCOVERY POST.—The locator shall also place a legal post at the point where he has found rock in place, on which shall be written discovery post. Provided, that when the claim is surveyed the surveyor shall be guided by the records of the claim, the sketch plan on the back of the declaration made by the owner when the claim was recorded, posts 1 and 2, and the notice on No. 1, the initial post.

EXAMPLES OF VARIOUS MODES OF LAYING OUT CLAIMS.

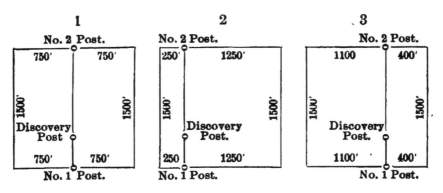

IT SHALL NOT BE LAWFUL TO MOVE NO. 1 POST, but No. 2 post may be moved by the Provinicial Land Surveyor when the distance between Nos. 1 and 2 posts exceeds 1,500 feet in order to place No. 2 post 1,500 feet from No. 1 post on the line of location. When the distance between posts Nos. 1 and 2 is less than 1,500 feet, the Provincial Land Surveyor has no authority to extend the claim beyond No. 2.

THE "LOCATION LINE" shall govern the direction of one side of the claim, upon which the survey shall be extended according to this act.

(*a*) THE HOLDER OF A MINERAL CLAIM shall be entitled to all minerals which may lie within his claim, but he shall not be entitled to mine outside the boundary lines of his claim continued vertically downwards.

(*b*) THIS ACT SHALL NOT PREJUDICE THE RIGHTS OF CLAIM OWNERS nor claim holders whose claims have been located under former acts.

(*c*) NO MINERAL CLAIM OF THE FULL SIZE SHALL BE RECORDED without the application being accompanied by an affidavit or solemn declaration in the Form S, made by the applicant or some person on his behalf cognizant of the facts. That the legal notices and posts have been put up; that mineral has been found in place on the claim proposed to be recorded; that the ground applied for is unoccupied by any other person as a mineral claim, and is not occupied by any building, or any land falling within the curtilage of any dwelling house, or any orchard, or any land under cultivation, or any Indian reservation. In the said declaration shall be set out the name of the applicant, the number and date of his free miner's certificate, and the name of the place where the said certificate was issued, and the date of the location of the claim. The words written on the No. 1 and No. 2 posts shall be set out in full, and as accurate a description as possible of the position of the claim given, having special reference to any prior locations it may join.

NO MINERAL CLAIM which at the date of its record is known by the locator to be less than a full sized mineral claim, shall be recorded without the word "fraction" being added to the name of the claim, and the application being accompanied by an affidavit or solemn declaration in the Form T, made by the applicant or some person on his behalf cognizant of the facts. That the legal posts and notices have been put up; that mineral has been found in place on the fractional claim proposed to be recorded; that the ground applied for is unoccupied by any other person as a mineral claim, and is not occupied by any building, or any land falling within the curtilage of any dwelling house, or any orchard, or any land under cultivation, or any Indian reservation.

FRACTIONAL DESCRIPTION.—In the said declaration shall be set out the name of the applicant, the number and date of his free miner's certificate, and the name of the place where the said certificate was issued, and the date of the location of the claim. The words written on the No. 1 and No. 2 posts shall be set out in full, and as accurate a description as possible of the position of the claim given. A description of the land bounding the fractional claim on all sides shall state whether it is vacant Crown land or land occupied by mineral claims, with the names of the claims. A sketch plan shall be drawn by the applicant on the back of declaration, showing as near as may be the position of the adjoining mineral claims, and the shape and size, expressed in feet, of the fraction desired to be recorded.

(*d*) PROVIDED THAT THE FAILURE on the part of the locator of a mineral claim to comply with any of the foregoing provisions of this section shall not be deemed to invalidate such location, if upon the facts it shall appear that such locator has actually discovered mineral in place on said location, and that there has been on his part a bona fide attempt to comply with the provisions of this act, and that the non-observance of the formalities hereinbefore referred to is not of a character calculated to mislead other persons desiring to locate claims in the vicinity.[5] 1897, c. 28, s. 4.

17. LOCATION MADE ON SUNDAY.—Any location made upon Sunday or any public holiday shall not for that reason be invalid, any law or statute to the contrary notwithstanding.

18. WHERE STAKING OUT CANNOT BE ·PROPERLY DONE.—In cases where, from the nature or shape of the ground, it is impossible to mark the location line of the claim, as provided by this act, then the claim may be marked by placing legal posts as nearly as possible to the location line, and noting the distance and direction such posts may be from such location line, which distance and direction shall be set out in the record of the claim.

19. RECORD OF CLAIM.—Every free miner locating a mineral claim shall record the same with the Mining Recorder of the district within which the same is situate, within fifteen days after the location thereof, if located within ten miles of the office of the said Mining Recorder. One additional day shall be allowed for such record for every additional ten miles, or fraction thereof. Such record shall be made in a book to be kept for the purpose in the office of the said Mining Recorder, in which shall be inserted the name of the claim, the name of each locator, the number of each locator's free miner's certificate, the locality of the mine, the direction of the location line, the length in feet, the date of location and the date of the record. Such record shall be, as near as may be possible, in the Form B in the schedule to this act, and a certified copy thereof shall be given by the Mining Recorder to the free miner or his agent. A claim which shall

5 Granger v. Fotheringham, 3 B. C. L. R. 590.

not have been recorded within the prescribed period shall be deemed to have been abandoned.

20. WHEN A FREE MINER IS ENTITLED TO RECORD.—A free miner shall not be entitled to a record of a mineral claim until he shall have furnished the said Mining Recorder with all the above particulars.

21. MINING RECORDER'S OFFICE.—Upon the establishment of a mining division and the opening of a Mining Recorder's office therein, under the authority of this act, such office and none other shall be the proper office for recording all mineral claims within such mining division, and making all records in respect thereof.

22. RECORDING CLAIM IN WRONG DISTRICT.—If through ignorance any free miner shall record a mineral claim in a different mining division to that in which such claim is situate, such error shall not affect his title to such claim, but he shall, within fifteen days from the discovery of his error, record such claim in the mining division in which it is situate, and such new record shall bear the date of the first record, and a note shall be made thereon of the error and of the date of the rectification of the same.

23. APPLICATION AT RECORDER'S OFFICE IN HIS ABSENCE.—If a free miner applies at the Mining Recorder's office during his absence to record a mineral claim, or any document or other matter required by this act to be recorded, and leaves the fee required by this act, and the particulars and information required to enable the Mining Recorder to make such record, with the officer or other person in charge of said office, he shall be entitled to have such record dated on the date of such application.

24. DURATION OF RECORD AND DUTY OF HOLDER.—Any free miner having duly located and recorded a mineral claim shall be entitled to hold the same for the period of one year from the recording of the same, and thence from year to year without the necessity of re-recording. Provided, however, that during each year, and each succeeding year, such free miner shall do, or cause to be done, work on the claim itself to the value of $100, and shall satisfy the Gold Commissioner or Mining Recorder that such work has been done, by an affidavit of the free miner or his agent, setting out a detailed statement of such work, and shall obtain from such Gold Commissioner or Mining Recorder, and shall record a certificate of such work having been done. Provided, also, that all work done outside of a mineral claim with intent to work the same shall, if such work have direct relation and be in direct proximity to the claim, be deemed, if to the satisfaction of the Gold Commissioner or Mining Recorder, for the purposes of this section, to be work done on the claim.

ADJOINING CLAIMS IN PARTNERSHIP.—Provided, further, that any free miner, or company of free miners holding adjoining mineral claims, or any two or more free miners who locate and record adjoining mineral claims, not exceeding eight in number, to be worked by them in partnership under the provisions of any act for the time being in force, shall, subject to filing a notice of their intention with the Gold Commissioner or Mining Recorder, be allowed to perform on any one or more of such claims all the work required to entitle him or them to a certificate for work for each claim so held by him or them. If such work shall not be done, or if such certificate shall not be so obtained and recorded in each and every year, the claim shall be deemed vacant and abandoned, any rule of law or equity to the contrary notwithstanding. 1897, c. 28, s. 5.

24a. LODES UNDER ALLUVIAL DEPOSIT. —When a lode is supposed to cross a valley or under an alluvial deposit, and where such lode is indicated by its appearance on the side of the mountain leading into such valley, any free miner upon making a sworn statement before the Mining Recorder or Gold Commissioner of the district that there is a lode which has indications of running through and under such alluvial deposit, shall be entitled to a permit for three months to search for such lode over the area of a mineral claim, with the privilege of having such permit extended, on his proving to the satisfaction of the Gold Commissioner that he has bona fide searched for such lode and has expended, either in cash or labor, or both, not less than $100 in such search. During the existence of such permit the ground covered by the same shall not be open to record by any other miner. The fee for such permit, and each renewal of the same, shall be the same as the fee for a record. 1897, c. 28, s. 13.

25. PAYMENT INSTEAD OF ASSESSMENT WORK.—The holder of a mineral claim may, in lieu of the work required to be done by Section 24 of this act, on a claim in each year, pay to the Mining Recorder in whose office the claim is recorded the sum of $100 and receive from such recorder and record a receipt for such payment. Such payment and the record thereof in any year shall relieve the person making it from the necessity of doing any work during the year in and for which and upon the claim in respect of which such payment is recorded.

26. SURFACE RIGHTS.—Notwithstanding anything to the contrary contained in any act, every

Crown grant hereafter issued of a mineral claim shall convey, and be deemed to convey, only the right to the use and possession of the surface of such claim, including the use of all the timber thereon, for the purpose of winning and getting from and out of such claim the minerals contained therein, including all operations connected therewith or with the business of mining, and the lawful holder by record of a claim shall, during the continuance of his record, be entitled to the same surface rights and no others, and all remaining surface rights shall be deemed to be vested in the Crown, and may be granted and disposed of as is provided by the land laws for the time being in force, but subject always to the rights of free miners as aforesaid. 1897, c. 28, s. 6.

27. PRIORITY OF LOCATION IN CASES OF DISPUTE.—In case of any dispute as to the location of a mineral claim, the title to the claim shall be recognized according to the priority of such location, subject to any question as to the validity of the record itself, and subject, further, to the free miner having complied with all the terms and conditions of this act.

28. IRREGULARITIES PREVIOUS TO LAST CERTIFICATES OF TITLE.—Upon any dispute as to the title to any mineral claim no irregularity happening previous to the date of the record of the last certificate of work shall affect the title thereto, and it shall be assumed that up to that date the title to such claim was perfect, except upon suit by the Attorney General based upon fraud.

29. NOT MORE THAN ONE CLAIM TO BE HELD BY FREE MINER.—No free miner shall be entitled to hold in his own name, or in the name of any other person, more than one mineral claim

on the same vein or lode, except by purchase, but such free miner may hold by location a claim upon any separate vein or lode.[6]

30. ABANDONMENT OF CLAIM.—A free miner may at any time abandon any mineral claim by giving notice in writing of such intention to abandon to the Mining Recorder, and from the date of the record of such notice all interest of such free miner in such claim shall cease. 1897, c. 28, s. 7.

31. MACHINERY ON ABANDONED CLAIM. —When a free miner abandons a mineral claim he shall have the right to take from the same any machinery and any personal property which he may have placed on the claim, and any ore which he may have extracted therefrom, within such time as shall be fixed by the Gold Commissioner or Mining Recorder.

32. RELOCATION OF ABANDONED CLAIM. —No free miner shall be entitled to relocate any mineral claim or any portion thereof which he shall have failed to record within the prescribed period, or which he shall have abandoned or forfeited, unless he shall have obtained the written permission of the Gold Commissioner to make such relocation; and he shall hold no interest in any portion of such mineral claim, by location, without such permission.[7]

33. RIGHT TO LODES DISCOVERED IN A TUNNEL.—Where a tunnel is run for the development of a vein or lode the owner of such tunnel shall, in addition to any mineral claim legally held by him, have the right to all veins or lodes discovered in such tunnel. Provided, that the ground containing such veins or lodes be marked out by

---

[6] Richards v. Price, 5 B. C. L. R. 362.
[7] Nelson v. Jerry, 5 B. C. L. R. 396.

him as a mineral claim, and be duly recorded within fifteen days after such discovery; and, provided further, that such veins or lodes are not included in any existing mineral claim. Any money or labor expended in constructing a tunnel to develop a vein or lode shall be deemed to have been expended on such vein or lode.

34. INTEREST IN CLAIM A CHATTEL INTEREST.—The interest of a free miner in his mineral claim shall, save as to claims held as real estate, be deemed to be a chattel interest, equivalent to a lease, for one year, and thence from year to year, subject to the performance and observance of all the terms and conditions of this act.

35. PURCHASE OF MINERAL CLAIM.—Any lawful holder of a mineral claim shall be entitled to a Crown grant thereof on payment to the Government of British Columbia of the sum of $500 in lieu of expenditure on the claim. The intending purchaser shall comply with all the provisions of Section 36 of this act, except such as have respect solely to the work required to be done on claims.

36. CERTIFICATE OF IMPROVEMENTS. — Whenever the lawful holder of a mineral claim shall have complied with the following requirements, to the satisfaction of the Gold Commissioner, he shall be entitled to receive from the Gold Commissioner a certificate of improvements in respect of such claim, unless proceedings by the person claiming an adverse right under Section 37 of this act have been taken.[8]

(a) WHAT WORK TO BE DONE BEFORE CERTIFICATE OF IMPROVEMENTS GRANTED.—Done or cause to be done work on the claim itself in developing a mine to the value of $500,

---

[8] Woodbury v. Hudmit, 1 B. C. L. R. 89.

exclusive of all houses, buildings and other like improvements. For the purpose of this section, work done on the claim by a predecessor or predecessors in title shall be deemed to have been done by the applicant who receives a transfer of such claim. (1897, c. 28, s. 8.)

(*b*) FOUND A VEIN.—Found a vein or lode within the limits of such claim.

(*c*) SURVEY REQUIREMENTS FOR CERTIFICATE OF IMPROVEMENTS.—Had the claim surveyed by an authorized Provincial Land Surveyor, who shall have made three plats of the claim, and who shall have accurately defined and marked the boundaries of such claim upon the ground, and indicated the corners by placing monuments or legal posts at the angles thereof, and upon such monuments or posts shall be inscribed by him the name and the official designation of the claim, and the corner represented thereby, and who shall have, on completion of survey, forwarded at once the original field notes and plan direct to the Lands and Works Department.

EVIDENCE OF LOCATION.—After a certificate of improvements has issued in respect of any claim so surveyed, prima facie evidence of its location upon the ground may be given by any person who has seen and can describe the position of such posts purporting to be so marked as aforesaid, and the said field notes, or a copy thereof certified in accordance with the "Evidence act," shall be received in all courts as prima facie evidence of the facts which they purport to set forth.

(*d*) NOTICE OF APPLICATION, ETC., TO BE POSTED.—Shall have posted on some conspicuous part of the land embraced in the survey a copy of the plat of the claim, and a legible notice in writing, in Form F of the schedule to this act, of his intention to apply for a certificate of improvements, and shall also have posted a similar notice in the Mining Recorder's office, and such notice shall contain:

(1) The name of the claim.

(2) The name of the lawful holder thereof.

(3) The number of such holder's existing free miner's certificate.

(4) His intention to apply for certificate of improvements at the end of sixty days, for the purpose of obtaining a Crown grant.

(5) The date of the notice.

(*e*) PUBLICATION OF SUCH NOTICE IN GAZETTE.—Inserted a copy of such notice in the British Columbia Gazette and in a newspaper published and circulating in the division in which the claim is situated, or, in the absence of such local paper, in the one nearest thereto, for at least sixty days prior to such application, which insertion can be made at any time after the posting of the notice on the claim. (1897, c. 28, s. 8.)

(*f*) FILED COPY OF ORIGINAL NOTES WITH RECORDER.—Shall have filed with the Mining Recorder a copy of the surveyor's original field notes and plat immediately after posting the notice on the claim of his intention to apply for a certificate of improvements.

(*g*) Filed with the Mining Recorder:

(1) AFFIDAVIT IN FORM G.—Affidavit of the holder of the claim, or his agent, in the Form G in schedule of this act.

(*h*) MINING RECORDER'S DUTIES THEREUPON.—At the expiration of the term of the said publication, provided no action shall have been commenced and notice thereof filed with the

Mining Recorder, he shall forward to the owner or agent, under Form I of the schedule to this act, the documents referred to above, together with a certificate that the notice provided by Section 36, sub-section (*d*), has been posted in his office, and the field notes and plan deposited for reference therein from the date of the first appearance of the said notice in the British Columbia Gazette and continuously therefrom for a period of at least sixty days. The recorder shall also set out in Form I the name of the recorded owner of the claim at the date of signing the same.

36a. COST OF SURVEY COUNTED AS WORK DONE ON CLAIM.—The owner of a mineral claim who has had his claim surveyed within one year from the date of the record of the claim, or if the claim was recorded before the passing of this act, then if surveyed within one year from the passing of this act, and has filed in the office of the Mining Recorder in the Mining Division in which the claim is situated, a declaration by a Provincial Land Surveyor, stating that he has surveyed the claim as required by sub-section (*c*) of Section 36, of the "Mineral act," and that he has delivered two plats of the claim and a copy of the original field notes to the owner of such claim, then the owner of such claim shall be entitled to have the cost of such survey, not to exceed $100, counted as work done on the claim. 1897, c. 28, s. 11.

37. CERTIFICATE OF IMPROVEMENTS NOT TO BE IMPEACHED EXCEPT FOR FRAUD.—(1.) A certificate of improvements when issued as aforesaid shall not be impeached in any court on any ground except that of fraud. [9]

ADVERSE CLAIMANT.—ACTION TO BE COMMENCED.—(2.) In case any person shall

[9] Nelson v. Jerry, 5 B. C. L. R. 396.

claim an adverse right of any kind, either to possession of the mineral claim referred to in the application for certificate of improvements or any part thereof, or to the minerals contained therein, he shall, within sixty days after the publication in the British Columbia Gazette of the notice referred to in Section 36 hereof (unless such time shall be extended by special order of the court upon cause being shown), commence an action in the Supreme Court of British Columbia to determine the question of the right of possession or otherwise enforce his said claim, and shall file a copy of the writ in said action with the Mining Recorder of the district or mining division in which the said claim is situate within twenty days from the commencement of said action, and shall prosecute the said suit with reasonable diligence to final judgment, and a failure to so commence or so to prosecute shall be deemed to be a waiver of the plaintiff's claim.

CERTIFIED COPY OF JUDGMENT MAY BE FILED.—After final judgment shall have been rendered in the said action the person or any one of the persons entitled to the possession of the claim or any part thereof, may file a certified copy of the same in the office of the Mining Recorder.

CERTIFICATE OF IMPROVEMENTS AFTER JUDGMENT.—After the filing of the said judgment, and upon compliance with all the requirements of the next preceding section, such person or persons shall be entitled to the issue to him or to them of a certificate of improvements in respect of the claim or the portion thereof which he or they shall appear from the decision of the court rightly to possess.

PENDING LITIGATION.—Provided, that this section shall not apply to any adverse claim filed or action to enforce the same commenced prior to the date of this act coming into force, but the same shall be continued in the same manner as if this act had not been passed.[10]

37a. ONUS OF PROOF ON CLAIMANT.—If any person shall in any suit or matter claim an adverse right of any kind to the mineral claim comprised in any record, or to any part thereof, or shall claim that any record is invalid or has been improperly obtained, or that the holder thereof has not complied with the provisions of the act under which the location and record were made, or has not prior to the obtaining of such record made a good and valid location of such mineral claim according to law, the onus of proof thereof shall be on the person so claiming an adverse right, or so claiming that such record is invalid and has been improperly obtained as aforesaid, and in default of such proof judgment shall be given for the holder of such prior record in so far as such action, suit or matter relates to any of the matters aforesaid. 1897, c. 28, s. 15.

38. EFFECT OF CERTIFICATE OF IMPROVEMENTS.—After the issuing and recording of such certificate of improvements, and while such certificate shall be in force it shall not be necessary to do any work on such claim.

39. RECORD OF CERTIFICATE OF IMPROVEMENTS ENTITLES OWNER TO CROWN GRANT.—On the granting and recording of such certificate of improvements in respect to a mineral claim situate outside of the Railway Belt, the holder thereof shall be entitled to a Crown grant of such claim without the payment of the $500 required by Section 35.

---

[10] Re Maple Leaf, Etc., 2 B. C. L. R. 323.

RAILWAY BELT.—And on the granting and recording of such certificate of improvements in respect of a mineral claim situate inside the Railway Belt, the holder thereof shall be entitled to a Crown grant of such claim on the payment of $5 per acre to the Mining Recorder.

40. APPLICATION FOR CROWN GRANT.— The holder of a mineral claim for which a certificate of improvements has been granted and recorded shall make application for a Crown grant to the Gold Commissioner, inclosing his certificate of improvements, the Crown grant fee of $5, the Mining Recorder's certificate, Form I, the field notes and plat and the affidavit, Form G, within three months from the date of such certificate of improvements, and in default of such application having been made within such time such certificate of improvements shall lapse and become absolutely void.

41. TRANSFER OF CLAIM AFTER APPLICATION FOR CERTIFICATE.—If the holder of a mineral claim, after applying for a certificate of improvements, shall sell and transfer such claim to another free miner, upon satisfactory proof of such sale and transfer being made to the Gold Commissioner, the new holder of the claim shall be entitled to a certificate of improvements in his own name. And if a sale and transfer shall be made to any person or company after a certificate of improvements shall have been issued, upon proper proof of such sale and transfer being made to the satisfaction of the Chief Commissioner of Lands and Works, the Crown grant shall issue to the new holder of the claim.

42. NOT TO TRANSFER AFTER CERTIFICATE UNTIL CROWN GRANT.—When a holder of a mineral claim has taken out his certificate of

improvements he shall not record any transfer of his rights in the said claim until he obtains his Crown grant.

43. CROWN GRANT DOES NOT INVALI-DATE A LIEN.—The issuance of a Crown grant shall not invalidate any lien which may have attached to any mineral claim previous to the issuance of such Crown grant.

44. WHAT PASSES BY CROWN GRANT ON WASTE LAND.—A Crown grant of a mineral claim located on any waste lands of the Crown shall be deemed to transfer and pass the right to all minerals within the meaning of this act (excepting coal) found in veins, lodes or rock in place, and whether such minerals are found separately or in combination with each other, in, upon or under the land in the said Crown grant mentioned. [11]

45. WHAT PASSES BY CROWN GRANT WHEN ALL MINERALS (SAVE COAL) HAVE BEEN RESERVED.—Crown grants of mineral claims located on lawfully occupied lands, the right whereon to enter, prospect and mine all minerals (other than coal) has been reserved to the Crown and its licensees, shall pass to the grantee all minerals within the meaning of this act (other than coal) found in veins or lodes or rock in place, and whether such minerals are found separately or in combination with each other, which may be in, upon or under the land in the said Crown grant mentioned, and including all the rights given to mineral claim holders of mineral claims so located, but such Crown grant shall expressly reserve the rights of such prior occupant.

---

[11] In re Good Friday, 4 B. C. L. R. 497; Trask v. Pellent, 5 B. C. L. R. 1; Kenney v. Harris, 5 B. C. L. R. 229; Kilbourne v. McGnigan, 5 B. C. L. R. 233; Corbin v. Lookout M. Co., 5 B. C. L. R. 281.

IN CASE OF TIMBER LEASE.—(Where the mineral claim is located on land lawfully occupied under a timber lease, the Crown grant shall convey the surface and minerals within the meaning of this act (save coal) found in veins or lodes or rock in place, but shall reserve the timber.)

46. WHAT PASSES BY CROWN GRANT WHEN GOLD AND SILVER HAS BEEN RESERVED.—Crown grants of mineral claims located on lawfully occupied lands, the right whereon to enter and mine gold and silver has been reserved to the Crown and its licensees, shall pass to the grantee all the gold and silver found in veins or lodes or rock in place, which may be in, upon or under the land in the said Crown grant mentioned, and including all the rights given to mineral claim holders of mineral claims so located; but such Crown grant shall expressly reserve the rights of such prior occupant.

46a. PURCHASE BY CROWN GRANTEE OF MINERAL CLAIM OF SURFACE RIGHTS ON WASTE LANDS.—The lawful holder of a Crown grant of a mineral claim issued under the provisions of this act shall, in cases where such mineral claim has been located on waste lands of the Crown or on lands not already lawfully occupied for other than mining purposes, be entitled to receive a Crown grant of all the surface rights of such mineral claim on payment to the Government of British Columbia of the sum of $5 per acre for such land, and of the fee of $5 for the Crown grant. 1897, c. 28, s. 12.

46b. REPEAL OF ACTS DEEMED TO HAVE CLAUSES SAVING RIGHT OF MINERAL CLAIM HOLDERS TO OBTAIN CROWN GRANTS.—Notwithstanding the repeal of any acts relating to mineral claims or the saving clauses of any such repealing acts, all such repealing acts shall be deemed to have contained provisions declaring the holders of records of mineral claims entitled to apply for Crown grants thereof under the provisions of the law in force at the time of such applications, and that the procedure upon any such applications shall be that prescribed by the statutes in force at the time of such applications, the grants thereafter vesting in the holders such rights as were declared by the statutes in force at the date of record of such mineral claims. Provided, however, that nothing contained in this section shall impair or in any way restrict the rights and privileges conferred on owners of mineral claims by the preceding section of this act. 1897, c. 28, s. 16.

46c. VALIDATION OF CROWN GRANTS HERETOFORE ISSUED. — All Crown grants heretofore issued to the holders of mineral claim records shall be deemed to have been validly issued so far as relates to the procedure upon the application to obtain same, if in the application therefor the holder thereof observed either the procedure prescribed by the statutes in force at the time of the record of such mineral claims, or the procedure prescribed by the statutes in force at the time of the applications for Crown grants thereof. 1897, c. 28, s. 17.

47. ADVERSE CLAIM AFFECTING ONLY PORTION OF CLAIM.—If an adverse claim shall only affect a portion of the ground for which a certificate of improvements is applied, the applicant may relinquish the portion covered by the adverse claim, and still be entitled to a certificate of improvements for the undisputed remainder of his claim, upon complying with the requirements of this act.

48. AFTER JUDGMENT IS GIVEN.—When

judgment in such case is rendered by the court, a memorandum of such judgment shall be entered in the "Record Book;" and if by any judgment the original boundaries of any claim shall be changed, a plat made by a Provincial Land Surveyor, and signed by the judge by whom the judgment has been given, shall be filed in the office of the Mining Recorder.

49. RECORD OF TITLE NOT REAL ES-TATE.—Every conveyance, bill of sale, mortgage or other document of title relating to any mineral claim, not held as real estate or mining interest, shall be recorded within the time prescribed for recording mineral claims. Provided, always, that the failure to so record any such document shall not invalidate the same as between the parties thereto, but such documents as to third parties shall take effect from the date of record, and not from the date of such document.

AFTER CROWN GRANT. — And provided further, that after the issuance of a Crown grant for any mineral claim it shall not be necessary to register any transfer or other document of title executed subsequent to such Crown grant with the Mining Recorder of the district in which the said claim is situated, but all documents relating to the same may thereafter be registered in the same manner as are other documents of title relating to the transfer of real estate.

"LAND REGISTRY ACT."—And all the provisions of the "Land Registry act," and any amendments thereto, shall apply to such registration.[12]

50. TRANSFERS TO BE IN WRITING.—No transfer of any mineral claim, or of any interest

---

12 Atkins v. Coy, 5 B. C. L. R. 8.

therein, shall be enforceable unless the same shall be in writing, signed by the transferrer or by his agent authorized in writing, and recorded by the Mining Recorder.

AGENT.—And if signed by an agent, the authority of such agent shall be recorded before the record of such transfer.

"LAND REGISTRY ACT."—All mineral claims derived under Crown grant, and every transfer thereof, or any interest therein, shall be registered under the provisions of the "Land Registry act."

50a. LOCATOR TO ASSIGN INTEREST IN CLAIM IN WRITING.—No free miner shall be entitled to any interest in any mineral claim which has been located and recorded by any other free miner unless such interest is specified and set forth in some writing signed by the party so locating such claim. 1897, c. 28, s. 14.

51. TRANSFERS UNDER "GOLD MINING AMENDMENT ACT, 1873."—The transfer of any real estate acquired under the provisions of the "Gold Mining Amendment act, 1873," shall be in writing, signed by the transferrer or his agent authorized in writing, and need not be by deed or under seal.

52. CLAIM OF MINER DURING ILLNESS AND AFTER DEATH.—No mineral claim shall be open to location by any other person during the last illness, nor, unless with the permission in writing of the Gold Commissioner, for twelve months after the death of the lawful holder.

53. FAULTS OF GOVERNMENT OF-FICIALS.—No free miner shall suffer from any acts of omission, or commission, or delays on the

part of any Government official, if such can be proven.[18]

54. LOCATION OF MILL SITES.—A free miner may locate any unoccupied and unreserved Crown land not known to contain mineral, and not exceeding five acres, as a mill site. No free miner shall be entitled to obtain and hold under this section more than one mill site for each mineral claim lawfully held by him. Such mill site shall be as nearly as possible in the form of a square. On locating a mill site, the free miner shall comply with the following requirements:

(*a*) Mark out the land by placing a legal post at each corner.

(*b*) Post a notice on each post, stating—

1. The name of such free miner.

2. The number of his free miner's certificate.

3. His intention, at the expiration of sixty days from the date of the notice, to apply for the land as a mill site.

4. The date of the notice.

(*c*) Post a copy of such notice on the office of the Mining Recorder.

55. RECORDER MAY GRANT LEASE FOR ONE YEAR.—On the expiration of sixty days after the fulfillment of the above requirements, the free miner shall deposit, in duplicate, in the office of the Mining Recorder, a plat of the said land made by an authorized Provincial Land Surveyor, and prove by affidavit that he has complied with the above requirements, and that the said land is not known to contain minerals, and shall furnish such other proof of the non-mineral character of the land as the Gold Commissioner may require; the free miner shall then be entitled to a lease, for one year, of the said

---

[18] Granger v. Fotheringham, 8 B. C. L. R. 590.

land, which lease shall be executed by the Gold Commissioner.

CROWN GRANT.—PRICE.—If, during the continuance of such lease, such free miner shall prove to the satisfaction of the Gold Commissioner that he has put or constructed works, or machinery for mining or milling purposes, on the said mill site, of the value of at least $500, he shall be entitled to a Crown grant of such mill site upon payment of $5 per acre for such land. Any free miner now having a lease of a piece of land for a mill site, upon proving to the satisfaction of the Gold Commissioner that he has put or constructed works, or machinery for mining or milling purposes, on the said mill site of the value of at least $500, shall, on payment of $5 per acre, be entitled to a Crown grant of such mill site.

56. APPLICATION FOR CROWN GRANT OF MILL SITE.—On applying for a Crown grant of a mill site, the free miner shall—

(1) Pay the sum of $5 per acre to the Mining Recorder.

(2) Deposit with the Mining Recorder the following documents:

(*a*) Lease of the mill site.

(*b*) Plat of the mill site.

(*c*) Surveyor's original field notes.

(*d*) A certificate from the Gold Commissioner that works or machinery for mining or milling purposes have been put or constructed on the mill site to the value of at least $500.

(*e*) Application for the Crown grant.

57. WHAT PASSES BY CROWN GRANT OF MILL SITE.—Crown grants of mill sites shall pass to the grantee all the surface of the land in the said Crown grant mentioned, but all such Crown grants

shall expressly reserve all minerals under the said land, and the right to the Crown and its licensees to enter and mine the said minerals.

58. LICENSE TO RUN TUNNELS AND DRAINS.—Any free miner, being the holder of a mineral claim or mine held as real estate, may, at the discretion of the Gold Commissioner, obtain a license to run a drain or tunnel, for drainage or any other purpose connected with the development or working of such claim or mine, through any occupied or unoccupied lands, whether mineral or otherwise, upon security being first deposited or given to such Gold Commissioner to his satisfaction for any damage that may be done thereby, and upon such other terms as he shall think expedient.

[Sections 59 to 79, inclusive, repealed by 1897, c. 28, s. 19.]

PART III.

Mining Partnership.

80. MINING PARTNERSHIPS; APPLICATION.—All mining partnerships shall be governed by the provisions hereof, unless they shall have other and written articles of partnership.

81. PARTNERSHIP TO BE ANNUAL.—A mining partnership shall, unless otherwise agreed upon, be deemed to be a yearly partnership, renewable from year to year by tacit consent.

82. SCOPE OF PARTNERSHIP.—The business of the partnership shall be mining and such other matters as pertain solely thereto.

83. RECORD OF MINING PARTNERSHIPS.—Mining partnerships can locate and record in the partnership name a mineral claim for each partner, but the name of every partner, and the number of every partner's free miner's certificate shall be on the record of every such claim. The partnership name must appear on every such record, and all the claims so taken up shall be the property of the partnership: Provided, always, that no free miner who is the member of a mining partnership, holding by right of location a mineral claim, shall be entitled to hold by right of location in his own name or in the name of any other partnership any interest in any other mineral claim on the same vein or lode on which the partnership claim is situate.

84. ONE PARTNER FAILING TO KEEP UP FREE MINER'S CERTIFICATE.— Should any partner fail to keep up his free miner's certificate, such failure shall not cause a forfeiture, or act as an abandonment of the partnership claim, but the share of the partner who shall so fail to keep up his free miner's certificate shall, ipso facto, be and become vested in his partners, pro rata, according to their former interests, on the said partners paying the free miner's certificate for the year.

85. PARTNER'S RIGHT TO VOTE.—A partner in any mining partnership or his agent authorized in writing shall, at any meeting thereof, be entitled to vote upon any interest or fraction of an interest which he may hold therein; but the result of the votes given shall be determined by the number of the full interests voted upon, and not by the number of partners voting at such meeting.

86. MAJORITY TO MAKE ASSESSMENTS. —A majority of such votes may decide when, how long, and in what manner to work the partnership claim, the number of men to be employed, and the extent and manner of levying the assessments to defray the expenses incurred by the partnership:

Such majority may also choose a foreman or manager, who shall represent the partnership, and sue and be sued in the name of the partnership for assessments and otherwise; and he shall have power to bind them by his contracts: Every partner, or his duly authorized agent, shall be entitled to represent his interest in the partnership property by work and labor so long as such work and labor be satisfactory to the foreman , or manager. In the event of such workman being discharged by the foreman or manager, the Court having jurisdiction in mining disputes may, if requested, summon the foreman or manager before it, and upon hearing the facts make such order as it shall deem just.

87. ASSESSMENTS TO BE PAID WITHIN THIRTY DAYS.—All assessments shall be payable within thirty days after being made.

88. DEFAULT IN PAYMENT OF ASSESS-MENT BY PARTNER.—Any partner making default in payment after receiving a notice specifying the amount due by him, shall, if such amount be correct, be personally liable therefore to the partnership, and his interest in the partnership property may be sold by the partnership for the payment of the debt, and any further assessment which may have accrued thereon up to the day of sale, together with all costs and charges occasioned by such default; and if the proceeds of the sale be insufficient to pay off the several sums mentioned, the court having jurisdiction in mining disputes, upon being applied to, shall issue an order directed to the sheriff to seize and sell any other personal property of the debtor. Notices of sale shall, in either of the above cases, be conspicuously posted thirty clear days prior to the day of sale in the vicinity of such mining or other property, and on the Court House or Mining Recorder's office nearest thereto. But if

such partner be absent from the district such notices
shall be posted as aforesaid sixty clear days before
the day of sale, and a copy of such notice shall be
published in some newspaper circulating in the district wherein such mining or other property is
situate.   Such sale shall be by public auction to the
highest bidder.   The purchaser shall be entitled to
possession of the property sold, and to a bill of sale
therefor signed by the auctioneer; such bill of sale
shall confer such title upon the purchaser as the
owner had.   And for the purpose of carrying out
the provisions of this section the Mining Recorder of
the mining division in which the property to be sold
is situate, or some one appointed by him, may act
as auctioneer.

89. EFFECT OF NOTICE OF ABANDON-
MENT.—After a notice of abandonment in writing
shall have been served on the foreman or manager
of a partnership by any member thereof, and duly
recorded, such member shall not be liable for any
debts or other liabilities of the partnership incurred
after service and record of such notice, and no
member shall be deemed to have abandoned an interest until service and record of such notice.

90. TITLE TO ABANDONED SHARE VESTS
IN   CONTINUING   PARTNERS.—Upon   the
abandonment of any share in a mining partnership,
the title to the abandoned share shall vest in the
continuing partners, pro rata, according to their
former interests.

91. PARTNER MAY SELL HIS INTEREST.
—Any partner shall be entitled to sell, or contract
for the sale of, his interest in the partnership property, but such interest shall continue liable for all
the debts of the partnership.

92. AFTER SALE, PARTNER NOT LIABLE FOR DEBTS OF PARTNERSHIP.—No partner shall, after a bill of sale conveying his interest has been recorded, be liable for any indebtedness of the partnership incurred thereafter.

93. LIMITED LIABILITY.—Any mining partnership composed of two or more free miners may limit the liability of its members, upon complying with the requirements following, that is to say:

Upon filing with the Mining Recorder a declaratory statement containing the name of the partnership, the location and size of every partnership claim, and the particular interest of each partner; and also placing upon a conspicuous part of every such claim, in large letters, the name of the partnership, followed by the words "Limited Liability."

94. ADDITION OF LIMITED LIABILITY TO COMPANY'S NAME.—The words "Limited Liability" shall thereupon become part of the partnership name.

95. EFFECT OF LIMITED LIABILITY.— After such conditions shall have been complied with, no member of such partnership shall be liable for any indebtedness incurred thereafter beyond an amount proportioned to his interest in the partnership.

96. ACCOUNTS TO BE KEPT.—Every such partnership shall keep a correct account of its assets and liabilities, together with the names of the partners, and the interest held by each, and shall make out a monthly balance sheet showing the names of the creditors, and the amounts due to each, and file the same among the papers of the partnership; and such balance sheet and all the books of the partnership shall be open to the inspection of creditors at all reasonable hours.

97. PARTNER MAY SELL.—Every partner in such partnership shall be at liberty to sell or dispose of his interest therein, or of any part thereof, to any other free miner.

98. AFTER SALE, PARTNER NOT LIABLE FOR DEBTS OF PARTNERSHIP.—No member of such partnership, after a bill of sale conveying his interest has been duly recorded, or after he has served a notice of abandonment of his interest on the foreman, and left a copy thereof with the Mining Recorder, shall be liable for any indebtedness of the partnership incurred thereafter.

99. DIVIDENDS.—No such partnership shall declare any dividend until all its liabilities have been paid.

100. APPOINTMENT OF FOREMAN.—Every such partnership shall appoint a foreman or manager, who shall represent the partnership, who shall sue and be sued in the name of the partnership, and his contracts in relation to the business of the partnership shall be deemed to be the contracts of the partnership.

101. TO WHAT PARTNERSHIP IS LIABLE. —No such partnership shall be liable for any other indebtedness than that contracted by its foreman or manager, or by his agent duly authorized in writing.

102. FAILURE TO COMPLY WITH PROVISIONS.—Should any such partnership fail to comply with any of the provisions of this act relating exclusively to "limited liability" partnerships, such partnerships shall, from the date of such failure, cease to be a "limited liability" partnership.

PART IV.

103. APPOINTMENT OF MINING RE-CORDER.—The Lieutenant Governor in Council may appoint any person to be a Mining Recorder in and for any part of the Province.

104. ELECTION OF RECORDER BY MIN-ERS.—Where mineral land is discovered in a part of the Province so situate that the provisions of this act as to free miners' certificates and records of mining property cannot be justly applied or enforced by reason of there being no Gold Commissioner or Mining Recorder in the locality, it shall be lawful for the miners of such locality to hold meetings at such times and places as may be agreed upon, and at such meeting, by a two-thirds vote, to appoint one of their number to issue free miners' certificates and to enter records of mining property; and such certificates and records shall be valid, notwithstanding any informality therein: Provided that all records so made, and all fees for the same in accordance with the schedule to this act, and a list of all free miners' certificates issued, and the date and term thereof, and the fees for the same, be forwarded to the nearest Gold Commissioner or Mining Recorder as soon thereafter as practicable.

105. RECORDER TO ISSUE CERTIFI-CATES.—Every Mining Recorder shall issue free miners' certificates and "substituted certificates" to all persons and companies entitled thereto.

106. BOOK OF FORMS, COUNTERFOILS, ETC.—Such free miners' certificates shall be taken from a printed book of forms, with duplicate counterfoils, one of which counterfoils shall be filed in the office of the Mining Recorder.

107. BOOKS TO BE KEPT BY MINING RE-CORDER.—Every Mining Recorder shall keep the following books:

(*a*) A book to be known as the "Record book."

(*b*) A book to be known as the "Record of Abandonments."

(*c*) A book to be known as the "Record of Affidavits."

(*d*) A book to be known as the "Record of Conveyances."

(*e*) A book to be known as the "Record of Free Miners' Certificates."

108. ISSUE OF CERTIFICATE.—Upon receipt of an affidavit setting forth a detailed statement of work, as required by Section 24, the Mining Recorder shall issue a certificate of work in the Form E in the schedule to this act.

109. FILING AND RECORD OF AFFIDAVIT AND CERTIFICATE.—Upon issuing such certificate of work, the Mining Recorder shall file such affidavit in the Record of Affidavits, and also record such certificate of work in the Record Book.

110. RECORD OF CERTIFICATE OF IM-PROVEMENTS.—Upon receiving a certificate of improvements, the Mining Recorder shall record the same verbatim in the Record Book.

111. WHAT RECORDER MUST RECORD.—The Mining Recorder must record all extensions of time, licenses, permits and other privileges granted by the Gold Commissioner or Mining Recorder, and all forfeitures declared by the Gold Commissioner, and a memorandum of every judgment affecting a mineral claim or other mining property, in the Record Book. 1897, c. 28, s. 9.

112. CERTAIN PARTICULARS TO BE EN-TERED IN FREE MINERS' CERTIFICATE

BOOK.—Upon any Mining Recorder issuing a free miner's certificate, or upon any free miner applying to record any mineral claim, bill of sale or other instrument, the Mining Recorder shall enter in the free miners' certificate book the particulars of such free miner's certificate, giving number of certificate, date, place of issue, and to whom issued.

113. RECORD OF ABANDONMENTS.—Upon the receipt of a notice of abandonment, the Mining Recorder shall record the same in the Record of Abandonments, and file such notice, and write across the record of the claim affected by such notice, in the Record Book, the word "Abandoned," and the date of the receipt by him of the notice. If only an interest in a mineral claim is abandoned, and not the entire claim, the memorandum in the record shall show which interest is abandoned.

114. HOW RECORDS ARE TO BE MADE.— The Mining Recorder shall record, by copying out verbatim all affidavits and declaratory statements required to be recorded in connection with his office, in the Record of Affidavits.

115. HOW RECORDS ARE TO BE MADE.— The Mining Recorder shall record, by copying out verbatim, in the Record of Conveyances, all conveyances, mortgages, bills of sale, contracts for sale, and other documents of title, including powers of attorney, or other authorities, to execute all or any of the above description of documents when brought to him for that purpose.

116. RECORD OF DOCUMENTS.—The Mining Recorder shall record in the Record Book all other documents relating to mining property which may be brought to him for record, and shall file all such documents which may be brought to him to be filed.

117. DATE OF ENTRY.—Every entry made in any of the above books shall show the date on which such entry was made.

118. BOOK TO BE OPEN FOR INSPECTION.—All books of record and documents filed shall, during office hours, be open to public inspection free of charge.

119. OFFICE COPY TO BE EVIDENCE.—Every copy of, or extract from, any entry in any of the said books, or of any document filed in the Mining Recorder's office, certified to be a true copy or extract by the Mining Recorder, shall be received in any court as evidence of the matters therein contained.

120. DUTY OF GOLD COMMISSIONER ON RECEIVING APPLICATION FOR CROWN GRANT.—Upon receipt from the holder of a certificate of improvements of an application for a Crown grant in the proper form, and all moneys payable in respect of the claim for which a Crown grant is applied, the Gold Commissioner shall send such moneys, together with the under-mentioned papers, to the Chief Commissioner of Lands and Works:

(1) The certificate of improvements.

(2) Affidavit of the holder of the mineral claim, or his agent—Form G.

(3) A copy of the plat of the mineral claim.

(4) The copy of the surveyor's original field notes.

(5.) Mining Recorder's certificate—Form I.

121. DUTIES WITH REFERENCE TO MILL SITES.—Upon receipt from the lessee of a mill site of all the moneys and documents mentioned in Section 56, the Mining Recorder shall send the same to the Gold Commissioner.

122. RECORDER TO COLLECT FEES.—Before issuing any free miner's certificate, or substituted certificate, or certificate of work, or making any entry in any book of record, or filing any document, or making any copy or extract therefrom, the Mining Recorder shall collect the fees payable in respect thereof.

Mining Divisions.

123. MINING DIVISIONS.—It shall be lawful for the Lieutenant Governor in Council to divide and subdivide any district into mining divisions and to establish in each mining division a Mining Recorder's office.

124. EFFECT OF ESTABLISHMENT OF RECORDER'S OFFICE IN MINING DISTRICT.—Upon the establishment of a mining division, and the opening of a Mining Recorder's office therein, under the authority of the last preceding section—

(*a*) Such office, and none other, shall be the proper office for recording all claims, records, certificates, documents or other instruments affecting claims, mines or mining property situate within such mining division not held as real estate; and whenever, by this act, or any act amending the same, anything is required to be done at or in the office of the Gold Commissioner or Mining Recorder of the district, it shall, if the same affects or concerns any claim, mine or mining property situate within a mining division not held as real estate, be done at or in the office of the Mining Recorder of the mining division wherein such claim or mine, or other mining property, is situate.

(*b*) Upon the district or division of any Mining Recorder being divided or subdivided into mining divisions, it shall be the duty of such Mining Recorder to make, or cause to be made, a transcript of all the entries in all the books mentioned in Section 107, affecting claims, mines or mining property situate in each newly created mining division not held as real estate, and to forward the same to the Mining Recorder of such mining division, and such transcript shall be kept in such office as part of the records of such office, and all transcripts of such records, certificates, documents or other instruments shall prima facie be deemed to be true copies of the several records, certificates, documents or other instruments of which they purport to be transcripts; and such transcripts or copies thereof, when certified by the Mining Recorder of the mining division in whose office they are kept, shall be admissible in evidence in all Courts of Judicature in this Province. 1897, c. 28, s. 10.

125. GOLD COMMISSIONER HAS ALL POWERS OF MINING RECORDER.—When there shall be no Mining Recorder for a district or division, the duties of the Mining Recorder shall devolve upon the Gold Commissioner, and it shall at all times be lawful for the Gold Commissioner to perform the duties of the Mining Recorder, and the Gold Commissioner shall have all the powers of a Mining Recorder.

126. OFFICE HOURS.—The Mining Recorder's office shall be open upon such days and hours as the Lieutenant Governor in Council may from time to time appoint, and failing any particular appointment shall be kept open upon all days, excepting public holidays, from 9 a. m. to 4 p. m., and such times shall be deemed the office hours of such office.

PART V.

Gold Commissioners.

126a. GOLD COMMISSIONERS TO BE APPOINTED BY THE LIEUTENANT GOVERNOR.—The Lieutenant Governor in Council may from time to time appoint such persons as he shall think proper to be respectively Chief Gold Commissioner and Gold Commissioners, either for the whole Province or for any particular districts therein, and from time to time in like manner fix and vary the limits of and subdivide such districts, and make and revoke all such appointments. C. A. 1888, c. 82, s. 4.

Tunnels and Drains.

127. COMMISSIONER MAY GRANT LICENSES FOR TUNNELS.—It shall be lawful for, but not incumbent upon, the Gold Commissioner to grant a license to any free miner, being the lawful holder of a mineral claim or mine held as real estate, to run a drain or tunnel, for any purpose connected with the development or working of such claim or mine, through any occupied or unoccupied lands, whether mineral or otherwise, upon security being deposited or given to him, to his satisfaction, for any damage that may be done thereby, and upon such other terms as he shall think fit.

[Sections 128 to 134, inclusive, repealed by 1897, c. 28, s. 19.]

Working of Mines or Claims, and Other Powers.

135. RELOCATION OF CLAIM.—The Gold Commissioner may, in his discretion, permit a free miner to relocate a mineral claim, or any part thereof, which may have been abandoned or forfeited by such free miner: Provided that such re-locations shall not prejudice or interfere with the rights or interests of others.

136. MARKING OUT SPACE FOR DEPOS-ITS.—The Gold Commissioner may mark out a space of ground for deposits of leavings and deads from any tunnel, claim or mining ground, upon such terms as he may think just.

137. COMMISSIONER TO PROVIDE FOR PUBLIC SAFETY.—The Gold Commissioner shall have the power to summarily order any mining works to be so carried on as not to interfere with or endanger the safety of the public, any public work or highway, or any mining property, mineral claims, mining claims, bed-rock drains, or bed-rock flumes; and any abandoned works may by his order be either filled up or guarded to his satisfaction, at the cost of the parties who may have constructed the same, or, in their absence, upon such terms as he shall think fit.

138. CROWN GRANTS UNDER "GOLD MIN-ING AMENDMENT ACT, 1873."—Notwithstand-ing anything contained in the "Gold Mining Amend-ment act, 1873," or in any Crown grant issued under the said act, or under this or any other act, it shall be lawful for the Gold Commissioner, in his discretion, and with or without any terms or condi-tions, to allow to the owners of mineral claims all such rights or privileges in and over mineral or other claims held as real estate as may be allowed in and over claims not so held; and owners of claims held as real estate shall be entitled to the same rights and privileges as owners of claims not so held.

139. ISSUE OF LEASE OF MILL SITE.—Upon receiving an application for a mill site from

any free miner, and upon proof being furnished to
his satisfaction of the non-mineral character of the
land applied for, and the deposit in duplicate of a
plat of said land, and upon proof by affidavit that
the applicant has complied with the requirements of
Section 54 of this act, the Gold Commissioner shall
issue to the applicant a lease of such land for one
year, in the form of the schedule to this act.

140. CERTIFICATE OF WORK ON MILL
SITE.—Upon being satisfied that the lessee of a
mill site has put or constructed thereon works or
machinery for mining or milling purposes to an
amount of not less than five hundred dollars, the
Gold Commissioner shall issue his certificate to that
effect.

141. RECORDER TO FORWARD DOCU-
MENTS, ETC., TO C. C. OF LANDS AND
WORKS.—Upon receipt from the Mining Recorder
of the moneys and documents mentioned or referred
to in Section 121, the Gold Commissioner shall sat-
isfy himself that the same are in order, and then
forward the same to the Chief Commissioner of
Lands and Works.

142. POWER TO CARRY OUT ACT.—The
Gold Commissioner shall have power to do all things
necessary or expedient for the carrying out of the
provisions of this act.

Administration.

143. COMMISSIONER TO ADMINISTER ES-
TATE OF INTESTATE DECEASED MINER.
—The Gold Commissioner, or any person authorized
by him, shall take charge of all the property within
the district of such commissioner, of any deceased
free miner, until the issue of letters of administration
or probate of the will, if any, and may cause any

mineral claims held or owned to be duly represented or dispense therewith at his option: Provided, however, that where any free miner shall die intestate, and the value of the personal estate of such deceased free miner is less than three hundred dollars, it shall not be necessary for the Gold Commissioner to obtain from any court letters of administration, but in such case the Gold Commissioner may administer and wind up the personal estate of the deceased, and do all things necessary and proper therefor, and act in all respects as if letters of administration to the personal estate of such deceased free miner had been granted to such Gold Commissioner, and the Gold Commissioner shall produce and pass his accounts, in each estate of which he shall undertake the administration, before a judge of the County Court of the district.

(*a*) APPLICATION OF "OFFICIAL ADMINISTRATOR'S ACT."—The Gold Commissioner or person authorized by him as aforesaid shall be governed by the provisions of the "Official Administrator's act," and amending acts, and any rules and regulations thereunder.   1897, c. 28, s. 20.

PART VI.

County Courts.

Jurisdiction, Procedure, Forms and Costs.

144. JURISDICTION OF COUNTY COURTS IN MINING MATTERS.—In addition to the jurisdiction and powers given to county courts by the "County Courts' Jurisdiction act," and other acts, every County Court shall have and exercise, within the limits of its district, all the jurisdiction and powers of a Court of Law and Equity—

(1) IN ALL PERSONAL ACTIONS, where

the debt or damages claimed arise directly out of the business of mining (other than coal mining), or from the exercise of or interference with any right, power or privilege given, or claimed to be given, by this act or any other act relating to mining (other than coal mining).

(2) IN ALL ACTIONS BETWEEN EM-PLOYERS AND EMPLOYES, where the employ-ment is directly connected with the business of mining (other than coal mining).

(3) IN ALL ACTIONS FOR SUPPLIES to persons engaged in mining, where such supplies were bought, contracted for or supplied, or were alleged to have been bought, contracted for or sup-plied for mining purposes, or for consumption by persons engaged in mining or prospecting.

(4.) IN ALL ACTIONS OF TRESPASS on or in respect of mineral claims or other mining prop-erty, or upon or in respect of lands entered or tres-passed on, or claimed to have been entered or tres-passed on, in searching for, mining or working minerals (other than coal), or for any other purpose directly connected with the business of mining (other than coal mining), or in the exercise of any power or privilege given, or claimed to be given, by this act, or any other act relating to mining (other than coal mining).

(5) IN ALL ACTIONS OF EJECTMENT from mineral claims or other mining property, or from lands entered, or claimed to have been entered, in searching for, mining or working min-erals (other than coal), or for any purpose directly connected with the business of mining, or entered, or claimed to have been entered, under some power, right or authority given or obtained under the pro-

visions of this act, or any other act relating to mining (other than coal mining).

(6) IN ALL SUITS FOR FORECLOSURE or redemption, or for enforcing any charge or lien, where the mortgage, charge or lien shall be on mineral claims, mines or other mining property.

(7) IN ALL SUITS FOR SPECIFIC PERFORMANCE OF, or for reforming or delivering up, or canceling any agreement for sale, purchase or lease of any mineral claim, mine or other mining property.

(8) IN ALL SUITS FOR THE DISSOLUTION or winding up of any mining partnership, whether registered or not, under the provisions of this act.

(9) IN ALL SUITS RELATIVE TO WATER RIGHTS claimed under this act, or any other act relating to mining (other than coal mining).

(10) IN ALL PROCEEDINGS FOR ORDERS IN THE NATURE OF INJUNCTIONS, where the same are requisite for the granting of relief in any matter in which jurisdiction is given to the County Court by this act.

(11) TRANSFER TO SUPREME COURT.— Provided, always, that at any time during the progress of any action, suit or matter relating to or concerning any of the classes of subjects in this section before referred to and enumerated, any of the parties to such action, suit or matter may apply by summons to any judge of the Supreme Court at Chambers for an order directing the transfer of such action, suit or matter into the Supreme Court, and upon such summons any judge of the Supreme Court may, if satisfied that it is expedient such action, suit or matter should be so transferred, make

an order directing the transfer of such action, suit or matter into the Supreme Court, and may in and by such order give all necessary directions for effectually procuring and completing such transfer, and may make such order as to costs, as well as of the proceedings theretofore had and taken in the County Court as of such summons, as he may think fit, and from and after the making of any such order for transfer into the Supreme Court all proceedings in respect of such action, suit or matter, shall be had and determined in the Supreme Court, and the jurisdiction of the County Court in respect thereof shall absolutely cease and determine. The Supreme Court, or a judge thereof, shall have discretion to order that any case so transferred shall be heard, tried or disposed of without pleadings.

145. "MINING JURISDICTION."—The jurisdiction given to County Courts by this act shall be known as the "mining jurisdiction" of the County Court, and the words "mining jurisdiction" shall be written or printed on all summonses, writs and other process, and all other documents in every action or cause brought under the mining jurisdiction of the County Court.

146. POWERS OF COUNTY COURTS AND OFFICERS.—County Courts and County Court judges, registrars, sheriffs, and other officers, shall have the same duties, powers, privileges and authorities in all actions and suits, and other proceedings brought under the mining jurisdiction of the County Court, as they now have, or at any time hereafter may have, in actions and suits and other proceedings brought under the ordinary jurisdiction of the County Court, and the provisions of all acts for the time being in force regulating the duties and powers of County Courts and County Court judges, registrars, sheriffs, and other officers, and regulat-

ing the practice and procedure in County Courts, and all rules and orders for the time being applicable to the ordinary jurisdiction of the County Court shall, so far as practicable and not inconsistent with this act, apply to the mining jurisdiction of the County Court.

147. ADJOINING DISTRICTS.—Where disputes arise concerning mining property, portions whereof are situated in adjoining or different districts, the County Court of either of such districts before which the dispute is first brought shall determine it.

148. SUMMONSES RETURNABLE FORTH-WITH.—The hearing of any summons, plaint or other process in any County Court shall not be deferred beyond the shortest reasonable time necessary in the interests of all parties concerned, and it shall be lawful for the registrar to make summonses or other proceedings returnable forthwith, or at any other time.

149. COURT MAY DECIDE ON THE GROUND.—In all mining actions or suits the court may decide the question at issue upon the ground in dispute, and such decision shall be entered as in ordinary cases, and have the same virtue and effect as if rendered in court.

150. ISSUES OF FACT MAY BE FOUND BY A JURY.—In any mining cause or suit either party may require that the issues of fact shall be tried by a jury, and the judge may, before delivering judgment in any action, suit or other proceeding, direct all or any issues of fact to be found by a jury.

151. COSTS.—In all actions, suits and other proceedings within the mining jurisdiction of the

County Court, the judge may order that costs be taxed on the higher or lower scale allowed by the County Court rules; or if he shall consider the case of sufficient importance, he may order that costs be taxed as in the Supreme Court, and the costs so ordered shall be the costs recoverable in such action, suit or other proceeding.

152. COUNTY COURT HAS JURISDICTION OVER LAND IN CERTAIN CASES.—Every County Court having jurisdiction in mining disputes shall, with reference to real estate held under the "Gold Mining Amendment act, 1873," or under this act, and notwithstanding any law to the contrary, have the same powers and authorities to decide all matters or disputes arising between the owners thereof, or between the owners thereof and any third person, or between mining joint stock companies, or between shareholders therein, or between them and the company, in the same way and as fully as it might do concerning claims not being real estate; and actions, suits and other proceedings relating to such matters or disputes shall be brought and had in the same manner as actions, suits or proceedings relating to mining claims not being real estate.

153. WRITS OF CAPIAS AND RESPONDEN-DUM, NE EXEAT REGNO AND CAPIAS AD SATISFACIENDUM.—Any County Court judge having jurisdiction in mining causes may direct the issuing of writs of capias ad respondendum, ne exeat regno, and capias ad satisfaciendum in all cases in which by law he has jurisdiction over the subject matter of the suit, but under and subject to such conditions as a judge of the Supreme Court might usually require in applications of a similar nature.

PART VII.

154. PENALTY FOR CONTRAVENTION OF ACT.—Any person willfully acting in contravention of this act, or refusing to obey any lawful order of the Gold Commissioner or of any judge presiding in a court shall, on conviction thereof in a summary way before any two justices of the peace or a stipendiary magistrate, or before any judge of a court having jurisdiction in mining disputes, be liable to a fine not exceeding two hundred and fifty dollars, or to imprisonment, with or without hard labor, for any term not exceeding three months.

155. RECOVERY OF PENALTIES.—All fines and penalties imposed or payable under this act may be recovered by distress and sale of any mining or other personal property of the offender; and in default of sufficient distress by imprisonment, with or without hard labor, not exceeding three months.

156. FINES, ETC., TO BE PAID INTO CONSOLIDATED REVENUE.—All fines, fees and penalties collected under this act shall be paid into the Consolidated Revenue Fund of British Columbia.

157. SAVING RIGHTS EXISTING BEFORE THE PASSING OF THIS ACT.—Nothing herein contained shall, save where such intention is expressly stated, be so construed as to affect prejudicially any mining rights and interests acquired prior to the passing of this act; and all mining rights and privileges heretofore and hereunder acquired shall, without the same being expressly stated, be deemed to be taken and held subject to the rights of Her Majesty, her heirs and successors, and to the public rights of way and water.

158. COPIES OF ACT.—Every free miner, on

application to the Mining Recorder of the district, shall be entitled to a printed copy of this act on payment of the sum of twenty-five cents.

159. BEFORE WHOM AFFIDAVITS MUST BE MADE.—Affidavits and declarations made under the provisions of this act shall be made before some judge or registrar of a Court of Record, or before some Gold Commissioner, Mining Recorder, stipendiary magistrate, justice of the peace, notary public, or commissioner for taking affidavits.

160. MINISTER OF MINES AND PROVINCIAL INSPECTOR OR MINERALOGIST MAY EXAMINE ANY MINERAL CLAIM.—The Minister of Mines and the Provincial Inspector or Mineralogist shall have the right to enter into or upon and examine any mineral claim or mine within the meaning of this act.

161. LIEUTENANT GOVERNOR MAY MAKE RULES, ETC.—TO RELIEVE AGAINST FORFEITURES UNDER SECTION 9.—PUBLICATION.—The Lieutenant Governor in Council may make such orders as are deemed necessary from time to time to carry out the provisions of this act according to their true intent, or to meet the cases which may arise and for which no provision is made in this act, or when the provision which is made is ambiguous or doubtful; and may also make regulations for relieving against forfeitures arising under Section 9 of this act; and may further make and declare any regulations which are considered necessary to give the provisions contained in this clause full effect; and from time to time alter or revoke any order or orders or any regulations made in respect of the said provisions, and make others in their stead; and further impose penalties not exceeding two hundred dollars, or not exceeding three months' imprisonment, for violation of any regulations under this act; and further provide that any statement or returns required to be made by said regulations shall be verified on oath. Every order or regulation made by virtue of the provisions of this section shall have force and effect only after the same has been published for two successive weeks in the British Columbia Gazette; and such orders or regulations shall be laid before the Legislative Assembly within the first fifteen days of the session next after the date thereof.

162. TAXATION OF MINES AND MONEYS INVESTED THEREIN.—Notwithstanding anything contained in this act, mines and moneys invested therein shall not be exempt from taxation, but shall bear such rate as may be imposed by any law in the Province.

163. ANNUAL TAX OF TWENTY-FIVE CENTS PER ACRE TO BE LEVIED ON EVERY CLAIM HELD UNDER CROWN GRANT.—There shall be levied and collected from the owner or occupier of every mineral or placer claim of which a Crown grant has issued, including Crown grants issued under authority of an act made and passed in the 36th year of Her Majesty's reign, entitled "An act to amend the 'Gold Mining Ordinance, 1867,' and the 'Gold Mining Amendment act, 1872,'" an annual tax of twenty-five cents for every acre and fractional part of an acre of land conveyed by the grant, payable on the thirtieth day of June in each year. Such tax shall form a charge upon the claim. The assessor appointed under or by virtue of any existing Assessment act, or any collector appointed under the "Provincial Revenue Tax act," is hereby authorized, as to the mineral or placer claims situate within the district for which he is appointed, to collect and receive the tax.

IN DEFAULT OF PAYMENT, CLAIM MAY BE SOLD.—HOW PURCHASE MONEY APPLIED.—In the event of the tax not being paid to the assessor or collector, the Gold Commissioner may in his discretion cause the claim upon which the tax is charged to be offered for sale by public auction, of which sixty days' notice shall be posted upon the principal court house of the district in which the claim is situate, and in one newspaper, if any, published in such district, and may sell such claim, receive the purchase money, and execute a conveyance thereof to the purchaser. The purchase money shall be applied in payment of the expenses of advertising and the payment of the tax, and any surplus shall be paid into the treasury in trust for the owner of the claim. In the event of there being no purchaser, or if the price offered shall not be sufficient to pay 'the tax and expenses of advertising, the land shall absolutely revert to the Province, and the Crown grant thereof shall be deemed void.

OWNER MAY BE SUED FOR TAX.—The assessor or collector may, before offering the claim for sale, sue the owner or occupier for the tax, in a summary manner, before any justice of the peace, who may adjudge the same to be paid; and in default of payment the amount due, together with costs, may be recovered by distress of the goods and chattels of the person against whom the tax may be recovered.

PROVISO FOR REMISSION OF TAX ON TWO HUNDRED DOLLARS HAVING BEEN EXPENDED ON CLAIM.—Provided, that if the owner of any such mineral or placer claim shall establish, to the satisfaction of the Gold Commissioner, Mining Recorder, or assessor and collector of the district in which the claim lies, that the sum of two hundred dollars has been expended thereon in labor or inprovements in any one year, then the tax shall not be levied in respect of such claim for such year.

164. CHANGE OF NAME.—Where a claim has been recorded under any name, and the owner or his agent is desirous of changing the same the Recorder of said mining division may, upon application being made by such owner or agent, and upon payment of a fee of twenty-five dollars, amend the record accordingly: Provided, however, that such change of name shall not in any way affect or prejudice any proceedings or execution against the owner of the said claim.

165. WHERE EVIDENCE OF LOCATION, ETC., EFFACED THROUGH FAULTS OF OTHERS.—Whenever through the acts or defaults of any person other than the recorded owner of a mineral claim or his agent by him duly authorized, the evidence of the location or record on the ground, or the situation of a mineral claim, has been destroyed, lost or effaced, or is difficult of ascertainment, nevertheless, effect shall be given to same as far as possible, and the court shall have power to make all necessary inquiries, directions and references in the premises, for the purpose of carrying out the object hereof, and vesting title in the first bona fide acquirer of the claim.

PART VIII.

Repealing Clause.

166. REPEALING CLAUSE.—The acts and parts of acts mentioned in this section shall stand repealed and be repealed; but such repeal shall not be deemed to imply that any of the said acts or parts of acts which have been repealed at any time

prior to the passing of this act have been in force since such appeal: Provided further, that such repeal shall not affect any rights acquired, or any liabilities or penalties incurred, or any act or thing done, under any of the said acts or parts of acts. .

The "Mineral Act, 1891," the "Mineral Act (1891) Amendment act, 1892," the "Mineral Act (1891) Amendment act, 1893," the "Mineral Act Amendment act, 1894," and the "Mineral Act Amendment act, 1895," are hereby repealed. 1891, c. 25; 1892, c. 32; 1893, c. 29; 1894, c. 32; 1895, c. 39.

167. PENDING LITIGATION NOT AF-FECTED.—Nothing herein contained or enacted shall affect any litigation pending at the time of the passage of this act.

169. REPEALS CERTAIN PROVISIONS C. A. 1888, C. 82.—Sections 5, 6, 13, 19, 20, 22, 27, 28 and 29 of the "Mineral act," being chapter 82 of the "Consolidated acts, 1888," are hereby repealed. 1897, c. 28, s. 21.

SCHEDULES.

Form A.
Location Notice.

Mineral Claim.
I,   , have this day located this ground as a mineral claim, to be known as the
        Mineral Claim,   feet in length
by   feet in breadth. The direction of
No. 2 post is   , and   feet of
this claim lie to the right and   feet to the left
of the location line.

Dated this   day of   , 189

Take care to number the posts 1, 2, }
making the initial post 1.   }

1897, c. 28, c. 23.

FORM B.
Record of Mineral Claim.

Mineral Claim.

No. of certificate,

Located by—

{ Set out the name of claim and number of receipt form of payment of the record fee of each locator, and the No. of each locator's Free Miner's Certificate opposite such name. }

The claim is situate

The direction of the location line is

The length of the claim is   feet.

The claim was located on the   day of

, 189 .

Recorded this   day of   , 189 .

Mining Recorder.

[If the stakes are not on the location line, comply with Section 18.]

1897, c. 28, s. 23.

FORM C.
Record of Partnership Mineral Claim.

Mineral Claim.

Located in the partnership name of

The members of the partnership and the Nos. of their respective free miner's certificates are—

The receipt form of payment of the record fee.

The claim is situate

The direction of the location line is

The length of the claim is   feet.

The claim was located on the   day of

189 .

Recorded this   day of   , 189 .
                                 Mining Recorder.
[If the stakes are not on the location line, comply
with Sec. 18.]

Form D.
Application for Certificate of Work.
Affidavit.

I,   , of   , in the District of   ,
free miner, make oath and say:
I have done, or caused to be done, work on the
                Mineral Claim, situate at
in the District of   , to the value of at least
$100, since the   day of   , 189 .   The
following is a detailed statement of such work:
[Set out full particulars of the work done in the
twelve months in which such work is required to be
done by Sec. 24.]
Sworn, etc.
[This affidavit may be made by an agent, and can
be altered to suit circumstances.]

Form E.
Certificate of Work.
(Name of Claim)

                        Mineral Claim.
This is to certify that an affidavit setting out a
detailed statement of the work done on the above
claim since the   day of   , 189 , made
by   , has this day been filed in my office, and
in pursuance of the provisions of the act in that behalf, I do now issue this certificate of work in respect of the above claim to
Dated
            Gold Commissioner or Mining Recorder.

Form F.
Certificate of Improvements.
Notice.

Mineral Claim.

Situate in the   Mining Division of
District.

Where located.

Take notice that I,   , free miner's certificate
No.   intend, sixty days from the date hereof, to
apply to the Mining Recorder for a certificate of improvements, for the purpose of obtaining a Crown grant of the above claim.

And further take notice that action, under Section 37, must be commenced before the issuance of such certificate of improvements.

Dated this   day of   , 189 .

Form G.

Application for Certificate of Improvements.
Applicant's Affidavit.

I,   , of   , in the District of
make oath and say:

1. I,   , the recorded holder, and am in undisputed possession of the   Mineral Claim, situated at   , in the District (or Division) of

2. I,   , have done, or caused to be don , work on the said claim in developing a mine to the value of at least $500, full* particulars whereof are hereunto annexed and marked "A."

---

*Particulars must be exclusive of all houses and other like improvements.

This affidavit may be made by an agent, duly authorized, in writing, and can be altered to suit circumstances.

3. I,   , found a vein or lode within the limits of the said claim.

4. I,   , had the claim surveyed by who has made three plats of the said claim.

5. I,   , placed one such plat on a conspicuous part of the land embraced in such plat on the   day of   , 189 .

6. I,   , posted a copy of the notice hereunto annexed, and marked "B," at the same place as said plat is posted, on the   day of   , 189 , and another copy on the Mining Recorder's office at   , on the   day of   , 189 , which said notice and plat have been posted, and have remained posted, for at least sixty days concurrently with the publication of the said notice in the British Columbia Gazette.

7. I,   , inserted a copy of the said notice in the British Columbia Gazette, where it first appeared on the   day of   , 189 , and in the   , a newspaper published in the Province and circulating in the district in which the said claim is situated, where it first appeared on the   day of   , 189 , and was continuously published for sixty days concurrently with the publication of the said notice in the British Columbia Gazette prior to the date of this affidavit.

8. I,   , deposited a copy of the field notes and plat in the Record office at   , on the   day of   189 , and they remained there for reference for sixty days concurrently with the publication of the said notice in the British Columbia Gazette.

Sworn and subscribed to   ,
    at   , this   day
    of   , 189 , before me.

Form H.

Certificate of Improvements.

Mineral Claim.

This is to certify that   , of   , in the District of   , free miner's certificate No.   , has proved to my satisfaction that he has complied with all the provisions of the "Mineral act" to entitle him to a certificate of improvements in respect of the   Mineral Claim, situate at   , in the District of   ; and in pursuance of the provisions of the said act I do now issue this certificate of improvements, in respect of the above claim, to

Dated

Gold Commissioner.

This certificate will become void unless a Crown grant is applied for within three months from its date.

[Form may be altered to suit circumstances.]

Form I.

Mining Recorder's Certificate.

Mining Division.
District.
Mineral Claim.

Date located,   Date recorded,

To

Sir—I herewith inclose the following documents relating to your application for a certificate of improvements to the above claim:

Affidavit of   , applicant (Form G).

Copy of plat of claim.

Copy of surveyor's field notes.

And I hereby certify that   has published

a notice of his intention to apply for a certificate of improvements for sixty days in the British Columbia Gazette, from the　　　　day of　　　, 189 , and　　　　newspaper from the day of　　　　, 189 . That during the above period a notice in accordance with Section 36, subsection (*d*), has been posted, and a copy of the field notes and plat of the said claim deposited for reference in my office, and that no notice of any action having been commenced against the issuance of a certificate of improvements to the said claim has been filed in this office up to this date.

The recorded owner of the said claim at this date is

Dated　　　　　　　　, 189 .

　　　　　　　　　　, Mining Recorder.

Form J.
Mill Site.
Notice.

Take notice that I,　　　　, of　　　　in the District of　　　　, free miner's certificate No.　　　, intend, sixty days from the date hereof, to apply for　　　acres of land for a mill site, situate at　　　, in the District of　　　, as a mill site.

Dated

Form K.
Mill Site.
Affidavit of Applicant Prior to Lease.

I,　　　　, of　　　　, in the District of free miner, make oath and say:

1. I have marked out the land required by me for a mill site, by placing a legal post at each corner.

2. I have posted a notice on each such post, and on the Mining Recorder's office at   , a copy of which notice is hereunto annexed, and marked "A."

3. The said land is not known to contain minerals, and is not, to the best of my knowledge and belief, valuable as mineral land.

FORM L.

Lease of Mill Site.

This indenture, made the   day of   , 189 , between   , the Gold Commissioner for the District of   (hereinafter called the lessor), of the one part, and   , of   , in the District of   , free miner (hereinafter called the lessee), of the other part, witnesseth, that in exercise of the powers vested in him by the "Mineral act," he, the said lessor, doth hereby demise unto the said lessee, his executors, administrators and assigns, all that
[Describe the mill site.]
for the term of one year from the date hereof, subject to the provisions and conditions of the "Mineral act" relating to mill sites.

In witness whereof, the said parties have hereunto set their hands and seals.

Signed, sealed and delivered

FORM M.

Mill Site.

AFFIDAVIT OF APPLICANT PRIOR TO CROWN GRANT.

I,   , of   , in the District of   free miner, make oath and say:

1. I am the lawful holder of the mill site mentioned in indenture of lease dated and made between

2. During the year mentioned in such lease as the term thereof, I put or constructed works or machinery, for mining or milling purposes, on the said mill site, of the value of at least $500.

Sworn, etc.

Form N.

Mill Site.

CERTIFICATE OF IMPROVEMENTS.

This is to certify that   has put or constructed works or machinery, for mining or milling purposes, to the value of at least $500, on the mill site described in and demised by indenture dated the   day of   , 189 , and made between   during the existence of such lease.

Gold Commissioner.

Form O.

Tunnel or Drain License.

To all whom it may concern:

Take notice that   , a free miner and the owner of   , having given security to the amount of   for any damage he may do, has this day obtained a license from me to run a tunnel (or drain) from   to his said claim (or mine).

The said license is granted on these express conditions:

[Set out conditions, if any.]

Dated

Gold Commissioner.

Form P.

Mill Site.

Application for Crown Grant.

To the Mining Recorder at   .

Sir—I inclose herewith the sum of   dollars and the undermentioned documents:

Lease of mill site.

Plat of mill site.

Surveyor's field notes.

Certificate of improvements.

Affidavit of applicant.

And I now apply for a Crown grant of the mill site demised by the abovementioned lease.

Yours respectfully,

[Forms Q and R, repealed by 1897, c. 28, s. 19.]

Form S.

For a Full Claim.

Mining Division,   District.

I, A. B., of   , in the   Mining Division of   District, free miner, make oath and say:

1. I am the holder of Free Miner's Certificate No. , dated   day of   , 18 , and issued at

2. On the   day of   , 18 , I located the   Mineral Claim, situated [here describe position of claim as near as possible, giving the name or names of any mineral claim or claims it may join.]

3. I have placed a No. 1 and a No. 2 and a discovery post of the legal dimensions on the said claim, with the legal notices on each post.

4. I have written on the No. 1 post the following words:

5. I have written on the No. 2 post the following words:

6. That I have found mineral in place on the said claim.

7. That I have marked the line between No. 1 and No. 2 posts as required by Section 16 of this act.

8. That to the best of my knowledge and belief the ground comprised within the boundaries of the said claim is unoccupied by any other person as a mineral claim; that it is not occupied by any building or any land falling within the curtilage of any dweling house, or any orchard, or any land under cultivation or any Indian reservation.

Note.—This declaration may be made by an agent.

Form T.

For Fractional Claim.

Mining Division,　　　　　　　　District.

I, A. B., of　　　　　　in the　　　　　　Mining Division of　　　　　　District, free miner, make oath and say:

1. I am the holder of Free Miner's Certificate No.　, dated　　　　day of　　　　　, 18 , and issued at

2. On the　　　　　day of　　　　　, 18 , I located　　　　the　　　　fractional mineral claim, situated

3. This is a fractional claim bounded on the north by　　　, on the south by　　　, on the east by　　　, and on the west by　　　, and is more particularly described on the sketch plan on the back of this declaration.

4. I have placed a No. 1 and a No. 2 and a discovery post of the legal dimensions on the said claim, with the legal notices on each post.

5. I have written on the No. 1 post the following words:

6. I have written on the No. 2 post the following words:

7. I have found mineral in place on the said fractional claim.

8. I have marked the line between No. 1 and No. 2 posts as required by Section 16 of this act.

9. That to the best of my knowledge and belief the ground comprised within the boundaries of the said fractional claim is unoccupied by any other person as a mineral claim; that it is not occupied by any building or any land falling within the curtilage of any dwelling house, or any orchard, or any land under cultivation, or any Indian reservation.

Note.—This declaration may be made by an agent.

———

Schedule of Fees to Be Charged.

For every free miner's certificate issued to an individual.............................$	5 00
For every free miner's certificate issued to a joint stock company—	
(*a*) Having a nominal capital of $100,000 or less.................................	50 00
(*b*) Having a nominal capital exceeding $100,000	100 00
[1897, c. 28, s. 22.]	
Every substituted certificate...............	1 00
Recording any claim......................	2 50
Recording every certificate of work........	2 50
Recording any "lay over," or every other record required to be made in the "Record Book"	2 50

Recording every abandonment, including the memorandum to be written on the record .... $ 2 50

For any other record made in the "Record of Abandonments"...................... 2 50

For recording every affidavit, where the same does not exceed three folios of 100 words.. 2 50

For every folio over three, 30 cents per folio. The above rate shall be charged for all records made in the "Record of Affidavits."

For all records made in the "Record of Conveyances," where the same do not exceed three folios............................. 2 50

For every folio over three, a further charge of 30 cents per folio.

For all copies or extracts from any record in any of the abovenamed books, where such copy or extract shall not exceed three folios, per copy........................ 2 50

Where such copies or extracts exceed three folios, 30 cents per folio for every folio over three.

For filing any document.................. 25

For a Crown grant....................... 5 00

PLACERS AND WATER RIGHTS.

From lack of space, the author has been compelled to omit the *"Placer Mining Act of 1891"* (Laws of 1891, c. 26; 1894, c. 33; 1895, c. 40; 1896, c. 35; 1897, c. 29), and the *"Water Clauses Consolidation Act, 1897"* (c. 45), of *British Columbia.*

Complete references to the provisions of those acts are, however, above noted.

PART II.

MINING LAWS OF CANADA.

ONTARIO.

THE MINES ACT.

Information for Applicants.

1. **MINES AND MINERALS** upon land located, sold or granted within the limits of the Free Grant Territory are reserved from the location and are the property of the Crown.

2. **IN ANY LETTERS PATENT** for lands granted under the Public Lands act for agricultural purposes after May 4, 1891, mines, minerals and mining rights are reserved and are constituted a property separate from the surface of the soil, unless otherwise provided in the patent or grant from the Crown.

3. **MINING LANDS MAY BE ACQUIRED** from the Crown either by purchase or lease under The Mines act. Applications should be made to the Department of Crown Lands, Toronto, and should be accompanied by an affidavit showing the discovery of valuable ore or mineral upon the land by or on behalf of the applicant, and the affidavits of at least two credible and disinterested parties showing that the land is unoccupied and unimproved (except by or on behalf of the applicant), and that there is no claim thereto adverse to his on the ground of occupation, improvements or otherwise. Such affidavits may be made before any Crown Lands Agent, Commissioner for taking affidavits, Notary Public or Justice of the Peace, and should be in the form given hereafter.

4. **EVERY APPLICANT** is required within sixty days from the date on which the application has been filed in the Department to pay one-fourth of the purchase price or rental, and within three months from the same date the remaining three-fourths, and (if in unsurveyed territory) the surveyor's plan, field notes and description of a location applied for

must be furnished to the Department of Crown Lands within at least four months of the date of application; but in case of locations in surveyed townships the time for completing all requirements on the part of the applicant may be limited to thirty da at the discretion of the Commissioner of Crown Lands.

5. APPLICATIONS FOR MINING LANDS containing ores or minerals of the same class or kind are limited in the case of an individual to 320 acres, and in the case of a firm, partnership, syndicate or company to 640 acres within a radius of fifteen miles in any one calendar year, and such areas may be applied for in separate locations of not less than forty acres each.

6. ALL COMMUNICATIONS on official business should be addressed (prepaid) to the head of the Department, as follows:

The Honorable
The Commissioner of Crown Lands,
Toronto.

7. EACH LETTER should relate to one subject or one parcel of land only, the postoffice address should be given, and the signature distinctly written. In every subsequent letter the number of the lot and concession and the name of the township or the name and number of the mining location should be repeated.

8. WHERE APPLICATION IS MADE FOR LETTERS PATENT, or for lease of mining land, the applicant should give his name in full, with place of residence and occupation, so that they may be set out in the instrument; and, in case the applicant be a married woman, the name, residence and occupation of her husband should also be given.

9. REMITTANCES to the Department may be made by marked checks and drafts, or by postoffice and express orders, made payable in every case to the Treasurer of Ontario. Cash by letter is at the risk of the sender.

10. SECTION 42 OF THE MINES ACT contemplates that the locatee on Crown land, as well as the grantee or lessee, is entitled to compensation for injury or damage to the surface rights at the hands of the owner or lessee of the mining rights thereafter granted in respect of the same land, and it empowers the Director of the Bureau of Mines · to order and prescribe the manner in which such compensation shall be ascertained and paid or secured. The issuing of the grant depends on the completion of the settlement duties required by the Public Lands and Free Grants and Homesteads acts and the Orders and Regulations made thereunder, and until these duties are performed the locatee's interest in the surface rights is not complete. In the case of ungranted lands the compensation to be paid to the locatee or purchaser for injury or damage to the surface rights shall be calculated upon the injury or damage to the annual value only of the locatee's or purchaser's interest in the land, and shall be paid annually until the issue of the patent, but so long only as the locatee or purchaser shall be recognized as such by the Department of Crown Lands.

11. BY ORDER IN COUNCIL dated 9th September, 1897, the following territory was declared to be a Mining Division under the name of the Michipicoten Mining Division—namely, the tract limited upon its east side by the meridian of the east end of Dog Lake, or say eighty-four degrees west from Greenwich, on the south side by the latitude of Cape Gargantua, say forty-seven degrees thirty-six

minutes, on the north side by the latitude of forty-eight degrees thirty minutes, and between the westerly ends of these lines of latitude, where they touch Lake Superior, by the shore line of the said lake, containing about five thousand square miles. The lands in such Mining Division may be taken up and held as mining claims under the Provisions of Part III of The Mines act, section 44 et seq. Copies of Regulations for Mining Divisions may be had upon application to the Director of the Bureau of Mines, Toronto.

FORM OF APPLICATION FOR MINING LANDS AND OF AFFIDAVIT OF DISCOVERY.

The Commissioner of Crown Lands, Toronto:

Sir—I hereby apply for a (grant or lease) under the terms and provisions of The Mines act, R.S.O. 1897, of a mining location consisting of   acres, more or less, described as follows: (If in a surveyed township give name of township and number of concession and section or lot or part thereof. If in unsurveyed territory give locality as described by the plans and field notes of the surveyor, or, if the land applied for has not been surveyed, such other description as will enable the Director of Surveys to indicate the locality upon the office map.)

Dated at   , 189

District of   I,   of the

of   in the

To Wit: of   , make oath and

say:

1. That on the   day of   , 189 , I, or (Name of party) on my behalf, discovered valuable ore or mineral on the location named in the

above application, that is to say: (Particulars of discovery.)

2. That I have no knowledge and have never heard of any adverse claim to the said location by reason of prior discovery or otherwise.

Sworn before me at
in the district of
this   day of
A. D. 189 .

AFFIDAVITS IN SUPPORT OF APPLICATION FOR LAND UNDER THE MINES ACT.

Ontario, ⎫ I,   of the township of
District of ⎪   in the district of
           ⎬ and I   of the township of
To Wit: ⎪ in the district of   do solemnly
           ⎭ swear:

1. That on the   day of   I personally visited and carefully examined   lot number   in the   concession of the township of   and at that time there was no person residing on said lot and there were no improvements thereon (or according as the fact is).

2. That there was no visible trace nor indication of work having been done on said lot, by any person or persons, for mining or other purposes (as the fact is).

3. And that to the best of my knowledge and belief there is no claim to said location by any person or persons adverse to that of   the applicant, on the grounds of priority of discovery of mineral thereon, or otherwise.

Sworn before me at
in the district of   this
day of   A. D. 189 .

AFFIDAVIT OF ORIGINAL DISCOVERER IN SUPPORT OF APPLICATION FOR FREE LOCATION OF FORTY ACRES.

Ontario ⎫ I, of in
District of ⎬ the district of , do
To Wit: ⎭ solemnly swear:

1. That on the day of A. D. 189 , I discovered valuable mineral in a vein or lode on (Describe the location), such mineral consisting of , and that I have no knowledge or information of any previous discovery of valuable mineral on said location, and verily believe that I am the original discoverer of the same.

2. That by careful examination on the ground I have ascertained that the mineral so discovered by me on said location is (State the kind of metal, ore or mineral), and is on or in a vein, lode or deposit, at least ten miles from the nearest known occurrence of the same metal, ore or mineral.

3. That the nearest mine, vein or lode of the same metal, ore or mineral to the mineral so discovered by me of which I have any knowledge or information is situated (Describe the location).

Sworn before me at the ⎫
of in the of ⎬
this day of A. D. 189 . ⎭

A Commissioner in H. C. J.

The material portions of this affidavit are to be confirmed by the affidavits of two disinterested persons, stating the facts in their knowledge and their means of knowledge. It is desirable that one of the two should, where that is practicable, be an Ontario Land Surveyor. The form is given hereunder.

AFFIDAVIT OF ONTARIO LAND SUR-VEYOR RE APPLICATION FOR FREE LOCATION OF FORTY ACRES.

Ontario   }   I,   of the
District of   }   of   in the
   To Wit: }   of   do solemnly swear:

1. That I am a duly qualified Ontario Land Surveyor.

2. That on the   day of   A. D. 189 , I visited (Describe the location) and saw the valuable metal, ore or mineral on or in a vein, lode or deposit thereon, of which one   claims to be the original discoverer, such metal, ore or mineral consisting of   .

3. That on the said date I carefully examined the location of the said metal, ore or mineral, and that to the best of my knowledge and information the same is at least ten miles from the nearest known mine or occurrence of the same metal, ore or mineral.

4. That the nearest known mine, vein, lode or deposit of metal, ore or mineral of which I have any knowledge or information is situated (Describe its location).

Sworn before me at the   }
of   in the   of   }
this   day of   A. D. 189 . }

                   A Commissioner in H. C. J.

The above affidavit may be used by others than surveyors in proof of claim, striking out clause 1 in such case.

An Act Respecting Mines.

Her Majesty, by and with the advice and consent

of the Legislative Assembly of the Province of Ontario, enacts as follows:

1. SHORT TITLE.—This act may be cited as The Mines act. 55 V., c. 9, s. 1.

PART I.—GENERAL PROVISIONS.

Interpretation.

2. INTERPRETATION.—Where the following words occur in this act, and in orders in council or regulations under it, they shall be construed in the manner hereinafter mentioned unless a contrary intention appears:

(1.) THE NOUN "MINE" shall include every shaft in the course of being sunk, and every adit, level and inclined plane in the course of being driven for commencing or opening any mine, or for searching for or proving minerals, and all the shafts, levels, planes, works, machinery, tramways and sidings, both below ground and above ground, in and adjacent to a mine, and any such shaft, level and inclined plane belonging to any mine to which this act applies, together with all rocks, soils or strata containing any ore or minerals, and all roast yards, smelting furnaces and other places where the work of mining may be carried on. 55 V., c. 9, 2 (1); 57 V., c. 16, s. 2, part.

(2.) THE VERB "MINE" and the participle "mining" shall include any mode or method of working whatsoever whereby the soil or earth or any rock, stone or quartz may be disturbed, removed, carted, carried, washed, sifted, roasted, smelted, refined, crushed or otherwise dealt with for the purpose of obtaining any metal or mineral therefrom, whether the same may have been previously disturbed or not. 55 V., c. 9, s. 2 (2); 57 V., c. 16, s. 2, part; 59 V., c. 13, s. 1.

(3.) "MINING DIVISION" shall include any tract of country declared to be a mining division within this act.

(4.) "CROWN LANDS" shall include all crown lands, school lands or clergy lands not in the actual use or occupation of the Crown, or of any public department of the Government of the Dominion of Canada or of this Province, or of any officer or servant thereof, and not under lease or license of occupation from the Crown or the Commissioner of Crown Lands, and as to which no adverse claim exists which is subsequently recognized by the Commissioner of Crown Lands.

(5.) "SURFACE RIGHTS" shall mean lands granted, leased or located for agricultural or other purposes, and in respect of which the ores, minerals and mines thereupon or under the surface thereof are by statute, the patent or lease, or otherwise, reserved to the Crown. 55 V., c. 9, s. 2 (3-5).

(6.) "MINING RIGHTS" shall mean the ores, mines and minerals on or under any land where the same are dealt with separately from the surface of the land. 60 V., c. 8, s. 1.

(7.) "PARTY WALL" shall mean a bank of earth or rock left between two excavations.

(8.) "SHAFT" shall include pit, and "plan" shall include a map and section, and a correct copy or tracing of any original plan as so defined.

(9.) "MACHINERY" shall include steam or other engines, boilers, furnaces, stamps or other crushing apparatus, winding or pumping gear, chains, trucks, tramways, tackle, blocks, ropes or tools, and all appliances of whatsoever kind used in or about or in connection with the mine.

(10.) "OWNER" when used in relation to any mine shall mean any person or body corporate who is the immediate proprietor, or lessee, or occupier of any mine, or of any part thereof, and shall not include a person or body corporate who merely receives a royalty, rent or fine from a mine, or is merely the proprietor of a mine subject to any lease, grant or license for the working thereof, or is merely the owner of the soil and not interested in the minerals of the mine.

(11.) "AGENT" when used in relation to any mine shall mean any person having, on behalf of the owner, care or direction of any mine, or of any part thereof, and shall include "manager" and "superintendent."

(12.) "INSPECTOR" shall include any inspector appointed under this act, and whether for a mining division or any part thereof or for the Province. 55 V., c. 9, s. 2 (7-12).

3. ROYALTIES.—All royalties, taxes or duties which by any patent or patents issued prior to the 4th day of May, 1891, have been reserved, imposed or made payable upon or in respect of any ores or minerals extracted from the lands granted by such patents and lying within this Province, are declared to have been repealed and abandoned; and such lands, ores and minerals shall be free and exempt from every such royalty, tax or duty.

RESERVATIONS.—And all reservations of gold and silver mines contained in any patent issued prior to the date aforesaid, granting in fee simple lands situate within this Province, are hereby rescinded and made void, and all such mines in or upon such lands shall be deemed to have been granted in fee simple as part of such lands and to have passed with such lands to the subsequent and present proprietors or owners thereof in fee simple; but the provisions of this section shall not be construed to apply to lands patented or to be patented under The Free Grants and Homesteads act. 55 V., c. 9, s. 3.

4. ROYALTIES PAYABLE TO THE CROWN. —(1) All ores and minerals mined, wrought or taken from lands located, sold and granted or leased by the Crown on or after the 4th day of May, 1891, and before the 1st day of January, 1900, shall be subject to a royalty to the Crown for the use of the Province, to be reckoned at the following rates, whether such royalty be reserved in the grant, patent or lease, or not:

(*a*) On ores of silver, nickel, nickel and copper, and iron, two per cent.

(*b*) On all other ores and minerals, such royalty as shall be from time to time imposed by order in council, not exceeding two per cent.

(2) HOW CALCULATED.—The said royalties shall be calculated upon the value of the ores or. minerals at the pit's mouth, less the actual cost of labor and explosives for mining and raising the same to the surface, and the subsequent treatment thereof for the market, and shall be payable at such time and times, and the values shall be fixed and ascertained in such manner as shall be provided by regulation to be made by the Lieutenant Governor in Council in that behalf.

(3) AFTER SEVEN YEARS.—The said royalties shall not be imposed or collected upon any ores mined, wrought or taken until after seven years from the date of the patent or lease, and no higher rate of royalty shall be levied upon ores and min-

erals taken from land than that provided for by the statute in force at the time of the sale or lease of such land.

(4) IN LIEU OF OTHERS.— The royalties payable under this section shall be in lieu of the larger royalties reserved under Section 3 of the act passed in the 54th year of Her Majesty's reign intituled An act to amend the General Mining act, or under Section 4 of The Mines act, 1892. 55 V., c. 9, s. 4, part; 57 V., c. 16, s. 1, part; 60 V., c. 8, s. 2.

5. ROYALTIES PAYABLE TO THE CROWN.—(1) Subject to the provisions of Subsection 3 of the preceding section, which shall apply to all royalties reserved under this section, all ores and minerals mined, wrought or taken from lands located, sold and granted or leased by the Crown on or after the 1st day of January, 1900, shall be subject to a royalty to the Crown for the use of the Province, to be reckoned at the following rates, whether such royalty be reserved in the grant, patent or lease, or not:

(*a*) On ores of silver, nickel, or nickel and copper, three per cent.

(*b*) On iron ore, not exceeding two per cent.

(*c*) On all other ores and minerals, such royalty as shall be from time to time imposed by order in council, not exceeding three per cent.

(2) HOW ASCERTAINED. — Such royalties shall be calculated upon the value of the ores or minerals at the pit's mouth, less the actual cost of labor and explosives for mining and raising the same to the surface, and shall be payable at such time and times and the values shall be fixed and ascertained in such manner as shall be provided by regulation to be made by the Lieutenant Governor

in Council in that behalf. 55 V., c. 9, s. 4, part; 57 V., c. 16, s. 1, part; 60 V., c. 8, s. 2.

6. ORES TAKEN FOR EXPERIMENTAL PURPOSES MAY BE FREE FROM ROYALTIES.—The Lieutenant Governor in Council may, upon the recommendation of the Director of the Bureau of Mines, direct that the ores of any mine taken or to be taken out by way of experiment and for the purpose of ascertaining the quality and value of the mineral and mine shall be free from royalty. 55 V., c. 9, s. 5.

7. LIEUTENANT GOVERNOR IN COUNCIL MAY MAKE REGULATIONS AS TO ARBITRATORS OR MINING BOARDS.—The Lieutenant Governor in Council may from time to time make such regulations as he deems necessary or expedient for the appointment of Arbitrators or Mining Boards to hear and determine appeals from the decisions of inspectors of divisions; for the prescribing, defining and establishing of the powers, duties and mode of procedure of the Arbitrators or Mining Boards; for the opening, construction, maintenance and using of roads to, through or over mining claims, mining locations or lands hereafter sold as mining lands; for the opening, construction, maintenance and using of ditches, acqueducts or raceways through or over such claims, locations or lands for the conveyance and passage of water for mining purposes; and generally for the purpose of carrying out this act; and such regulations, after publication in the Ontario Gazette, shall have the force and effect of law. 55 V., c. 9, s. 6 (1); s. 28 (2); 60 V., c. 8, s. 4.

8. REGULATIONS TO BE LAID BEFORE ASSEMBLY.—Any regulations made under this act by the Lieutenant Governor in Council shall, if made when the Legislative Assembly is sitting, be laid upon the table of the House during the then session, and if made at any other time shall be laid upon the table of the House within fifteen days from the beginning of the next session thereof. 55 V., c. 9, s. 6 (2); 57 V., c. 16, s. 16.

9. CROWN LANDS MAY BE EXPLORED FOR MINES, ETC.—Any person or persons may explore for mines or minerals on any Crown lands, surveyed or unsurveyed, and not for the time being marked or staked out and occupied as hereinafter mentioned except on such lands as may by the Lieutenant Governor in Council have been withdrawn from sale, location or exploration as being valuable for their pine timber or for any other reason, and any person attempting to explore, occupy or work any lands so withdrawn shall incur a penalty of twenty dollars and costs and in default of payment of the fine and costs such person may be imprisoned for any period not exceeding one month. 55 V., c. 9, s. 7; 60 V., c. 3, s. 3, c. 8, s. 5.

10. CROWN LANDS MAY BE SOLD AS MINING LOCATIONS.—(1) Crown lands not situated within any Mining Division which are supposed to contain ores or minerals and mining rights in lands, the ores or minerals whereof have been reserved by the Crown, may be sold or leased as mining lands in blocks, sections or lots, to be called "mining locations."

(2) MINING CLAIMS.—Where such Crown lands are situated within a mining division they may be occupied and worked as "mining claims," under miners' licenses, as hereinafter provided. 60 V., c. 8, s. 6.

11. PAYMENTS OUT OF IRON MINING FUND.—(1) The Treasurer of the Province may,

under the authority of such regulations as may be made from time to time by the Lieutenant Governor in Council, pay out of the Iron Mining Fund, established by the act passed in the 57th-year of Her Majesty's reign, chapter 16, to the miners or producers of ore upon all iron ores which shall be raised or mined and smelted in the Province for a period of five years from the first day of January, 1896, the equivalent of one dollar per ton of the metallic iron product of such ores; but no part of said moneys shall be so paid until the said regulations so far as they govern payments have been approved by the Legislative Assembly. 57 V., c. 16, s. 12; 59 V., c. 13, s. 6.

(2) NOT MORE THAN $25,000 TO BE PAID OUT IN ANY YEAR.—Should so large a quantity of ore be raised or mined and smelted in any one year that the sum of $25,000 will be insufficient to meet the payments provided for in the preceding subsection, then payments to the miners or producers thereof shall be made upon a pro rata basis, so that no more than $25,000 shall be paid for the produce of ores in any one year. 57 V., c. 16, s. 13.

12. UNEXPENDED APPROPRIATION TO LAPSE AFTER FIVE YEARS.—Payments out of the appropriation of $125,000 for the Iron Mining Fund shall cease and determine with the payments of any sum or sums which shall have been earned during the said period of five years, and any part or balance of the said sum remaining thereafter shall be returned to and become part of the Consolidated Revenue Fund of the Province. 57 V., c. 16, s. 14.

13. PURCHASE OF DRILLS FOR EXPLORATORY PURPOSES.—(1) The Commissioner of Crown Lands may, out of the moneys voted for that purpose, purchase not more than two diamond drills

to be used in exploratory drilling of ores or minerals in the Province, under rules and regulations to be made by the Lieutenant Governor in Council.

(2) The regulations shall, amongst other things, provide:

(*a*) For the control and working of the drills under the direction of a person or persons employed for the purpose by the Bureau of Mines.

(*b*) As to the payment of freight charges where the drills are used upon mines or lands other than those owned by the Crown.

(*c*) As to the applications for the use of the drills and the method of dealing therewith.

(*d*) As to the charges for the use of the drills and for damages thereto, or wear and tear connected therewith, and otherwise as to the Lieutenant Governor in Council shall seem meet.　57 V., c. 16, s. 15.

14. APPOINTMENT OF DIRECTOR.—There shall be established in connection with the Department of Crown Lands a Bureau of Mines to aid in promoting the mining interests of the Province, and the Lieutenant Governor in Council may appoint an officer to be known as director of the Bureau of Mines, who shall act under the direction of the Commissioner of Crown Lands, unless and till otherwise ordered, and who shall be paid such salary as shall be voted by the Legislature, 55 V., c. 9, s. 22.

15. POWERS OF DIRECTOR.—The Director of the Bureau of Mines shall have all the powers, rights and authority throughout the Province which an inspector or local agent has or may exercise in any mining division or locality, and such other powers, rights and authority for the carrying out of the provisions of this act as shall be assigned to him by regulation.　55 V., c. 9, s. 23.

16. APPOINTMENT AND POWERS OF IN-
SPECTORS OF MINING DIVISIONS.—(1) The
Lieutenant Governor may appoint for the Province,
or any part thereof, and for every mining division
or for any part thereof, an inspector, who shall be an
officer of the Bureau of Mines, and may by order in
council prescribe the duties and fix the salary of
such inspector.   55 V., c. 9, s. 25 ; 60 V., c. 8, s. 12.

(2) INSPECTOR NOT TO BE INTERESTED
IN MINES.—No person shall be appointed or
authorized to act as an inspector who practices or
acts, or is a partner of any person who practices or
acts, as a mining agent, or who is employed by the
owners of or is interested in any mine.   55 V., c. 9,
s. 64; 60 V., c. 8, s. 26.

17. APPOINTMENT OF AGENTS FOR SALE
OF MINING LANDS.—The Lieutenant Governor
may from time to time appoint local officers or
agents to receive applications for the sale of mining
lands in their respective agencies and to carry out
the provisions of any regulations and orders in
council in that behalf, and to supply information to
intending purchasers, and such officers and agents
shall be paid in such manner and at such rates as
the Lieutenant Governor in Council may direct.   55
V., c. 9, s. 28 (1).

18. OFFICERS TO HAVE NO INTEREST
IN MINING CLAIMS, ETC.—No officer appointed
under this act shall, either directly or indirectly,
purchase or be or become proprietor of, or interested in, any Crown lands or mining claim; and any
such purchase or interest shall be void.

PENALTY.—And if any officer violates the provisions of this section he shall forfeit his office, and
in addition thereto shall be liable to a penalty of
$500 for every such offense, to be recovered in an

action by any person who sues for the same. 55 V., c. 9, s. 27.

19. POWERS OF INSPECTOR.—An inspector under this act shall have power to do all or any of the following things, namely:

(1.) To make such examination and inquiry as may be necessary to ascertain whether the provisions of this act relating to matters either above or below ground are complied with in the case of any mine.

(2.) To enter, inspect and examine any mine and every portion thereof, at all reasonable times by day or night, but so as not to impede or obstruct the working of the mine.

(3.) To examine into and make inquiry respecting the state and condition of any mine, or any portion thereof, and the ventilation of the mine, and all matters and things connected with or relating to the safety of the persons employed in or about the mine, or any mine contiguous thereto, and to give notice to the owner or agent in writing of any particulars in which he considers such mine or any portion thereof or any matter, thing or practice to be dangerous or defective, and to require the same to be remedied within the period of time named in such notice, and unless the cause of danger is removed or such defect is remedied within the time named, the owner or agent shall be guilty of an offense against this act.

(4.) To exercise such other powers as may be necessary for ensuring the health and safety of miners and all other persons employed in or about mines and mining works. 55 V., c. 9, s. 65 (1); 60 V., c. 8, s. 27.

20. REPORTS OF INSPECTOR.—Every inspector under this act shall make an annual report of his proceedings during the preceding year to the Director of the Bureau of Mines, which report shall

be laid before the Legislative Assembly. 55 V., c. 9, s. 67, part.

21. SERVICE OF NOTICES PENDING AP-POINTMENT OF INSPECTOR.—In the event of a vacancy in the office of Mining Inspector any notice by this act required to be given to such officer shall be given to the Director of the Bureau of Mines. 55 V., c. 9, s. 68.

22. PLANS TO BE PRODUCED ON INSPEC-TION OF MINE.—On the occasion of any examination or inspection of a mine the owner shall, if required so to do, produce to the inspector or any other person authorized by the Commissioner of Crown Lands, an accurate plan of the workings thereof; every such plan as aforesaid shall show the workings of the mine up to within six months of the time of the inspection, and the owner shall, if required by such inspector or other authorized person, cause to be marked on such plan the progress of the workings of the mine up to the time of such inspection, and shall also permit the inspector to take a copy or tracing thereof. 55 V., c. 9, s. 66.

23. INSPECTOR TO BE A JUSTICE OF THE PEACE.—Every inspector shall be *ex-officio* a justice of the peace of the county or united counties, district or districts which a mining division comprehends or includes, in whole or in part, or in which or in any portion of which a mining division lies, and it shall not be necessary that he shall reside therein or possess any property qualification whatever in order to enable him lawfully to act as such justice of the peace. 55 V., c. 9, s. 26 (1); 60 V., c. 8, s. 13.

24. POWER TO SETTLE DISPUTES BE-TWEEN LICENSEES.—Every inspector shall, as to the mining division for which he is appointed, have power to settle summarily all disputes between licensees as to the existence or forfeitures of mining claims, and the extent and boundary thereof, and as to the use of water and access thereto, and generally to settle all difficulties, matters or questions between licensees which may arise under this act; and the decision of such inspector, in all cases under this act, shall be final, except where otherwise provided by this act, or where another tribunal is appointed under the authority of this act; and no case under this act shall be removed into any court by *certiorari.*   55 V., c. 9, s. 26 (2).

25. APPOINTMENT OF CONSTABLES IN MINING DIVISIONS.—Every inspector appointed in and for a mining division under this act may appoint any number of constables not exceeding four; and the persons so from time to time appointed shall be and are hereby constituted, respectively, constables and peace officers for the purposes of this act, for and during the terms and within the mining divisions for which they are respectively appointed. 55 V., c. 9, s. 46.

PART II.—MINING LOCATIONS.

26. FORM AND SIZE OF MINING LOCATIONS.—Mining locations under this act shall conform to the following requirements:

(1.) IN UNSURVEYED TERRITORIES IN ALGOMA, ETC.   In the unsurveyed territory within the District of Algoma, Thunder Bay and Rainy River, and that part of the District of Nipissing which lies north of the French River, Lake Nipissing and the River Mattawa, every regular mining location shall be rectangular in shape, and the bearings of the outlines thereof shall be due north and south and due east and west astronomically.

DIMENSIONS.—And such location shall be of one of the following dimensions, namely, eight chains in length by forty chains in width, containing 320 acres, or forty chains square, containing 160 acres, or forty chains in length by twenty chains in width, containing eighty acres, or twenty chains in length by twenty chains in width, containing forty acres.

.(2.) WHEN LOCATIONS BORDER ON LAKES AND RIVERS IN SAID TERRITORY.—Where a mining location in the unsurveyed lands in the territory aforesaid borders upon a lake or river a road allowance of one chain in width shall be reserved along the margin of the lake or river, and the width of the location shall front on the road allowance, and the bearings of the other outlines of the location shall be due north and south and due east and west astronomically, and the location shall otherwise conform to the requirements of the preceding subsection as nearly as the nature of the land will admit.

ISLAND OF THIRTY ACRES. — Provided, that the Commissioner of Crown Lands may, where in his opinion the public interests will not be prejudiced, specially direct that such reservation shall not be made in the case of any island or islands which contain not more than thirty acres.

(3.) WHEN IN TOWNSHIPS IN SAID TERRITORY SURVEYED IN SECTIONS. — In the townships in said territory surveyed or hereafter to be surveyed into sections or lots, every mining location after such survey shall consist of a half, a quarter, an eighth or a sixteenth of a section or lot as the case may be, but so that the area of any such mining location shall not be less than forty acres.

(4.) RESERVATION FOR ROADS.—In all patents and leases for mining locations in the territory aforesaid there shall be a reservation for roads of five per centum of the quantity of land professed to be granted. 55 V., c. 9, s. 10 (1-4).

(5.) LOCATIONS IN OTHER UNSURVEYED TERRITORY.—In the lands not situate within the limits of the territory aforesaid mining locations shall be as may be defined by any order in council hereafter to be made, but so that the area of any such location shall be not less than forty acres. 55 V., c. 9, s. 10 (5); 57 V., c. 16, s. 3.

27. HOW MINING LOCATIONS IN UNSURVEYED TERRITORY TO BE SURVEYED.— Mining locations in unsurveyed territory shall be surveyed by an Ontario Land Surveyor, and shall be connected with some known point in previous surveys, or with some other known point or boundary (so that the tract may be laid down on the office maps of the Territory in the Department of Crown Lands) at the cost of the applicants, who shall be required to furnish within four months of the time of their application the surveyor's plan, field notes and description of the location, showing a survey in accordance with this act, and to the satisfaction of the Commissioner of Crown Lands, and such surveyor's plan, field notes and description shall not be regarded as constituting a claim to the location on behalf of the party for whom or at whose instance they have been prepared, unless they shall be filed in the Department of Crown Lands immediately upon completion of the survey. 55 V., c. 9, s. 11; 60 V., c. 8, s. 7 (1).

28. CONDITIONS OF APPLICATION FOR

MINING LOCATIONS.—In addition to the requirements of Sections 26 and 27, every application for a mining location shall be accompanied with an affidavit showing the discovery of valuable or or mineral thereon by or on behalf of the applicant, and that he has no knowledge and has never heard of any adverse claim by reason of prior discovery or otherwise, and every applicant shall within sixty days pay into the Department of Crown Lands one-fourth of the purchase price or rental, and within three months the remaining three-fourths, the time to be reckoned from the date on which the application has been filed in the department, and in case of failure in respect of any of these requirements the application shall lapse and be of no effect. Provided, however, that in no case shall a patent or lease for a location in unsurveyed territory issue until a survey has been filed as required by the next preceding section, and that in the case of locations in surveyed townships the time for completing all requirements on the part of an applicant may be limited to thirty days at the discretion of the Commissioner of Crown Lands. 60 V., c. 8, s. 7 (2).

29. LIMIT OF APPLICATIONS IN ANY COUNTY OR DISTRICT.—No application for mining lands containing ores or minerals of the same class or kind shall be entertained in any one calendar year from any person for more than 320 acres, nor from any firm, partnership, syndicate or incorporated company for more than 640 acres, within a radius of fifteen miles in any one district or county of the Province, and such areas may be composed of separate locations of not less than forty acres each; and in the event of an application lapsing or becoming abandoned, the applicant therefor may apply for other mining land in the same district or county in place thereof, but so as not to

exceed the limit herein provided; and where a locality or territory is reported or shown to be rich in ores or minerals, the Commissioner of Crown Lands may still further limit applicants to one or more locations of forty acres, at his discretion. 60 V., c. 8, s. 7 (3). ·

30. APPLICATIONS PRIOR TO 13th APRIL, 1897.—In the case of applications for mining lands made prior to the thirteenth day of April, 1897, and not prior to that day finally disposed of by the Commissioner of Crown Lands, the periods in which all requirements herein are to be completed shall date from the said thirteenth day of April; and, in all other respects, the provisions of Sections 27, 28 and 29 shall apply, except in cases where the surveys for the lands had prior to the said day been made and filed, or at least one-half of the purchase money paid thereon, in which cases the periods of time mentioned in Section 28 shall be deemed to run from the said thirteenth day of April. 60 V., c. 8, s. 7 (4).

31. PRICE OF MINING LOCATIONS.—(1) The price per acre of all Crown lands to be sold as mining lands or locations in the districts of Algoma, Thunder Bay, Rainy River and that part of the district of Nipissing which lies north of the French River, Lake Nipissing, and the River Mattawa shall be:

(a) If in a surveyed township and within six miles of any railway $3 00
(b) If elsewhere in surveyed territory, 2 50
(c) If within six miles of any railway but in unsurveyed territory... 2 50
(d) If situate elsewhere in unsurveyed territory.............. 2 00

(2) PRICE OF CROWN LANDS.—The price

per acre of all other Crown lands sold as mining lands or locations and lying south of the aforesaid lake and rivers shall be:

> (*e*) If in a surveyed township and
> within six miles of any railway $2 oo
> (*f*) If situate elsewhere............ 1 50

57 V., c. 16, s. 4 part.

(3) PRICE OF MINING RIGHTS.—The price per acre for a patent of mining rights shall be half of the above rates. (Order in council dated May 21, 1897.)

32. FIRST DISCOVERER OF MINERALS TO BE ENTITLED TO A FREE GRANT.—A prospector or explorer who is the first discoverer of valuable metals, ores or minerals shall be entitled, subject to the royalties provided by this act, to a free grant of one location of forty acres where the vein, lode or other deposit is not less than ten miles from the nearest known mine, vein, lode or deposit of the same metal, ore or mineral respectively; and proofs of his being the first discoverer and of the distance from the nearest known occurrence of the same metal, ore or mineral shall be made by affidavit to the satisfaction of the Commissioner of Crown Lands. 60 V., c. 8, s. 3.

33. WITHDRAWAL OF TERRITORY PENDING EXPLORATION, WITH POWER TO INCREASE THE PRICE OR RENT.—Where a part or section of the Province is shown or reported to be rich in ores or minerals the Lieutenant Governor in Council may withdraw the whole or a portion thereof from sale or lease, and set the same apart pending an exploration thereof or the prospecting of veins, lodes or other deposits of ores or minerals therein by the use of a diamond drill or otherwise, under direction of the Commissioner of

Crown Lands, and may fix the price per acre at any greater sum than is hereinbefore provided, or may offer the same for sale at public auction, on such terms and conditions as may be fixed by order in council. 60 V., c. 8, s. 8.

34. LOCATION SOLD TO BE HELD UNDER CONDITION OF CERTAIN EXPENDITURES IN MINING THEREON.—(1) The grantee or owner of any mining location sold and patented under Section 31 shall, during the seven years immediately following the issue of the patent therefor, expend in stripping or in opening up mines, in sinking shafts or in other actual mining operations, exclusive of all houses, roads and other like improvements, a sum not less than at the rate of one dollar per acre during the first two years, and a sum not less than at the rate of one dollar per acre during each remaining year of the said seven years, and the said expenditure may consist of labor actually performed by grown men to be computed at the rate of two dollars per man per day; but if two or more locations are contiguous, the whole of the mining work herein required may be done upon one of them.

(2) ON DEFAULT TO REVERT TO THE CROWN.—In default of such expenditure during the first two years or during any subsequent year of the said period of seven years all rights connected with any such mining location shall, upon an order in that behalf being made by the Lieutenant Governor in Council, upon the report of the Director of the Bureau of Mines that such expenditure has not been made, revert to, and be vested in, Her Majesty, her successors and assigns, for the public uses of the Province, freed and discharged of any interest or claim of any other person or persons whatsoever. 60 V., c. 8, s. 9.

35. LEASES OF MINING LANDS AUTHORIZED.—(1) Instead of granting any mining lands in fee simple the same may be leased or demised for a term of ten years, with the right of renewal for a further term of ten years at the same rental if the covenants and conditions have been performed and fulfilled.

(2) RENTAL.—Unless otherwise provided by regulation the rental for the first year shall be one dollar per acre, and for each year thereafter the sum of twenty-five cents per acre payable in advance, in respect of lands within the territory designated in the first subsection of Section 31 of this act; and sixty cents per acre the first year, and thereafter for each year fifteen cents per acre, payable in advance, in respect of lands situate elsewhere.

(3) RENEWAL OF LEASE.—Such lease may, at the expiration of the second term, if the covenants and conditions thereof have been performed and fulfilled, be renewed for a term of twenty years on such conditions and at such rent as the regulations shall provide, and may in like manner and subject to the like conditions be renewed from time to time at the expiration of every twenty years.

(4) CONDITIONS OF LEASE.—Every such lease shall be subject to such covenants and conditions on the part of the lessee, his executors, administrators and assigns, to be paid, observed and performed, as shall be provided by regulation.

(5) REMOVAL OF MACHINERY ON EXPIRY OF LEASE.—The said lease may among other things provide for the removal, in case of forfeiture or non-renewal of the lease, of any mining plant and machinery which the lessee, his executors,

heirs and administrators shall have placed or erected upon the said premises.

(6) EXPENDITURE UPON LANDS LEASED. —There shall be expended in stripping or in opening up mines or in sinking shafts or in other actual mining operations the like sums upon lands leased under the provisions of this act as it is provided by Section 34 hereof shall be expended in the case of sales or grants and within the like periods, and in default of such expenditure the lease shall be forfeited and become absolutely void, and the said lands, mines and minerals shall, upon an order in that behalf being made by the Lieutenant Governor in Council upon the report of the Director of the Bureau of Mines that such expenditure has not been made, revert to and become the property of and be vested in Her Majesty, her successors and assigns, and shall cease to be the property of any other person or persons whatsoever. 55 V., c. 9, s. 14.

(7) When mining rights are leased the rental shall be fifty per cent. of the rates fixed by Subsection 2. Order in council dated May 21, 1897.

36. FORFEITURE OF LEASES ON NON-PAYMENT OF RENT.—If default is made by the lessee in the payment of rent the lease shall be forfeited, but the lessee may defeat the forfeiture by payment of the full amount of rent within ninety days from the day when the same becomes payable; but unless the whole of the rent is paid within ninety days from the said day the lease shall be absolutely forfeited and void, any statute, law, usage or custom to the contrary notwithstanding, and all claims of any and every kind of the lessee or his assigns shall from and after such period forever cease and determine. 55 V., c. 9, s. 16.

37. FAILURE OF CO-OWNER OR CO-LESSEE TO CONTRIBUTE HIS SHARE.—(1)

Upon the failure of any one or more of several co-owners or co-lessees of a location to contribute his or their proportion of the expenditures or of the rental necessary to hold such location, the co-owners or co-lessees who have performed the labor or made the improvements or paid the rent as required by the provisions of this act may, at the expiration of the year, give such delinquent co-owner or co-lessee, or his personal representative in case of death, personal notice in writing, or notice by registered letter addressed to his last known place of abode, calling upon him to make the necessary payment; and if upon the expiration of three calendar months from such notice the delinquent co-owner or co-lessee or his said representative shall have failed to contribute his proportion to meet such expenditures or improvements or rental, as the case may be, upon report thereof by the Director of the Bureau of Mines, the Commissioner of Crown Lands may order that his interest in the location shall become the property of and be vested in his co-owners or co-lessees who have made the expenditures or improvements or paid the rent overdue as aforesaid; and the same shall vest in such co-owners or co-lessees accordingly; or if the commissioner thinks fit to refer the matter to the High Court, the Court shall have authority to make the like order.

(2) WHEN NOTICE MAY BE GIVEN TO HEIRS.—In case of the death of such person either before or after default in respect of his share, and no person has taken out administration to his estate or has obtained probate of his will, the notice provided for in the preceding subsection may be given to the heirs of such person. 60 V., c. 8, s. 10.

38. WHEN LESSEE MAY BECOME PURCHASER.—The lessee may at any time during the demised term, upon the payment of all rent

due and the performance and fulfillment of all other covenants and conditions, become the purchaser of the lands demised to him, and in such case the sum paid for the first year's rental shall be treated as part of the purchase money.   55 V., c. 9, s. 15.

39. PINE TREES RESERVED.—(1) The patents for all Crown lands sold as mining lands shall contain a reservation of all pine trees standing or being on the lands, which pine trees shall continue to be the property of Her Majesty, and any person holding a license to cut timber or sawlogs on such lands may at all times during the continuance of the license enter upon the lands and cut and remove such trees and make all necessary roads for that purpose.

(2) PATENTEES MAY USE TIMBER FOR BUILDING, FENCING, ETC., ON THE LAND. —The patentees or those claiming under them (except patentees of mining rights hereinafter mentioned) may cut and use such trees as may be necessary for the purpose of building, fencing and fuel on the land so patented, or for any other purpose essential to the working of the mines thereon, and may also cut and dispose of all trees required to be removed in actually clearing the land for cultivation.

(3) TIMBER CUT TO BE SUBJECT TO DUES.—No pine trees except for the said necessary building, fencing and fuel, or other purpose essential to the working of the mine, shall be cut beyond the limit of such actual clearing; and all pine trees so cut and disposed of, except for the said necessary building, fencing and fuel, or other purpose aforesaid, shall be subject to the payment of the same dues as are at the time payable by the holders of licenses to cut timber or sawlogs.   55 V., c. 9, s. 17.

40. APPLICATION OF SECTION 39 TO LEASES.—The preceding section shall apply to all leases issued under this act, other than leases of mining rights hereinafter mentioned, with the following limitations and variations, that is to say:

1. No pine trees shall be used for fuel other than dry pine trees, and (except for domestic or household purposes) only after the sanction of the timber licensee or the Department of Crown Lands is obtained.

2. In case it is intended to clear for cultivation any portion of the lands so leased it shall be the duty of the lessee to give the holder of the timber license three months' notice in writing of his intention to clear, and the area intended to be cleared, and its position, so that such timber licensee may remove any timber on the area intended to be cleared.

3. If at the expiry of the time limited by the notice such timber shall not have been removed from the area intended to be cleared, then the lessee shall be at liberty to cut and dispose of all trees required to be removed in actually clearing for cultivation the area specified in such notice, and all trees so cut and disposed of shall be subject to the payment of the same dues as are at the time payable by the holders of licenses.

4. If during the first ten years it is sought to cut timber, other than pine, on the lands so leased, beyond what is required for building, fencing or fuel, or in the course of actual clearing for cultivation, or for any other purpose essential to the working of the mines as hereinbefore provided, application shall first be made to the Commissioner of Crown Lands, who may grant authority to cut such timber and fix the rate of dues to be paid thereon. 55 V., c. 9, s. 18.

41. MINING RIGHTS RESERVED MAY BE SOLD OR LEASED.—The ores, minerals and mining rights that have in the patents been reserved to the Crown in any land may be granted or leased to the owner of the surface rights who applies therefor, unless a patent or mining lease has been previously applied for by a person who is the first discoverer of valuable ore or mineral in or upon the premises, when such applicant shall have priority. 60 V., c. 8, s. 11.

42. HOW COMPENSATION TO OWNER OF SURFACE RIGHTS SHALL BE ASCERTAINED.—(1) Where the surface rights have been granted, leased or located, and a patent or lease of mining rights shall thereafter be granted in respect of the same land, in the event of the parties failing to agree upon compensation for injury or damage to the surface rights either in the form of a specified interest in the mineral rights or ore or mineral, to be secured to the owner of the surface rights, or by payment or agreement to pay in money, or the giving of security, the Director of the Bureau of Mines shall order and prescribe the manner in which compensation for the damage or injury to the surface and surface rights shall be ascertained, paid or secured.

(2) For the purposes aforesaid the said director is empowered to appoint a valuator or valuators, arbitrator or arbitrators, who shall have all the powers for the purposes for which he or they shall be appointed of an arbitrator or arbitrators under any act of the Legislature, or he may direct that such compensation shall be ascertained by suit or action in any County or District Court. 55 V., c. 9, s. 20.

43. RIGHT OF ENTRY OF PROSPECTORS LIMITED.—No person shall have the right of entry as prospector or explorer upon the surface rights of that portion of any lot used as a garden, orchard, vineyard, nursery, plantation or pleasure ground, or upon which crops that may be damaged by such entry are growing, or on which is situated any spring, artificial reservoir, dam or waterworks, or any dwelling house, outhouse, manufactory, public building, church or cemetery, unless with the written consent of the owner, lessee or locatee, or of the person in whom the legal estate therein is vested. 55 V., c. 9, s. 21.

PART III.—MINING CLAIMS.

44. MINING DIVISIONS, HOW TO BE DECLARED.—The Lieutenant Governor in Council may from time to time by order in council declare any tract of country therein described to be a mining division; and by any subsequent order in council may from time to time extend, add to or diminish the limits of the division, or may otherwise amend any such order in council, or may cancel the same; and from and after the publication in the Ontario Gazette of an order in council declaring a tract of country to be a mining division, the mining division therein mentioned and described and all mines on Crown lands situate in the division shall be subject to the provisions of this act, and to any regulations to be made under this act. 55 V., c. 9, s. 24.

45. MINER'S LICENSE.—(1) The Director of the Bureau of Mines may, on payment of a fee of ten dollars, grant to any person applying for the same a license to be called a "miner's license."

(2) DURATION, ETC., OF LICENSE.—Every miner's license shall be in force for one year from the date thereof and shall not be transferable, ex-

cept with the consent of the Director of the Bureau of Mines; and only one person shall be named therein, who shall be called the licensee, and who, before the expiration of the license, or within ten clear days thereafter, and not afterward, shall have the right to a renewal of the license by the Director of the Bureau on payment to him of the like fee of ten dollars, or such other sum as may then be the fee fixed by law or regulation for a miner's license; but in the case of a remote mining division, the Commissioner of Crown Lands may authorize and empower the inspector of the division to issue or renew such license, subject to the conditions and requirements of this section or any regulation thereunder.

(3) FORM OF LICENSE.—A miner's license may be in the following form:

PROVINCE OF ONTARIO.

No.   (Name of division) Mining Division.   **$**
     Bureau of Mines.   (Date)   18

Miner's License.

Issued to A. B., in consideration of the payment of a fee of ten dollars, under the provisions of The Mines act, to be in force for one year from the date hereof.   C. D.,
                 Director.

(4) PAYMENT TO PRECEDE RENEWAL.— A miner's license shall not be renewed until the fee of ten dollars has been paid. 57 V., c. 16, s. 4, part.

46. POWERS OF LICENSEE UNDER LICENSE.—A miner's license shall authorize the licensee personally, and not through another, to mine during one year from the date of the license, and

from the date of any renewal thereof, on any mining claim marked or staked out by such licensee on Crown lands, as hereinafter provided; but any person or persons not occupying any other mining claim may be employed by the licensee to assist him in working such claim, or the licensee may organize a company to work the same. 55 V., c. 9, s. 30; 57 V., c. 16, s. 5.

47. RIGHT OF LICENSEE TO STAKE OUT CLAIMS AND WORK SAME.—A licensee who discovers a vein, lode or other deposit of ore or mineral within the division mentioned in his license, shall have the right to mark or stake out thereon a mining claim, providing that it is on Crown lands not withdrawn from location or exploration and is not included in a claim occupied by another licensee, or on lands the mines, minerals and mining rights whereof have been reserved by the Crown, and shall have the right to work the same or to transfer his interest therein to another licensee; and in case the surface rights have been granted, leased or located by the Crown to another person, the licensee must proceed as provided in Section 42 of this act. 60 V., c. 8, s. 14 (1).

48. HOW STAKED OUT.—A mining claim shall be deemed to be marked or staked out when a discovery post of wood or iron on which is written or stamped the name of the licensee is planted upon an outcropping or other indication of ore or mineral within the boundaries of the said claim, and a post of wood or iron is planted at each of the four corners in the order following, viz.: No. I at the northeast corner, No. II at the southeast corner, No. III at the southwest corner and No. IV at the northwest corner, the number in each case to be on the side of the post turned toward the post which follows in the order in which they are

named; and if one or more corners of a claim fall in any situation where the nature or shape of the ground renders the planting of a post or posts impracticable, such corner or corners may be indicated by placing at the nearest suitable point a witness post, which in that case shall contain the same marks as those prescribed herein for corner posts, together with the letters W. P. and an indication of the bearing and distance of the site of the true corner from such witness post. 60 V., c. 8, s. 14 (2).

49. NOT MORE THAN ONE CLAIM TO BE STAKED OUT ON SAME VEIN.—No more than one claim shall be staked out by any individual licensee upon the same vein, lode or deposit of ore or mineral, unless such claim is distant at least three miles from the nearest known mine or discovery on the same vein or lode. 60 V., c. 8, s. 14 (3).

50. DIMENSIONS OF MINING CLAIMS.— (1) A mining claim shall be a square of fifteen chains, or 990 feet, containing twenty-two and one-half acres.

(2) HOW TO BE LAID OUT.—Each mining claim shall be laid out with boundary lines running north and south and east and west astronomically, and the measurements of each claim shall be horizontal, and the ground included in each claim shall be deemed to be bounded under the surface by lines vertical to the horizon.

(3) WATER POWER NOT TO BE DEEMED INCLUDED.—A valuable water power lying within the limits of a claim shall not be deemed as part of it for the uses of the licensee. 60 V., c. 8, s. 14 (4).

51. FORFEITURE OF CLAIMS BY FAILURE TO NOTIFY INSPECTOR AND TO FURNISH PLAN.—(1) Every inspector appointed under this act shall keep a book for the recording

therein of mining claims, which book shall be open to inspection by any person on payment of a fee of twenty cents; and every licensee who has marked or staked out a mining claim under this act shall within thirty days thereafter supply to the inspector of the division an outline sketch or plan thereof showing the discovery post and the corner posts, and the witness posts (if any), and their distances from each other in feet, together with a notice in writing setting forth the name of the licensee and the number of his license, the name (if any) of the claim and its locality as indicated by some general description or statement, the time when the same was marked or staked out, the length of the boundary lines if for any cause they are not regular, and the nature of such cause, the situation of the discovery post as indicated by distance and direction from the first corner post, and the date of the record; and the inspector shall forthwith enter the particulars of the notice in his book, and shall file the notice and sketch or plan with the records of his office.

(2) If the licensee fails to comply with the provisions of this section so far as the same relate to him, the mining claim so marked or staked out shall be deemed to be forfeited and abandoned, and all right of the licensee therein shall cease. 55 V., c. 9, s. 34; 60 V., c. 8, s. 15, and c. 3, s. 3.

52. FORFEITURE BY ALLOWING CLAIM TO REMAIN UNWORKED.—(1) A mining claim shall also be deemed to be forfeited and abandoned, and all right of the licensee therein shall cease, in case the mining claim remains unworked for the space of three months after the same has been first marked or staked out as aforesaid, or if the same at any time after the expiration of three months, remains unworked for the period of fifteen days. [1]

---

[1] Brown v. Com'r for Railways, 15 App. Cas. 200; The Queen v. McCurdy, 2 Ex. C. H., 311.

(2) PROVISO.—Provided, however, that in case it is shown to the satisfaction of the inspector of the division, either before the expiration of the respective periods aforesaid or within fifteen days thereafter, that the non-working of such claim arose from the illness of the licensee, or other reasonable cause satisfactory to the inspector, he may extend the time during which the mining claim may remain unworked for such period as he thinks reasonable, and may in like manner thereafter, for reasonable cause established to his satisfaction, grant further extensions of the time during which the claim may remain unworked without being liable to forfeiture; and the inspector shall forthwith enter in the said book all such extensions of the time granted by him and shall report all such extensions.

(3) PROVISO AS TO NORTHERN DISTRICTS.—Provided also that in those parts of the Province lying to the north of French River, Lake Nipissing and Mattawa River, and extending thence to the western limits of the Province, no forfeiture shall be incurred by reason of the non-working of a mining claim between the first day of December and the first day of April following; but in any case actual mining operations must be carried on upon claims taken up in the said territory for at least eight months in every calendar year, saving as provided herein. 55 V., c. 9, s. 35; 57 V., c. 16, s. 6; 60 V., c. 8, s. 16.

53. EXCEPTION WHERE SUSPENSION OF WORK ORDERED.—No mining claim within a division shall be considered unworked within the meaning of the preceding section during the time that an order in council directs that work on mining claims within such mining division may be suspended. 55 V., c. 9, s. 36.

54. LICENSE TO BE EXHIBITED TO IN-SPECTOR ON DEMAND.—Every licensee shall produce and exhibit his license to the inspector for the division, and prove to the satisfaction of the inspector that it is in force, whenever required by him so to do. 55 V., c. 9, s. 38.

55. PARTY WALLS TO BE LEFT BE-TWEEN CLAIMS, AND KEPT CLEAR FOR USE AS ROADS.—PENALTY.—A party wall of at least fifteen feet thick shall be left between ad-joining claims on Crown lands, which party wall shall be used in common by all parties as a roadway for all purposes for which the same may be re-quired, and as a mode of access to the stream, lake or pond where one exists; and the party wall shall not be obstructed by any person throwing soil, stone or other material thereon; and every person so ob-structing the party wall shall be liable to a fine of not more than five dollars and costs; and in default of the payment of the fine and costs, to be imprisoned for any period not exceeding one month. 55 V., c. 9, s. 41; 60 V., c. 8, s. 18.

56. PERSON REMOVING PARTY WALL TO CONSTRUCT NEW ROADWAY.—If at any time it is found necessary or expedient to remove a party wall as aforesaid, the person so removing it shall, if required so to do, construct a new roadway in no wise more difficult as an approach than the one destroyed by the removal of the party wall, under a like penalty as provided in the next preced-ing section; and in case of a removal of a party wail the minerals found therein shall belong to the owners of the adjoining claims, each of whom shall own the half next his claim. 55 V., c. 9, s. 42; 60 V., c. 8, s. 19.

57. CROWN LANDS' LICENSEES NOT TO

DAMAGE OTHER CLAIMS. — PENALTY.—
No person mining upon Crown lands shall cause
damage or injury to the holder of any claim other
than his own by throwing earth, clay, stones or
other material upon such other claim, or by causing
or allowing water which may be pumped or bailed
or may flow from his own claim to flow into or
upon such other claim, under a penalty of not more
than five dollars and costs, and in default of payment of the fine and costs he may be imprisoned for
any period not more than one month. 55 V., c. 9,
s. 43.

58. ACT RESPECTING RIOTS NEAR PUB-
LIC WORKS TO BE IN FORCE IN MINING
DIVISIONS. — REV. STAT., C. 38. — (1) The
Lieutenant Governor in Council may, as often
as occasion requires, declare by proclamation
that he deems it necessary that The Act Respecting Riots Near Public Works shall, so far
as the provisions therein are applicable, be in
force within any mining division or divisions; and
upon, from and after the day to be named in any
such proclamation, Section 1 and Sections 3 to 11
inclusive of the said act shall, so far as the provisions thereof can be applied therein, take effect
within the mining division or mining divisions
designated in the proclamation; and the provisions
of the said act shall apply to all persons employed in
any mine, or in mining within the limits of such
mining division or divisions, as fully and effectually
to all intents and purposes as if the persons so employed had been specially mentioned and referred
to in the said act.

(2) The Lieutenant Governor in Council may in
like manner from time to time declare the said act
to be no longer in force in such mining division or
divisions; but this shall not prevent the Lieutenant

Governor in Council from again declaring the said act to be in force in any such mining division or mining divisions; but no such proclamation shall have effect within the limits of a city. 55 V., c. 9, s. 47.

PART IV.—MINING REGULATIONS.

59. APPLICATION OF PART IV.—This part shall apply to all mines, quarries and pits, and to oil, gas and salt wells, and other openings from which ores or minerals of any kind or class are raised or taken, and to all furnaces or works for smelting or otherwise treating ores, rocks, clays, sands, oils, brines or other minerals for any economic object; and all owners or agents of such mines, quarries, pits, wells, furnaces and works shall observe and keep the provisions of this Part, and in case of non-observance thereof shall incur the penalties provided therefor by Section 80. 59 V., c. 13, s. 2.

60. EMPLOYMENT OF WOMEN AND CHILDREN.—No boy under the age of fifteen years shall be employed in or allowed to be for the purpose of employment in any mine to which this act applies below ground; and no girl or woman shall be employed at mining work or allowed to be for the purpose of employment at mining work in or about any mine. 55 V., c. 9, s. 54.

61. HOURS OF EMPLOYMENT OF BOYS. —No boy or young male person of the age of fifteen and under the age of seventeen years shall be employed or allowed to be for the purpose of employment in any mine to which this part applies below ground on Sunday or for more than forty-eight hours in any one week, or more than eight hours in any one day.

(2) The period of such employment, and the time during which any such boy or person may be below ground for the purpose of employment, shall respectively be deemed to begin at the time of leaving the surface, and to end at the time of returning to the surface.

(3) A week shall mean the period between midnight on Sunday night and midnight on the succeeding Saturday night.   55 V., c. 9, s. 55; 60 V., c. 8, s. 22.

62. REGISTER TO BE KEPT OF LADS EMPLOYED.—The owner or agent of every mine to which this part applies shall keep in the office at the mine, or in the principal office of the mine belonging to the same owner in the district in which the mine is situated, a register, and shall cause to be entered in such register the name, age, residence and date of the first employment of all boys or young male persons of the age of fifteen and under the age of seventeen years who are employed in the mine below ground, and shall produce such register to any inspector at the mine at all reasonable times when required by him, and allow him to inspect and copy the same. The immediate employer of every boy or male young person of the age aforesaid, other than the owner or agent of the mine, before he causes such boy or male young person to be in any mine to which this Part applies below ground, shall report to the owner or agent of such mine, or some person appointed by such owner or agent, that he is about to employ such boy or young male person in the said mine.   55 V., c. 9, s. 56.

63. AGE AND SEX OF PERSONS IN CONNECTION WITH ENGINES.—Where there is a shaft, inclined plane, or level in any mine to which this Part applies, whether for the purpose of an entrance to such mine or of a communication from one part to another part of such mine, and persons are taken up, down or along such shaft, plane or level by means of any engine, windlass or gin, driven or worked by steam or by any mechanical power, or by an animal, or by manual labor, no person shall be allowed to have charge of such engine, windlass or gin, or of any part of the machinery, ropes, chains or tackle connected therewith, unless he is a male of at least twenty years of age. Where the engine, windlass or gin is worked by an animal, the person under whose direction the driver of the animal acts shall, for the purposes of this section, be deemed to be the person in charge of the engine, windlass or gin, and no person shall be employed as such driver who is under sixteen years of age. 55 V., c. 9, s. 57.

64. PENALTY FOR EMPLOYMENT OF PERSONS CONTRARY TO ACT.— If any person contravenes any provision of the four next preceding sections of this act, he shall be guilty of an offense against this act, and in case of any such contravention, by any person whomsoever in the case of any mine, the owner and the agent of such mine shall each be guilty of an offense against this act, unless such owner or agent proves that he had taken all reasonable means to prevent such contravention by publishing and to the best of his power enforcing the provisions of this act. 55 V., c. 9, s. 58 (1).

65. WHERE PERSON UNDER AGE EMPLOYED ON FALSE REPRESENTATION.—If it appears that a boy or young person or any person employed about an engine, windlass or gin, was employed on the representation of his parent or guardian that he was of an age at which his employment would not be in contravention of this act, and under the belief in good faith that he was of that age, the owner or agent of the mine and the imme-

diate employer shall be exempted from any penalty, notwithstanding such boy or other person was not of an age at which his employment as aforesaid is authorized by this act, provided such owner, agent or employer shall immediately, upon discovery of the fact, discharge such boy from such employment, but the parent or guardian shall for the misrepresentation aforesaid be deemed guilty of an offense against this act. 55 V., c. 9, s. 58 (2); 60 V., c. 8, s. 23.

66. PROHIBITION OF PAYMENT OF WAGES AT PUBLIC HOUSES, ETC.—(1) No wages shall be paid to any person employed in or about any mine to which this Part applies at or within any public house, beer shop or place for the sale of any spirits, wine, beer, or other spirituous or fermented liquor, or other house of entertainment, or within any office, garden or place belonging or contiguous thereto or occupied therewith.

(2) PENALTY.—Every person who contravenes, or permits any person to contravene this section, shall be guilty of an offense against this act, and in the event of any such contravention by any person whomsoever the owner and agent of the mine in respect of which the wages were paid shall each be guilty of an offense against this act, unless such owner or agent proves that he had taken all reasonable means to prevent such contravention by publishing and to the best of his power enforcing the provisions of this section. 55 V., c. 9, s. 59.

67. ANNUAL RETURNS BY OWNERS AND AGENTS OF MINES.—(1) The owner or agent of any mine, quarry or other works to which this Part applies shall on or before the fifteenth day of January in every year send to the Bureau of Mines a correct return for the year ending on the preced-

ing thirty-first day of December of the number of persons ordinarily employed in or about such mine below ground and above ground respectively, and distinguishing the different classes and ages of the persons so employed whose hours of labor are regulated by this act, the average rate of wages of each class and the total amount of wages paid during the year, the quantity in standard weight of the mineral dressed, and of the undressed mineral which has been sold, treated or used during such year, and the value or estimated value thereof.

PROVISION FOR MONTHLY OR QUARTERLY RETURNS.—And the owner or agent of every metalliferous mine shall, if required, make similar returns at the end of each month or quarter of the calendar year for such month or quarter in order that the same may be tabulated for publication by the Director of the Bureau under the instructions of the Commissioner of Crown Lands.

(2) SCHEDULES TO BE FURNISHED BY DIRECTOR OF BUREAU.--For the purpose of collecting the data of such statistics the Director of the Bureau of Mines shall prepare the required schedules in such forms as he may from time to time deem desirable, and send the same by mail to be filled up and returned by the owner or agent of every such mine, quarry or works in the Province. 55 V., c. 9, s. 60 (1, 2); 59 V., c. 13, s. 3 (1); 60 V., c. 8, s. 24.

(3) PENALTY.— Every owner or agent of a mine, quarry or other works who fails to comply with this section, or makes any return which is to his knowledge false in any particular, shall be guilty of an offense against this act.   55 V., c. 9, s. 60 (3); 59 V., c. 13, s. 3 (2).

68. FENCING OF ABANDONED OR UN-

WORKED MINES.—For the prevention of accidents where any mine has been abandoned or the working thereof has been discontinued, the owner or lessee, or other person interested in the minerals of the mine shall cause the top of the shaft and all entrances from the surface, as well as all other pits and openings dangerous by reason of their depth, to be and to be kept securely fenced; and if and person fails to act in conformity with this section he shall be guilty of an offense against this Part, and any shaft, entrance, pit or other opening which is not fenced as aforesaid shall be deemed to be a nuisance. 60 V:, c. 8, s. 25.

69. GENERAL RULES.—The following general rules shall, so far as may be reasonably practicable, be observed in every mine to which this Part applies.

1. VENTILATION.— An adequate amount of ventilation shall be constantly produced in every mine to such an extent that the shafts, winzes, sumps, levels, underground stables and working places of such mine and the traveling roads to and from such working places shall be in a fit state for working and passing therein.

2. GUNPOWDER AND BLASTING. — Gunpowder, dualin, dynamite or other explosive or inflammable substance shall only be used underground in the mine as follows:

(*a*) It shall not be stored in the mine in any quantity exceeding what would be required for use during six working days.

(*b*) It shall not be taken for use into the workings of the mine except in a securely covered case or canister, containing not more than eight pounds.

(*c*) A workman shall not have at any time at any

place where the same is being used more than one such case or canister.

(*d*) In charging holes for blasting, unless in mines excepted from the operation of this section by the Commissioner of Crown Lands, an iron or steel pricker shall not be used, and no person shall have in his possession in the mine underground any iron or steel pricker, and an iron or steel tamping rod or stemmer shall not be used for ramming either the wadding or the first part of the tamping or stemming on the powder.

(*e*) A charge of powder which has missed fire shall not be unrammed.

(*f*) A charge which has missed fire may be drawn by a copper pricker, but in no case shall any iron or steel tool be used for the purpose of drawing or drilling out a charge. 55 V., c. 9, s. 74 (1-2).

3. No gunpowder, dualin, dynamite or other explosive shall be used to blast or break up ore in roast heaps where, by reason of the heated condition of such ore or otherwise, there is any danger or risk of premature explosion of the charge. 57 V., c. 16, s. 10, part.

4. MANHOLES IN SELF - ACTING OR ENGINE PLANES.— Every underground plane on which persons travel which is self-acting, or worked by an engine, windlass or gin, shall be provided at intervals of not more than twenty yards with sufficient manholes for places of refuge, and every such plane which exceeds thirty yards in length shall also be provided with some proper means of signaling between the stopping places and the ends of the plane. 55 V., c. 9, s. 74 (3).

5. REFUGES IN TRAMROADS.—Every road on which persons travel underground where the produce of the mine in transit ordinarily exceeds ten tons in any one hour over any part thereof shall

be provided at intervals of not more than one hundred yards with sufficient spaces for places of refuge, each of which spaces shall be of sufficient length, and of at least three feet in width between the wagons running on the tramroad and the side of the road; and the Commissioner of Crown Lands may, if he sees fit, require the inspector to certify whether the produce of the mine in transit on the road aforesaid does or does not ordinarily exceed the weight as aforesaid, and such certificate shall be conclusive as to the matters therein stated. 55 V., c. 9, s. 74 (4); 60 V., c. 8, s. 28, part.

6. KEEPING REFUGES CLEAR. — Every manhole and space for a place of refuge shall be constantly kept clear, and no person shall place anything in a manhole or in such space in such a position as to prevent convenient access thereto. 55 V., c. 9, s. 74 (5); 60 V., c. 8, s. 28, part.

7. FENCING OF OLD SHAFTS AND OTHER OPENINGS.—The top of every shaft which was opened before the commencement of the actual working for the time being of the mine and has not been used during such actual working shall, unless the inspector otherwise permits, be securely fenced; and the top of every other shaft which for the time being is out of use, or used only as an air shaft, and all other pits or openings dangerous by reason of their depth upon which work has been discontinued, shall also be securely fenced. 55 V., c. 9, s. 74 (6); 60 V., c. 8, s. 28, part.

8. FENCING OF ENTRANCES TO SHAFTS. —The top and all entrances between the top and bottom of every working or pumping shaft shall be properly fenced, but this shall not be taken to forbid the temporary removal of the fence for the purpose of repairs or other operations, if proper precautions are used.

9. SECURING OF SHAFTS.—Where the natural strata are not safe, every working or pumping shaft, adit, tunnel, drive, roadway or other workings ·shall be securely cased, lined or timbered, or otherwise made secure.

10. SAFETY FROM WATER.— Every mine shall be provided with proper and sufficient machinery and appliances for keeping such mine free from water, the accumulation or flowing of which might injuriously affect any other mine.

11. DIVISION OF SHAFT.— Where one portion of a shaft is used for the ascent and descent of persons by ladders or by a man-engine, and another portion of the same shaft is used for raising the material being mined, the first mentioned portion shall be cased or otherwise securely fenced off from the last mentioned portion.

12. SIGNALING.—Every working shaft in which persons are raised which exceeds fifty yards in depth, shall, unless exempted in writing by the inspector, be provided with guides and some proper means of communicating by distinct and definite signals from the bottom of the shaft, and from every entrance for the time being in work between the surface and the bottom of the shaft, to the surface, and also of communicating from the surface to the bottom of the shaft, and to every entrance for the time being in work between thé surface and the bottom of the shaft.

13. COVER OVERHEAD.—A sufficient cover overhead shall be used when lowering or raising persons in every working shaft, except where it is worked by a windlass, or where the person is employed about the pump or some work of repair in the shaft, or where a written exemption is given by the inspector.

14. CHAINS.—A single linked chain shall not be used for lowering or raising persons in any working shaft or plane except for the short coupling chain attached to the cage or load.

15. SLIPPING OF ROPE ON DRUM.—There shall be on the drum of every machine used for lowering or raising persons such flanges or horns, and also, if the drum is conical, such other appliances as may be sufficient to prevent the rope from slipping.

16. BRAKE.—There shall be attached to every machine worked by steam, water or other mechanical power, and used for lowering or raising persons, an adequate brake, and also a proper indicator (in addition to any mark on the rope) which will show to the person who works the machine the position of the cage or load in the shaft.

17. INCLINATION OF LADDERS.—A proper footway or ladder, inclined at the most convenient angle which the space in which the ladder is fixed allows, shall be provided in every working shaft where no machinery is used for raising or lowering persons; and every such ladder shall have substantial platforms at intervals of not more than forty feet, and no such ladder shall be fixed for permanent use in a vertical or overhanging position unless in shafts used exclusively for pumping. In every mine in which vertical or overhanging ladders shall be in use in the shaft at the time these rules were first applied to it, such ladders may be retained if securely fixed platforms are constructed at intervals of more than thirty feet from each other, and such ladders have sufficient spaces for footholds of not less than six inches.

18. DRESSING-ROOM.—If more than twelve persons are ordinarily employed in the mine below

ground, sufficient accommodation shall be provided above ground near the principal entrance of the mine, and not in the engine house or boiler house, for enabling the persons employed in the mine to conveniently dry and change their clothes.

19. FENCING MACHINERY.—Every fly-wheel and all exposed and dangerous parts of the machinery used in or about the mine shall be kept securely fenced.

20. GAUGES TO BOILERS AND SAFETY VALVES.—Every steam boiler shall be provided with a proper steam-gauge and water-gauge, to show respectively the pressure of steam and the height of water in the boiler, and with a proper safety valve.

21. WILLFUL DAMAGE.—No person shall willfully damage, or without proper authority remove or render useless, any fencing, casing, lining, guide, means of signaling, signal, cover, chain, flange, horn, brake, indicator, ladder, platform, steam-gauge, water-gauge, safety valve, or other appliance or thing provided in any mine in compliance with this act. 55 V., c. 9, s. 74 (7-20).

70. NOTICE OF CHANGES IN CONNECTION WITH THE WORKING OF A MINE OR IN RESPECT OF ITS OFFICERS, ETC.— In any of the following cases, namely:

1. Where any working is commenced for the purpose of opening a new shaft for any mine to which this Part applies.

2. Where a shaft of any mine to which this Part applies is abandoned, or the working thereof discontinued.

3. Where the working of a shaft of any mine to which this Part applies is recommenced after an abandonment or discontinuance for a period exceeding two months; or

4. Where any change occurs in the name of a

mine, or in the name of the owner or agent of a mine to which this Part applies, or in the officers of any incorporated company which is the owner of a mine to which this Part applies.

The owner or agent of such mine shall give notice thereof to the inspector within two months after such commencement, abandonment, discontinuance, recommencement or change, and if such notice is not given the owner or agent shall be guilty of an offense against this act.   55 V., c. 9, s. 62; 59 V., c. 13, s. 4.

71. NOTICE OF ACCIDENTS IN MINES TO BE SENT TO BUREAU OF MINES.—(1) Where in or about any mine to which this act applies whether above or below ground, either

1. Loss of life or any personal injury to any person employed in or about the mine occurs by reason of any explosion of gas, powder or of any steam boiler; or

2. Loss of life or any serious personal injury to any person employed in or about the mine occurs by reason of any accident whatever,

THE OWNER OR AGENT of the mine shall, within twenty-four hours next after the explosion or accident, send notice in writing of the explosion or accident and of the loss of life or personal injury occasioned thereby to the Director of the Bureau of Mines, and shall specify in such notice the character of the explosion or accident and the number of persons killed and injured respectively.

(2) WHERE ANY PERSONAL INJURY, of which notice is required to be sent under this section, results in the death of the person injured, notice in writing of the death shall be sent to the inspector within twenty-four hours after such death comes to the knowledge of the owner or agent. Every owner or agent who fails to act in compliance

with this section shall be guilty of an offense against this act.   55 V., c. 9, s. 61.

72. SPECIAL REPORT.—The Commissioner of Crown Lands may at any time direct an inspector to make a special report with respect to any accident in a mine to which this act applies, which accident has caused loss of life or personal injury to any person, and in such case shall cause such report to be made public at such time and in such manner as he thinks expedient; and in conducting an inquiry into the cause of loss of life or of personal injury to any person in or about a mine, the inspector shall have power to take evidence upon oath.   55 V., c. 9, s. 67, part; 57 V., c. 16, s. 8.

PART V.—OFFENSES AND PENALTIES.

73. PENALTY FOR REMOVING PICKET.— Any person who removes, or disturbs with intent to remove, any stake, picket or other mark placed under the provisions of this act, shall forfeit and pay a sum not exceeding twenty dollars and costs; and in default of payment of the fine and costs, may be imprisoned for any period not exceeding one month.   55 V., c. 9, s. 45.

74. PENALTY FOR CONTRAVENING PART III.—Every person contravening Part III of this act or any rule or regulation made under it, in any case where no other penalty or punishment is imposed, shall, for every day on which such contravention occurs, or continues, or is repeated, incur a fine of not more than twenty dollars and costs; and in default of payment of the fine and costs, such person may be imprisoned for a period not exceeding one month.   55 V., c. 9, s. 48.

75. PUNISHMENT FOR DEFACING NO-
TICES.—Every person who pulls down, injures or
defaces any rules, notice or abstract posted up by
the owner or agent shall be guilty of an offense
against this act. 55 V., c. 9, s. 75.

76. PENALTY FOR OBSTRUCTING IN-
SPECTOR.—Every person who willfully obstructs
an inspector in the execution of his duty under this
act, and every owner or agent of a mine who refuses
or neglects to furnish to the inspector the means
necessary for making any entry, inspection, examination or inquiry under this act in relation to such
mine, shall be guilty of an offense against this act.
55 V., c. 9, s. 65 (2).

77. RESPONSIBILITY OF CONTRACTOR
TO PREVENT ACCIDENTS.—Where work of
any sort in or about a mine is let to a contractor, he
shall observe and carry out all the provisions of
Part IV for the prevention of accidents, and if he
contravenes any of such provisions he shall be
guilty of an offense against this act and shall be
liable to the same penalties and may be proceeded
against in the same way and to the same extent and
effect as if he were an owner or agent. 57 V.,
c. 16, s. 9.

78. CONTRAVENTION OF RULES TO BE
AN OFFENSE.—Every person who contravenes or
does not comply with any of the general rules contained in Section 69 shall be guilty of an offense
against this act, and in the event of any contravention of or non-compliance with any of the said general rules in the case of any mine to which this act
applies by any person whomsoever being proved,
the owner and agent of such mine, and any contractor and foreman employed in or about such mine,
shall each be guilty of an offense against this act

unless such contractor or foreman proves that he
had taken all reasonable means to prevent such contravention or non-compliance by publishing, and to
the best of his power enforcing, the said rules as regulations for the working of the mine.   55 V., c. 9,
s. 74 (21); 57 V., c. 16, s. 10, part.

79. WHERE EMPLOYES DEEMED GUILTY.
—Every person other than the owner or agent employed in or about a mine, who is guilty of any act
or omission which in the case of the owner or agent
would be an offense against Part IV shall be deemed
to be guilty of an offense against the said part.
55 V., c. 9, s. 69, part.

80. PENALTIES.—Every owner or agent guilty
of an offense against Part IV shall be liable to a
penalty not exceeding, except as in this section
hereinafter provided, fifty dollars, and any other person guilty of an offense against Part IV aforesaid shall
be liable to a penalty not exceeding, except as in this
section hereinafter provided, ten dollars: Provided
that if the Director of the Bureau of Mines or an inspector has given written notice of any such offense
having been committed, every such owner, agent or
other person shall be liable to a further penalty not
exceeding five dollars for every day that such offense
continues after such notice.   55 V., c. 9, s. 69, part;
59 V., c. 13, s. 5.

81. PROSECUTION OF OWNER OR AGENT.
—No prosecution shall be instituted against the
owner or agent of a mine to which this Part applies
for any offense under this act except by an inspect-
or, or by the county or district Crown attorney, or
with the consent in writing of the attorney general;
and in case the owner or agent of a mine is charged
with an offense under this act he shall not be found
guilty thereof if he proves that he had taken all

reasonable means to prevent the commission thereof, and an inspector shall not institute any prosecution against an owner or agent if satisfied that he had taken such reasonable means as aforesaid. 55 V., c. 9, s. 71.

82. INSPECTOR MAY CONVICT ON VIEW. —Every inspector for a mining division may convict upon view of any of the offenses punishable under the provisions of Part III of this act or any regulation made under it. 55 V., c. 9, s. 49.

83. MANNER IN WHICH PROSECUTION MAY TAKE PLACE.— REV. STAT., C. 90. — All prosecutions for the punishment of any offense under this act except under Section 18 may take place before any two or more of Her Majesty's justices of the peace having jurisdiction in the county or district in which the offense is committed, or before a police or stipendiary magistrate, or before an inspector of the mining division, under the provisions of The Ontario Summary Convictions act. 55 V., c. 9, s. 52; 60 V., c. 8, s. 21.

84. LIMITATIONS OF PROSECUTIONS AND FORM OF INFORMATION.—Any complaint or information made or laid in pursuance of this act shall be made or laid within three months from the time when the matter of such complaint or information respectively arose, and

1. The description of any offense under this act in the words of this act shall be sufficient in law.

2. Any exception, exemption, proviso, excuse or qualification, whether it does or does not accompany the description of the offenses in this act, may be proved by the defendant, but need not be specified or negatived in the information, and if so specified or negatived no proof in relation to the matter so specified or negatived shall be required on the part of the prosecutor or informant. 55 V., c. 9, s. 70.

85. PROSECUTION UNDER OTHER ACTS.
—Nothing in this act shall prevent any person from
being indicted or liable under any other act or
otherwise to any other or higher penalty or punishment than is provided for any offense by this act,
provided that he shall not be punished twice for the
same offense.　55 V., c. 9, s. 72 (1).

86. WHERE PROSECUTION SHOULD BE
UNDER ANOTHER ACT.—If the court before
whom a person is charged with an offense under this
act thinks that proceedings ought to be taken
against such person for such offense under any other
act or otherwise, the court may adjourn the case to
enable such proceedings to be taken.　55 V., c. 9,
s. 72 (2).

87. APPLICATION OF FEES, FINES AND
PENALTIES.—Fees, penalties and fines received
under this act, and the costs of all such convictions
as take place before any inspector or magistrate
appointed under this act, shall form part of the
Consolidated Revenue Fund of this Province, and
be accounted for and dealt with accordingly; and
the expenses of carrying this act into effect in any
mining division shall be paid by the Lieutenant
Governor out of the said Consolidated Revenue
Fund.　55 V., c. 9, s. 51.

MICHIPICOTON MINING DIVISION.

Copy of an order in council approved by His Honor
the Lieutenant Governor, the 9th day of September, A. D. 1897.

Upon consideration of the annexed memorandum
of the Director of the Bureau of Mines, dated September 8, 1897,* and upon the recommendation of

*Not printed.

the Honorable the Commissioner of Crown Lands, the committee of council advise that the tract first mentioned in the said memorandum, namely, the tract limited upon its east side by the meridian of the east end of Dog Lake, or say eighty-four degrees west from Greenwich, on the south side by the latitude of Cape Gargantua, say forty-seven degrees thirty-six minutes, on the north side by the latitude of forty-eight degrees thirty minutes, and between the westerly ends of these lines of latitude, where they touch Lake Superior, by the shore line of said lake, containing about five thousand square miles, be so declared a mining division, and that the name thereof be the "Michipicoton Mining Division."

Certified,

J. R. CARTWRIGHT,
Clerk, Executive Council.

REVISED AND AMENDED REGULATIONS FOR MINING DIVISIONS.

Approved by the Lieutenant Governor in Council, January 29, 1898.

1. ANY PERSON MAY EXPLORE FOR MINERALS on any Crown lands not for the time being marked or staked out and occupied, except on such lands as by the Lieutenant Governor in Council may have been withdrawn from sale, location or exploration as being valuable for their pine timber or for any other reason.

2. WHERE CROWN LANDS are situated within a mining division they may be occupied as mining claims under miners' licenses.

3. THE LIEUTENANT GOVERNOR may

appoint for every mining division or for any part thereof an inspector, who shall be an officer of the Bureau of Mines.

4. EVERY INSPECTOR shall have power to enter, inspect and examine any mine or portion thereof or works connected therewith relating to the health and safety of the persons employed in or about the mine or works, and to give notice to the owner or agent in writing of any particulars in which he considers such mine or works, or any portion thereof, or any matter, thing or practice, to be dangerous or defective, and to require the same to be remedied within the period of time named in such notice; and on the occasion of any examination or inspection of a mine the owner shall produce to the inspector, if required so to do, an accurate plan of the workings thereof up to the time of such inspection, and shall also permit the inspector to take a copy or tracing thereof.

5. EVERY INSPECTOR SHALL BE EX-OF-FICIO A JUSTICE OF THE PEACE of the county or united counties, district or districts which a mining division comprehends or includes, in whole or in part, or in which or in any portion of which a mining division lies.

6. EVERY INSPECTOR SHALL HAVE POWER, within the mining division for which he has been appointed, to settle summarily all disputes between licensees as to the existence or forfeiture of mining claims, and the extent and boundary thereof, and as to the use of water and access thereto, and generally to settle all difficulties, matters or questions which may arise between licensees; and the decision of the inspector in all such cases shall be final except where otherwise provided by the Mines act, or where another tribunal is appointed

under authority of the act; and no case under the act shall be removed into any court by certiorari.

7. EVERY INSPECTOR of a mining division appointed under the Mines act may appoint any number of constables not exceeding four; and the persons so appointed shall be constituted constables and peace officers for the purposes of the act for and during the terms and within the mining divisions for which they are appointed.

8. NO PERSON SHALL BE APPOINTED or authorized to act as an inspector who practices, or acts, or is a partner of any person who acts as a mining agent, or who is employed by the owners of or is interested in any mine.

9. THE DIRECTOR OF THE BUREAU OF MINES shall have all the powers, rights and authority throughout the Province which an inspector has or may exercise in any mining division, and such other powers, rights and authority for the carrying out of the provisions of the Mines act as shall be assigned to him by regulation.

10. NO DIRECTOR, inspector or other officer appointed under the Mines act shall directly or indirectly purchase or become interested in any Crown lands or mining claim; and any such purchase or interest shall be void; and if any officer violates this regulation he shall forfeit his office and be liable in addition to a penalty of five hundred dollars for every such offense, to be recovered in an action by any person who sues for the same.

11. THE LIEUTENANT GOVERNOR in Council may by order declare any tract of country therein described to be a mining division; and by any subsequent order in council may add to or diminish the limits of the division, or may otherwise amend any such order, or may cancel the same.

12. ON PAYMENT OF A FEE OF TEN DOLLARS, or such other sum as may be fixed by regulation, the Director of the Bureau of Mines (or the inspector of a division when so authorized by the Commissioner of Crown Lands) may grant to any person registered partnership, or mining company incorporated under the laws of the Province applying therefor, a license to be called a "miner's license," which shall be in force for one year from the date thereof, and shall not be transferable except with the consent of the director of the bureau or the inspector of the division.

13. THE PERSON, PARTNERSHIP OR COMPANY named in a license shall be called the "licensee," and upon payment of the fee fixed by law or regulation, and production of proof under oath that the mining conditions have been duly performed upon the claim or claims staked out and held, such licensee shall have the right to renewal if application is made therefor before the expiration of the license or within ten days thereafter.

14. EVERY LICENSEE shall produce and exhibit his license to the inspector for the division, and prove to the satisfaction of the inspector that it is in force, at the time of recording his claim, and at any other time when required by the inspector so to do.

15. A MINER'S LICENSE shall authorize the licensee to explore any portion of the mining division named in his license, and to mine during one year from the date of the license on any mining claim marked or staked out by such licensee on Crown lands, and he may employ any person to assist him in working such claim, or may organize a company to work the same, and in either case the working conditions shall be deemed to be complied with

when the equivalent of one man's labor for the year in actual mining has been performed as hereinafter required; but no licensee shall have the right to cut down or use any timber which may be upon his claim except for purposes of building, fencing or fuel, or other purposes necessary for working the mine upon the said claim.

16. A LICENSEE WHO DISCOVERS A VEIN, lode or other deposit of ore or mineral in place within the division mentioned in his license shall have the right to mark or stake out thereon a mining claim, providing that it is not included in a claim occupied by another licensee, or is not on Crown lands withdrawn from location or exploration, or on lands the minerals and mining rights whereof have been reserved by the Crown; and he shall have the right to work the same, or he may transfer his interest therein to another licensee upon payment of a fee of five dollars to the inspector of the division, who shall record the transfer in his book.

17. IF THE WORKING CONDITIONS have been complied with as hereinafter required for a period of three years on a claim of twenty chains square, or for two years on a claim of fifteen chains square or less, or when the equivalent of such working conditions has been complied with in a less period of time in the respective cases, the licensee may apply for and obtain a patent or lease for the land embraced in the claim, free from any further working conditions, upon a survey thereof being made and filed according to Section 27 of the Mines act, R.S.O. 1897, and upon payment therefor to the Department of Crown Lands of the purchase price or first year's rental at a rate per acre as provided in Sections 31 and 35 respectively of the said act; and the time when the royalties may begin to be

imposed or collected upon ores or minerals mined, wrought or taken from a claim so patented or leased shall be reckoned from the date of recording such claim in the inspector's office.

18. A MINING CLAIM shall be marked or staked out by planting a discovery post of wood or iron (on which is written or stamped the name of the licensee, number of his license, and date of his discovery) upon an outcropping or show of ore or mineral in place within the boundaries of the claim, and by planting at each of the four corners a post of wood or iron in the order following, viz.: No. I at the northeast corner, No. II at the southeast corner, No. III at the southwest corner, and No. IV at the northwest corner, the number in each case to be on the side of the post toward the post which follows it in the order in which they are named. See Fig. 1.

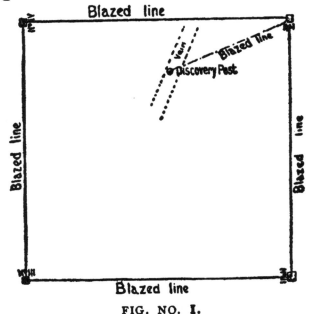

FIG. NO. I.

19. IF ONE OR MORE CORNERS OF A CLAIM fall in any situation where the nature or shape of the ground renders the planting of a post or posts impracticable, such corner or corners may be indicated by placing at the nearest suitable point a witness post, which in that case shall contain the same marks as those prescribed for corner posts, together with the letters "W. P." (witness post), and an indication of the bearing and distance of the site of the true corner from such such witness post. See Fig. 2.

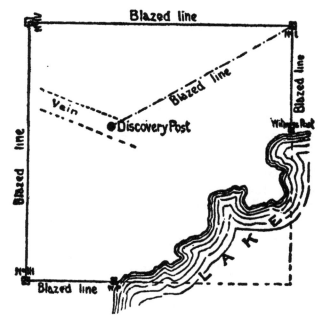

FIG. NO. 2.

20. WHERE THERE ARE STANDING TREES upon a mining claim so staked out, the licensee shall be required to blaze the trees and cut the underbrush along the boundary lines of the claim, and also along the line from the first corner post to the discovery post.

21. A MINING CLAIM SHALL BE A SQUARE of fifteen chains or 990 feet, horizontal measurement, containing twenty-two and one-half acres, or of such other extent, greater or less, but so as not to exceed a square of twenty chains or 1,320 feet, containing forty acres, and shall be laid out with boundary lines running north and south and east and west astronomically, and the ground included in each claim shall be deemed to be bounded under the surface by lines vertical to the horizon: but an irregular portion of land lying between two or more claims may be staked out with boundaries conterminous thereto, provided that its area shall not exceed forty acres. A valuable water power lying within the limits of a claim shall not be deemed as part of it for the uses of the licensee.

22. NO MORE THAN ONE CLAIM shall be staked out by any individual licensee upon the same vein, lode or deposit of ore or mineral, unless such claim is distant at least sixty chains from the nearest known mine, claim, or discovery on the same vein, lode or deposit, but no licensee shall stake out and record in the same mining division, within a radius of fifteen miles, more than four claims in one calendar year.

23. FOR EACH ADDITIONAL MINING CLAIM after the first marked or staked out by a licensee, whether upon the same vein, lode or deposit, or upon another, he shall pay to the inspector of the division a fee of ten dollars a year in advance when recording the same if the area is more than twenty-two and one-half acres and six dollars if it is twenty-two and one-half acres or less, and a like fee in each case shall be paid for every additional claim so held at the time of renewal of the license.

24. EVERY INSPECTOR OF A MINING DIVISION shall keep a book for the recording of mining claims therein, and such book shall be open to inspection by any person on payment of a fee of twenty cents.

25. EVERY LICENSEE who has marked or staked out a mining claim shall, within thirty days thereafter, supply under oath to the inspector of the division an outline sketch or plan thereof, showing the discovery post and corner posts, and the witness posts (if any) and their distances from each other in feet, together with a notice in writing setting forth under oath the name of the licensee and the number of his license, the name (if any) of the claim and its locality as indicated by some general description or statement, the length of the boundary lines if for any cause they are not regular and the nature of such cause, the situation of the discovery post as indicated by distance and direction from the first corner post, the time when discovery of ore or mineral was made and when the claim was marked or staked out and the date of the said notice; and every licensee shall accompany his sketch or plan and notice with an affidavit showing the discovery of valuable ore or mineral upon the claim by or on behalf of such licensee, and that he has no knowledge and has never heard of any adverse claim by reason of prior discovery or otherwise.

26. THE INSPECTOR shall forthwith enter in his book the particulars of the notice of claim presented by every licensee, and shall file the notice, sketch or plan and affidavit with the records of his office, and if there is no dispute as to the rights of the licensee to the claim by reason of prior discovery or otherwise, the inspector may, at the expiration of ninety days from the date of the record

thereof, grant to the licensee a certificate of such record.

27. IF THE LICENSEE FAILS TO COMPLY with the provisions of Regulation 25 so far as they relate to him, or if, having complied with them, he or any person in his behalf shall remove any post for the purpose of changing the boundaries after the plan and notice have been filed, the mining claim marked or staked out by him shall be deemed to be forfeited and abandoned, and all right of the licensee therein shall cease.

28. A MINING CLAIM shall also be deemed to be forfeited and abandoned and all right of the licensee therein shall cease in case the miner's license has run out and has not been renewed, or if the annual fee for a claim has not been prepaid, or if actual mining operations shall not be carried on upon each claim taken up except as provided in Regulation 29 for at least five months of one man's time, or an equivalent if more than one man is employed on the same claim, in every calendar year.

29. FOR EVERY FOUR CLAIMS or less held by the same licensee or by different persons agreeing to combine their mining operations within a radius of one mile, all such mining operations may be carried on upon one of the claims; but notice of an intention to carry on such operations must be filed with the inspector, and a record of all mining operations carried on by a licensee during his license year verified by oath shall be filed with the inspector, who shall enter an abstract thereof in his book.

30. A LICENSEE may at any time abandon a mining claim by giving notice in writing to the inspector of the mining division of his intention so to do, and from the date of the record of such notice

In the inspector's book all interest of the licensee in such claim shall cease.

31. A PARTY WALL at least fifteen feet thick (seven and one-half feet on each side of the boundary lines) shall be left between adjoining claims on Crown lands, which shall be used in common by all parties as a roadway for all purposes, and shall not be obstructed by any person throwing soil, stone or other material thereon; and if it is found necessary or expedient to remove such party wall the person so removing it shall if required construct a new roadway in no wise more difficult of approach than the one destroyed by the removal of the party wall; and every person obstructing a party wall or failing to construct a new roadway in place of the one destroyed shall be liable to a fine of not more than five dollars and costs, or in default to be imprisoned for any period not exceeding one month.

32. NO PERSON MINING UPON CROWN LANDS shall cause damage or injury to the holder of another claim, by throwing earth, clay, stones, or other material thereon, or by causing or allowing water to flow into or upon such other claim from his own, under a penalty of not more than five dollars and costs, and in default of payment he may be imprisoned for any period not more than one month.

33. ANY PERSON WHO REMOVES OR DISTURBS with intent to remove any stake, picket or other mark placed under the provisions of the Mines act shall forfeit and pay a sum not exceeding twenty dollars and costs; and in default of payment may be imprisoned for any period not exceeding one month.

34. ANY PERSON CONTRAVENING PART III of the Mines act or any rule or regulation made under it, in any case where no other penalty or punishment is imposed, shall, for every day on which

such contravention occurs, or continues, or is repeated, incur a fine of not more than twenty dollars and costs; and in default of payment may be imprisoned for a period not exceeding one month.

35. EVERY PERSON WHO PULLS DOWN, injures or defaces any rules, notice or abstract posted up by the owner or agent of a mine, shall be guilty of an offense against the Mines act.

36. EVERY PERSON WHO WILLFULLY OBSTRUCTS an inspector in the execution of his duty under the Mines act, and every owner or agent of a mine who refuses or neglects to furnish to the inspector the means necessary for making an entry, inspection, examination or inquiry under the Mines act in relation to such mine, shall be deemed to be guilty of an offense against the act.

37. EVERY INSPECTOR OF A MINING DIVISION may convict upon view of any of the offenses punishable under the provisions of Part III of the Mines act or any regulations made thereunder.

38. THE LIEUTENANT GOVERNOR in Council may, as often as occasion requires, declare by proclamation that he deems it necessary that the act respecting Riots Near Public Works (R. S. O. 1897, Chap. 38) shall, so far as the provisions therein are applicable, be in force within any mining division; and upon and after the day to be named in any such proclamation Section 1 and Sections 3 to 11 inclusive of the said act, so far as the provisions thereof can be applied therein, shall take effect within the mining division designated in the proclamation; and the provisions of the said act shall apply to all persons employed in any mines, or in mining within the limits of such division, as fully and effectually to all intents and purposes as if the

persons so employed had been specially mentioned and referred to in the said act.

39. ALL THE PROVISIONS OF PART IV of the Mines act, R. S. O. 1897, being the part under the heading of Mining Regulations, shall apply in every particular to all mines and other openings from which ore or mineral of any kind or class is raised or taken, and to all works for smelting, milling or otherwise treating ores or mineral for any economic object, which are situated within the limits of a mining division.

INDEX TO PART II.

MINING LAWS OF CANADA.

Lightning Source UK Ltd.
Milton Keynes UK
UKHW010007160219
337399UK00011B/850/P